Praise for Len Gaby
and
THE ART OF THE MENSCH

"Forty years ago, when Len was just starting to amass his wealth, I suggested that he share his business insights with the world. We both went our separate ways and 40 years later he finally got the time to do it. Bravo, Len, you are certainly an insightful business Mensch!"

— Dr. Charles Lusthaus Ph.D. | Professor McGill University
Montreal (retired) and Founder, Universalia Management Group

"When I first met Len Gaby, I knew that he was a man who could get things done. He and Debbie built a business that was among Arizona's most admired and in The Art of the Mensch Len shares the stories and experiences and lessons that have shaped his life... all in the hope of enriching yours."

— Rita Davenport | Author, Speaker, Trainer

"Len and I started college together at the University of Buffalo in 1963, and travelled different roads to find our own joy in life. What a great ride."

— Shep Gordon | Agent, Manager, Producer, and Author of
They Call Me SuperMensch

the art of the mensch

my theory of infinite wealth

LEONARD S. GABY

the art of the
mensch
my theory of infinite wealth

LEONARD S. GABY

Published by Brisance Books Group LLC

Cover Design by PCI Publishing Group LLC

Visit www.TheArtoftheMensch.net
for special sales, events and speaker inquiries.

Printed in the United States of America

First Edition: 2017   Hardcover

ISBN: 978-1-944194-16-1

012017

TABLE OF CONTENTS

DEDICATION

To my wonderful wife Debbie and our beautiful children
who have always inspired and encouraged me
to be the best I can be.

And to all those who have had an influence on me
throughout my life,
whether you know it or not.

FOREWORD

When spouses are or become business partners there are typically two outcomes. One: it's a constant battle, head-butting and bickering and power plays. Or, two: it's a scenario in which your strengths compliment each other, your different perspectives and experiences help you see and appreciate multiple points of view, and you know that the person you trust most in the world has your back.

It's my nature to find something good in everyone I meet. And while that may be an admirable quality... it wasn't one that made me immune to being fired—even from my own company.

My position as co-founder, co-owner and spokesperson of *Sleep America*, as well as the Founder of *Debbie Gaby Charities* did not insulate me from being fired. I like to think of this aspect of our business life together not as being 'fired,' but of playing to our strengths. It didn't take long to find the areas of the business in which each of us excelled— Len as the behind-the-scenes guy who kept operations running smoothly, and me as the face and voice of Sleep America. And while building a profitable business was important to us that the business was a part of our local community—and that Len and I made keeping our relationship and our marriage a high priority. And today, 20 years after we said our "I dos," we are enjoying each other and our life more than ever.

We're often asked how a husband and wife create a successful business, working together 24/7, *and* maintain a happy marriage. I'm not going to say it is easy, because it's not. But the effort that it takes is well worth the rewards. It begins with a solid foundation based on the fact that we truly love each other and are dedicated to one another's success. And when two strong people—with different outlooks and opinions—come together there are both fireworks and compatibilities. Raised in the traditions of the South, it has always been my natural instinct to allow Len to take the lead role in our business. But I can tell you that I have never been shy when it came to sharing what was important to me.

It has always been my belief that *Sleep America* was so successful because, together, we were stronger than we would have been individually. Len is a brilliant businessman and I've learned so much from him. He has a knack for keeping me grounded, while I have the ability to help him view situations through a softer, more compassionate lens. Don't let him fool you though, under that shrewd business sense there is the heart of a romantic who once hid a gorgeous gold necklace—in a bread basket in a restaurant in Chicago—as a surprise that he knew would delight me!

Len has been such a blessing in my life and I was excited when he told me that he was going to share his experiences in this book. As you will see, life with Len Gaby is never dull. Not only is he full of energy, but he has an extraordinary talent for paying attention. Throughout his life he has learned from observing and interacting with many different people. His keen observational skills did not stop with individuals, displaying his natural instinct to understand how culture plays such a pivotal part in shaping all aspects of our lives. This afforded him the ability to be the architect of his life. To me, Len radiates *infinite wealth* because he did not pass up any of the learning opportunities that life placed in front of him. I think people will find his life fascinating and discover so much from his personal stories... because experience is one of our greatest teachers.

For as long as I can remember, I have embraced the teachings of Anthony Robbins, especially these two thoughts: "Follow your passion" and "What the mind can perceive, the body can achieve." Len Gaby embodies both, living his life as testament to these concepts. Len is a man who is bigger than life—and I've never met anyone who knows how to travel or celebrate in a grander fashion. When he is in charge of the agenda, you are guaranteed to be exposed to the best life has to offer.

While reading a great book, I like to turn back the corners and highlight what's most important to me. I imagine you might do the same.

There is no doubt in my mind that there will be quite a few folded corners and highlighted passages in your copy of this book. I hope you enjoy sharing Len's adventures—and how his experiences not only shaped his life, but gave him so much to share with others.

Many Blessings,
Debbie Gaby

INTRODUCTION

Each of us, with our unique perspectives and varied exposures and experiences, is likely to define *success* somewhat differently.

For some, it's about notoriety or wealth. For others success is measured by the impact we've had on the world we live in or how well we've used the talents we were given. For me, success is achieving the goals in life that you have set for yourself. More specifically, by focusing on the details of your aspirations, business ventures, and personal relationships, I define success as having the opportunity to create what I like to refer to as *infinite wealth*.

Many people create their goals entirely from a monetary standpoint, measuring their success based solely upon how much money or "stuff" they have acquired. This can lead to disappointment because, even if someone reaches their financial goal and if that is the only criteria with which they measure, they typically find that they're still not happy and fulfilled. You could liken this to a person who has been overweight their entire life and who believes when they finally get to that magic number on the scale, all of their problems will be solved. Maintaining an ideal weight may help them feel a bit better, but it will not solve the issue that initially led to their unhappiness.

In my experience, financial success alone is seldom fulfilling in a truly deep and profound sense. And I've found that the most successful people in all facets of life are the ones who are most grateful, whatever their current situation. It seems to me that there is a direct correlation between a person's level of happiness and their level of gratitude. There are many people with modest financial resources who are totally happy. Typically they have a wonderful, cohesive family unit, make the most with whatever they have, and don't anguish over the fact that they don't have more. Conversely, you find people who have abundant financial resources, who have *not* achieved infinite wealth and definitely aren't happy because they are always wanting more or desiring something other than what they *do* have.

You may find yourself asking, as I've asked myself, *How do I get there and how do I reach my pinnacle of infinite wealth?* All that is required is for you to pay attention to the opportunities, lessons, and wisdom you are already encountering every day.

In this book, I share stories about the people and experiences that helped me to realize what was truly important to me, and how I used these moments to create the life I wanted. All it takes is mindfulness to make your dreams a reality for yourself and those with whom you choose to build your life.

I believe that there is enough opportunity—especially in the United States' capitalistic society, even with all of its flaws and challenges—for you to achieve whatever it is you really want. We are indeed fortunate because this isn't the case in other parts of the world today. Which is another yet reason for us to be grateful...

Whether you are motivated to start your own business, take a leadership role in an entrepreneurial company, or choose to lead a nonprofit, club or a youth baseball team culture always plays a role. And it can be a defining, pivotal role in the life of any venture or enterprise. If you are a person who can influence that culture, you have an opportunity to achieve great things by positively affecting not only the lives of those you come into contact with, but future generations as well. I believe it is imperative to look at culture as a way of defining the environment that you are trying to create in your organization. It has been my experience that culture flows from the Top-Down, exuding from the Inside-Out. If you are going to be the architect of that culture, you need to understand its power, because the road to infinite wealth is guided by the map of culture.

Most of us have heard sports commentators talk about the chemistry of the locker room? My interpretation is that it is not so much chemistry, as it is culture. A glimpse into what we value and aspire to. You see the NFL struggling with it today. Will it continue to embrace a culture in which it tolerates famous athletes and celebrities doing things that are totally offensive to the rest of the population? Would we tolerate such behavior from our neighbors—or even our friends and family? Of course not. The bar, I believe, should be higher for the "rich and famous." For me, culture can be likened to the flow of a river. In every river there is a current that says "This is the way we go." When you have someone who tries going the other way, what do you do with him or her? Do you given them second chances... based upon what your culture dictates? Or take a hard line: "We don't tolerate that—ever"? Those are the issues that organizations and companies struggle with, and it is in this arena that you find out how strong a culture is and how committed the organization is to a positive culture. I would submit that organizations and enterprises that have explicit values of what's acceptable and what's not acceptable, with clearly-defined boundaries, are the ones that will be most successful in today's world. The ones with poorly defined parameters are likely to have more people testing the boundaries. Whether it's a drug or domestic violence policy, or simply whether team members are on time and reliable.

If an organization is structured so the culture flows down river with clear goals and common values, it creates infinite wealth with no limit to how good things can get. Isn't that a wonderful concept? Hope is what drives people. The hope that they can get to a point where everything is as they wish... with the added bonus that they have the good judgment to appreciate it. It's a quality of life issue to which we can all aspire. You don't even have to be a businessperson to accept these concepts and benefit from them in your life.

All of us are the product of our environments and cultures, whether we recognize it or not. The question is, will you simply float down whatever stream you are in without conscious thought, or will you shape that current, your culture, for your own benefit and that of everyone else around you?

Most of us have a self-image built, unconsciously, through life experiences and the influence of our family, education, neighbors, and friends. However, if you want to enjoy the best life possible, it is imperative to achieve your own culture and personal values. You may have heard this concept called *inner speak*. Have you asked yourself: *What are those conversations you have with yourself? What are those things that you tell yourself? How do they impact your behavior and choices in life? What do you do when nobody is looking?* These are the things that create your own personal integrity and character. And these are the things that define a mensch.

I'll never forget when Martin Luther King Jr. said, "I want my children to be judged by the quality of their character, rather than the color of their skin." To me, that is a significant and meaningful statement about the role that quality of our character plays in our lives. It's reflected in how we treat others, and the choices we make throughout our lives. We are all unique—motivated and satisfied by different things—but each of us has the power to not only positively affect our lives with our choices, but we have the power to influence our families, communities, organizations, countries, and the world... simply by how we approach them.

If you want to experience "infinite wealth" you need only to become the architect of your culture, not a victim of it. Commit yourself to creating the life—the culture and the values—that is aligned with how you define success.

Soon you'll meet some of the interesting people who taught me the secrets of infinite wealth...

Chapter 1

ROOTS IN CULTURAL DIVERSITY

"For me, Jewish culture was less about religion and more about the customs, food, family and a deep sense of community."

R eaching my 60th birthday in 2005 was a significant milestone. If somebody had asked me, at 40, if I was going to live to be 60 my answer probably would've been, "Not likely." Although it has always been my nature to be grateful for each and every day, it was actually a surprise to me to make it. My father only lived to be 47 and with my significant health issues over the years—open heart surgery, liver problems, and so forth—there were a few times when it occurred to me that I might not make it into my Golden Years.

Feeling nostalgic for the first time about a birthday, I said to my wife Debbie, "I think I'd really like to get my friends together and mark this one."

On a trip to Hawaii, years before, we were lucky enough to meet Michael Cairns, the executive chef at the esteemed Biltmore Hotel in Phoenix, Arizona, at the time. After contacting Michael with my birthday celebration plan, he completely surprised me with his approach. Typically, a chef tells you, "Here are the menus I have and here's what I can do. Choose from this menu and we'll go from there."

Instead, to my delight, Michael asked me, "What's your favorite dish? What do you really like?"

"I don't know. I love hearty food and Italian dishes," I told him.

"Well, what Italian dish do you like the most?" he asked.

"Osso buco is one of my favorites," I told him. I could almost smell that veal shank and vegetables after hours of slow cooking in a cast-iron crock.

"Well," he said. "We'll make you osso buco."

"There may be 60 to 70 people..." I cautioned.

He was unflappable. "I'll figure it out," he said.

He was on to the next menu-planning item. "We could have a big birthday cake for you, but what's your favorite dessert? Over your lifetime, what is the best dessert you ever had?"

"It has to be one I had at the Buckhead Diner in Atlanta, Georgia. It was a banana cream pie topped with shaved white chocolate—and it was phenomenal."

"Done," Michael said. "Favorite wine?"

He made that banana cream pie with shaved white chocolate for all the guests and it was as wonderful as my memory of that sensational dessert 20 years ago in the South.

The evening was filled with all of my favorites and not only was it delicious, every last morsel was as good, if not better than I'd ever had. As I looked around the private room in the Valley Cottage off of the Biltmore Hotel, I knew that this night would become one of my fondest memories. Friends and family came from all over the country—from New York to California and dozens of cities in between—to celebrate with me. Everyone who had been invited accepted the invitation, flew into

Phoenix, and helped to create a truly magical evening. My good friend Dan Voetmann, a wonderful singer and guitar player, entertained us throughout the evening, even singing a whimsical song he wrote about me.

Very informally, and as the spirit moved them, many people stood up and reminisced about their "times with Len Gaby." We shared many laughs, as well as a few tears. Although I was hoping the guests would just roast me all night—with taunts and jabs and good-humored ribbing—they mostly shared how they felt about me and our experiences throughout the years.

Finally, I had to put a stop to all the sentimentality. At one point it almost sounded like they were eulogizing me!

"This is too serious!" I said. "We need some funny stories." We laughed for hours as many of the guests talked about whimsical moments we shared. But, inevitably, some just couldn't seem to resist the temptation to say something kind and sweet.

It was surreal to spend an evening with so many people that I loved and respected over the years. And heart-warming to have my wife, children, sister, and so many friends from across the country come together. Listening to them speak about how much I meant to them or how much they enjoyed having me in their lives was an extraordinary gift. My sister Susan, always the thoughtful and creative one, gave me a nostalgic gift she created from an early childhood memento she'd kept from my late mother's belongings. In a beautiful shadowbox sat a tiny shoe. My shoe. It had been run over by a trolley car... decades ago. Engraved below, it read: Len Gaby – *Life on the Fast Track*.

It was hard to believe that so much time had gone by so fast. Even Arthur Goldman, who'd become a friend back in the mid-1970s when I worked for Simmons, came and shared the evening with us. When we met he was an assistant buyer for Abraham & Straus, a department store in Brooklyn, New York. By the time he became the mattress buyer, we had already built a great relationship. My company clearly and sincerely wanted to do business with "A&S," as we called them, so Arthur helped me approach his management and we ended up doing many memorable things together.

I remember asking Arthur, "What can I do to get your management involved in this process?" He said, "Just start by taking them to lunch and build a relationship."

Keep in mind that this was Brooklyn, the most populous borough of New York City, so there were numerous options—a great steakhouse called Peter Luger's, delicious delicatessens, and places to get New York cheesecake. But I knew just the place to go. A new restaurant that had recently opened called The River Café. It was literally a barge converted into a restaurant that sat in the East River in Brooklyn. It offered the most spectacular and unobstructed views of Manhattan. A limo took me, Arthur, and his two senior managers to lunch one beautiful summer day. To create a bit of mystery, we hadn't told them where we were going, so they were in the dark until we arrived. The River Café was a big deal at the time and they were thoroughly impressed because it was the best new restaurant at the time. I definitely had their attention.

Over the years, Arthur has mentioned that not one person, among all the people they did business with, ever thought of doing something like that. And that relationship-building gesture became an important event for them to rally around and feel, *We're really important because we went to lunch at The River Café in a limo.* This was the late 1970s and taking a limo to lunch was not quite as common in those days as it might be today. Ultimately, we ended up building a great business with Abraham & Straus because, I believe, that initial meeting set the tone for our relationship. Arthur shared that story at my party and it was obvious to me that it was an experience he had never forgotten... even after almost 40 years.

THE PALM

Years later, Arthur joined Robinsons-May, a regional department store based in Southern California. By then we had both moved up the food chain. My title at the time was Executive Vice-President at Simmons and he was General Merchandise Manager. On a business trip to California, we met for dinner at a classic restaurant called The Palm. Priding themselves on being a New York restaurant transplanted in Beverly Hills, The Palm truly exuded New York's distinct culture. With its obnoxious waiters and minimalist style, it was *the* place to get your New York "fix" while in Los Angeles.

The original restaurant was a unique restaurant located on 2nd Avenue in New York City near the newspaper publishing offices of the *Daily News* and *The New York Times*. Many of the newspaper writers ate at The Palm because they catered to the late hours the writers and artists kept. At the time, many newspapers used caricatures—cartoons and so forth—and the walls of the restaurant were covered with original caricature sketches of the famous people in New York. Even today, you can see these exclusive drawings adorning the walls at The Palm.

When the restaurant opened up in Beverly Hills, the idea was to bring a slice of New York and its one-of-a-kind culture to LA. It featured wood floors covered in sawdust and genuinely obnoxious waiters who had actually relocated from The Big Apple. The only difference was that, on the walls, they showcased caricatures of local celebrities from California. Keeping with the original theme, it was very exclusive and expensive. There wasn't a menu—but people like me loved it because it was akin to going home to New York, at least for a little while. The waiter we encountered at The Palm in California did not disappoint.

Our waiter came over and said, "What do you want?"

I asked, "What do you have?"

"Well, we got lobsters, sirloin steak, steak and peppers, and filet mignon. We've got a porterhouse that's 32 ounces and we have sea bass."

Arthur asked, "How big are the lobsters?"

"They're 4- to 5-pound lobsters."

"Good," he said. "I'll have lobster."

"I'll try the sea bass," I said.

The waiter glared at me and said: "This is a steak and lobster joint. Do you want steak or lobster?"

"Is the sea bass fresh?" I asked.

"Of course it's fresh," he said.

"I'll try the sea bass," I repeated.

He said to me, "Sir, you're not paying attention. I said this is a steak and a lobster joint. Do you want steak or lobster?"

I said, "I think you're the one who's not paying attention. I'll have the sea bass."

He sulked away disgruntled, but later brought out a phenomenal portion of fresh sea bass that was perfectly prepared and delicious.

If you aren't from New York, you would've probably thought: *Oh, he's trying to tell me something. He's warning me to stay away from the sea bass because it's not fresh, or the steak is much better.* We both knew that there was nothing wrong with the sea bass, but I had to fight him to get it because, at that time, that entrée was maybe $25—and everything else was priced at $40 and higher.

The Palm did well in California because there were many transplanted New Yorkers in Los Angeles who were doing very well so they could afford an expensive restaurant. They came to get that "fix" of New York City and a dose of that city's culture that they craved.

When you grew up with that kind of adversarial (and seemingly combative) banter, it was refreshing to experience it on the West coast— where everyone else in the Los Angeles area was refined and pleasant. For people like myself, The Palm was a little oasis in Beverly Hills where you could experience New York at its most authentic. There was always a waiter ready and willing to verbally abuse you a bit... for old times' sake. The culture of New York was transmitted through the restaurant, its ambiance and its people.

CLASHING CULTURES

Born in the midst of New York's rich cultural diversity, growing up there gave me unparalleled exposure to what brought people together.

For me, Jewish culture was less about religion and more about the customs, food, family and a deep sense of community.

There's nothing religious about chicken soup or kosher foods. Similarly, if you look at the Italian community, it was more about cultural ties, not religious beliefs, that bound people together. In New York, there's a wonderful area called *Little Italy* where many of the Italian immigrants have congregated over the years. They felt the connection to each other because they spoke a common language, cooked and enjoyed the same types of foods, and shared similar communication styles and customs. That's culture.

The Jewish immigrants that came over from Russia, Poland, Germany, and other parts of the world in the early 1900s all gathered in the Lower East Side of New York City. There was this whole Jewish community that gravitated toward each other, again, because they spoke the same language, ate the same types of foods, and understood one another's mannerisms and innuendos. Many of them spoke Yiddish, a combination of Hebrew and Slavic languages. Today, there are people who actually study Yiddish, although it is not *technically* a language. My paternal grandmother actually ran a Yiddish Theater in New York, which staged plays in Yiddish.

There was also a Greek population, and Polish neighborhoods—all rich in traditions and customs. This all had to do with immigration. People coming to America as a land of opportunity and a home to freedoms that so many of the immigrants sought. Today, we see it in Hispanic communities across the United States. The food, language, faith, and customs brought here from their homelands have become the cultural center for these populations. In New York, this was very visible and tangible to me while growing up. You could see, hear, feel, smell, and taste it. A favorite sensory memory of mine is going to Ferrara's in Little Italy, where they had the most amazing Italian desserts—cannoli and tiramisu, beautifully displayed and mouth-wateringly delicious.

New York City's Chinatown is a wondrous place as well. The streets are unusually narrow and there are many spectacular restaurants. We used to go to one called Hung Fat on Mott Street. There was no waiting area inside the restaurant, so the line formed down the sidewalk outside. The weather wasn't always great, but you would stand outside anyway, sometimes for hours, waiting to get into this tiny, spectacular restaurant. There were probably 20 restaurants within a hundred yards of it, but everybody wanted to go to Hung Fat because it served the most delicious Chinese food. The waiters didn't speak English so you had to point to what you wanted or try to communicate with gestures. One of the greatest aspects about New York was even though there were these separate ethnic communities, there was no sense of being uncomfortable when you entered a culture experience different from your own.

Little Italy, Chinatown, the Lower East Side of Manhattan, and the Greek neighborhoods are all within blocks of each other. Chinatown and Little Italy are literally right next to each other with only a single street dividing them. On one side of that street you were in Chinatown, and on the other you were in Little Italy. I feel fortunate to have grown up in a multicultural city where such a rich mix of nationalities and traditions could exist in relative harmony. Much of my education about culture was born from living there.

When we lived in the Bronx it was in an extremely diverse area which afforded me the opportunity to live my formative years interacting with many different people and avoiding some of the stereotyping and prejudices that so many people in this country experienced during that era.

My best friend at the time was an African-American boy named Cuba. This is my earliest recollection of a friend and it left a strong impression on me. I recall playing stickball in the street with Cuba in the Bronx. A car door became first base... a manhole cover second, and so forth.

Recently I was trying to get closer to the concept of this 'friend' named Cuba because it was such an unusual name and experience. I found out that Cuba Gooding Sr. grew up in the Bronx at the same time I was there and that his name was bestowed on him by his father who actually came from Cuba. I'm sure that this is more than a coincidence, and that the wonderful actor Cuba Gooding Jr.'s father and I were friends 65 years ago on the streets of the Bronx in New York.

When I was about seven years old, we moved to Bayside, Queens and although most would consider that a short distance from our home in the Bronx, the diversity and richness was not the same. My parents always strived to provide us with an assortment of experiences—from attending symphonies and jazz concerts to the ballet—and life in Queens seemed almost rural compared to the Bronx. Concerts and the ballet helped me to cultivate a deep appreciation for the arts, music, and cultural diversity.

My mother had a story that she loved to tell about when I was a very young child, still in a highchair. While dining at a Chinese restaurant, the waitress brought out a round scoop of white rice in a small dish and placed it in front of me. After lunging into that rice face first, like a typical toddler, I evidently spit it out and made a monstrous mess because it didn't meet my expectation. It must have appeared to me to be a bowl of sweet vanilla ice cream and when it wasn't, it ended up everywhere except in my stomach. My mom told me that they left a tip at the table and another one on the highchair so the waiter knew that tip came from me for making such a colossal mess. There was one great lesson there for me: Exposure comes in all shapes and forms—and flavors... often when we least expect it.

As a young boy it was a ritual for me to walk from our apartment in Queens to the delicatessen three blocks away to buy the Sunday edition of *The New York Times* along with lox, bagels, and cream cheese for my family's breakfast. It was my Sunday tradition. It still makes me smile to remember how I struggled to get home with all of the food because of how huge the Sunday edition of the *Times* was. Even if you've never pondered it before, think back and I bet you will find cultural influences from your childhood that had a hand in molding your view of your neighborhood, city, country, and the world.

Chapter 2

THE JOY OF FAILURE

*"Always keep your goal in mind
while remaining creative
about the route to getting there."*

You're not always going to be successful in life, but you certainly don't have to see any situation as impossible. That is one of the challenges many people face when they think that their aspirations are unattainable. They envision something that they want to achieve and then they create a path to achieve that vision that didn't previously exist. The first path is not always the right path and you have to be okay with trying again if that doesn't work out. One of the most important things I've learned is to always keep your goal in mind while remaining creative about the route to getting there.

The sooner we start working on that, the better off we are. That is why the little failures and successes in the early stages of my life had a big impact later on. My teenage years taught me that being told *No* is not the end of the road or the end of the world, but instead an opportunity to look at the situation from a new perspective and try a different approach.

Yes means Yes. No means maybe. Maybe can become Yes.

OFF THE RAILS

Although I have no personal recollection of it, my 60th birthday present from my sister Susan commemorated the story told to me many times by my parents.

One day I was out for the day with my father and his life-long friend Joe Feinman. Apparently, it was unusual for him to take me out without my mother when I was a very small child and still in diapers. For whatever reason, we were having a day out, running around town. At some point, while walking across a street, my father noticed me limping, and couldn't figure out why. When he realized that—somehow—I was missing one shoe, he turned around to see where I had lost it. It seemed that my shoe had gotten caught in the trolley track causing me to step out of it, leaving it stuck in the track. Just as he spotted it and went to retrieve it, the trolley came by and ran over the little shoe, crushing it and cutting it almost in half.

My parents kept the shoe, thinking it was a wonderful story to share with me some day in the future. But that's not the end of the story that day. Now I was short one shoe and my father, who was a brilliant man, but not very comfortable handling a young child, decided he'd better get me a new pair of shoes. After buying them, and while still in the shoe store, I soiled my diaper. Ill-equipped to handle the situation, he didn't have a fresh diaper with him so he took me to the restroom and very uncomfortably wiped my bottom, threw my diaper in the trash, and put my shorts back on without a diaper. Apparently, I hadn't fully completed my "business" because, while walking back with him into the shoe store, I dropped little turds along the way. Somebody said to my father, "Look what your son is doing in the store." Grabbing a newspaper, he picked up those little turds and threw the smelling bundle away in the restroom. We walked out with my new shoes—but no diaper—and headed home.

After arriving home, my mother asked, "Why does Lenny have new shoes?"

"Don't ask," my father said. He wasn't in the mood to recount the day's events.

HUSKIES... THIRD FLOOR

A vivid memory of shopping with my father that I've never forgotten was when I was 12 years old and preparing for my Bar Mitzvah. He took me to Barney's, the place to go for boys and men's clothing, located at 7th Avenue & 17th Street in Manhattan. This was 1957, before department stores really became important. We walked into Barney's, and I can still see the salesman leaning on the wall as if he had been on his feet all day. My father, again a little awkward and uncomfortable in his parental role, walked up to him and pointed to me. He started to say, "I need a..." but never got the word *suit* out of his mouth. Without hesitating, the salesman screamed, "Huskies! Third floor!"

To me, it seemed that he yelled the word *Huskies* so loud that everyone in the entire store heard that I had been directed to the Husky department. I should point out that I interpreted the term *husky* as a euphemism for *fat*. As we made our way to the third floor to the Husky department for clothing for overweight boys, I felt awkward and "labeled" for the first time in my life. It was obvious that I was not alone (and certainly not the only "husky" young boy in NYC) because there was a whole department for kids like me. But it still hit me that I was being judged as somebody who was less than perfect and less than desirable. Every kid feels out of place in some way, I think, but at that point in my life—when I, like most kids, wanted to feel *average* or *normal* or *typical*—I was reminded that I was *husky*. I wished I wasn't; I wanted to be *average*.

The remark didn't seem to faze my father, and it seemed to have gone in one ear and out the other. He didn't show any signs of being particularly offended or the least bit concerned. He was extremely impatient at times, and he probably just wanted to get to the third floor, find a suit, and get out of there. This experience opened my eyes to an awareness that previously hadn't existed for me. Obviously it was pretty painful because it was so many years ago, but I can still clearly hear him screaming, "Huskies... third floor."

Several years passed from my Bar Mitzvah and I got taller, growing out of the Husky suit from Barney's. My teen years were ripe for conflict with my father as we both had strong personalities; but he always maintained control of the situation.

THE ART OF MOWING

Even at 15 years old, giving up easily wasn't part of my nature. Let's use a weekly allowance as an example. Although it was definitely not from a lack of asking on my part, my dad *never* gave me any money. Throughout years of my relentless pestering, he always said "*No.*"

"Why?" I wailed, on countless occasions. I needed to understand his adamant refusals.

In retrospect, it was probably much more difficult for him to say "No" to my constant badgering. I am convinced that it would have been a whole lot easier for him to have said, "*Yes, here are a couple of bucks for you, kid, now run along and have a good time.*" He might have added: "*You're not such a bad young man.*" I would have liked that, but it didn't happen. He kept saying "No"—and he was adamant about it. Obviously he was trying to instill a work ethic in me. At the time I recall being resentful and disappointed. Today, I fully "get it."

At that time, we had just moved into a very modest home in Buffalo with a beautiful front lawn. It was nothing fabulous, but to us (and compared to what we had come from) it definitely felt like we had moved up. The only thing my dad asked me to do around the house was to cut the lawn. That's when my plan to persuade him to give me some money—by withholding my lawn mowing services—was hatched. My theory was that if I wasn't cutting the grass he would get upset about it, presenting me with the opportunity to plead my case for a few dollars. The lawn grew longer and longer and taller and taller until, at one point, he convinced me that it was time to cut it. Not by giving me the money, but by telling me the strike was over.

As I recall it went something like, *"Get out there and cut the lawn. NOW!"*

When cutting a lawn that's pretty short, mowing it is hardly even noticeable. But because the grass in my yard was so high, I realized that, as I mowed, a design was being created. My creative side kicked in, driving me to meticulously mow a dollar sign across the full length of the yard. When complete, the $ sign was about 50 feet long. After I completed my "work of art," I invited him out to see the lawn. The front door was a little bit elevated, so my father had a great view of my masterpiece. To put it mildly, he had no sense of humor that day—and there was no way to convince him that letting my creative side run wild was funny. He made me cut the rest of the lawn and that was the end of it.

Do you remember those old cartoons—the ones in which a character became extremely angry and you'd hear a train whistle as their cheeks puffed out and became beet red, just before steam came shooting out of their ears? Well, there was a level of red that rose up and replaced the whites of my dad's eyes one day...and I remember thinking, *there is no question his head is going to explode.* He was livid! And, not for the first time, I was the source of his frustration and anger.

Although he didn't say a word when he saw it, it was obvious that he did not share my amusement about having used the lawn mower to create a dollar sign on our front lawn. With a nervous chuckle I said, "Dad, relax. It's just for the planes...so they know where to drop the money." To restate the obvious: He wasn't amused.

Although my stubbornness drove me to keep asking, he never cracked and gave me any money. Eventually, I stopped asking because my money came from cutting other people's lawns instead. In hindsight, I don't think my dad was being unreasonable, but it sure would have been nice for him to throw me a couple of bones once in a while.

Which takes us back to money... and the fact that I've always had a taste for the finer things. It never crossed my mind to modify my tastes to accommodate my means. It made more sense to me to increase my means by working harder to afford the things I wanted. For me, one of the key attributes of an entrepreneur is being a problem solver. Many people think that a goal they have in mind may seem unattainable, and therefore, they can't achieve it. The question I always ask is not, *can I* or *can't I*, but how? How can I do what I want, achieve what I desire? How do I make that happen?

PILES OF... MANURE

Like many 16-year-old boys, along with driving a car comes certain financial needs—like gas and dating and eating out. But job hunting at 16 isn't always easy. As a football player in high school, lifting weights and staying in shape was important to me, so finding a job that kept me active was appealing. One day, shortly after meeting the owner of the Wayside Nursery in Buffalo, I asked him for a job. He told me he didn't have anything for me, citing my youth and lack of experience. My first inclination was to accept that answer. But after thinking about it, days later, I returned to him with a proposal.

Knowing that he wouldn't be assuming any risk, because technically I wouldn't be an employee, I offered to work in the back of the nursery where shipments arrived and customers loaded their cars with peat moss, fertilizer, topsoil, grass seed, and all kinds of large, heavy bags. I said, "Let me work out back and see if I can earn tips by loading people's cars. When you have trucks that come in, I'll help unload them to get the physical workout I'm seeking and help you out as much as I can." I continued to make my case: "By helping people, I'll earn some tip money. And if my contribution is substantial enough...you'll want to pay me." He still wasn't convinced, so I kept on talking... "If for some reason that doesn't work, then I'll just go away. And you will probably never know that I was there because my presence didn't make an impression or add value."

To my amazement, he listened quietly to my proposal then answered, "Great idea, that's a good proposition. I'll give you a chance."

Grateful—and thrilled to have a job, even without compensation—I may have overdone it a bit with the customers, but I figured out pretty quickly how to ingratiate myself to them so they'd want to tip me. Although never trained to do so, it became clear to me that looking people in the eye, smiling, and using the respectful words—*Sir, Ma'am, please,* and *thank you*—went a very long way. It also gave me real world practice in learning the art of small talk... what worked and what didn't.

Before the summer was over, the owner appointed me as the manager of the backend of the nursery. Everything outside the physical boundaries of the nursery itself was my domain. He left it up to me saying, "You take care of it and make sure that everything is in place." That was my first experience with real responsibility. I remember vividly the sense of pride I felt the first few times I heard, *What's next?* and *What do we do now?* from employees waiting for my directives.

Making money while staying physically active was my original goal, but having some responsibility and accountability was exhilarating to me. Loving the fact that this entrepreneur trusted and believed in me, I would have never let him down. At the time, it all seemed very natural and logical, however, looking back at that experience some 50+ years later, it is clear to me that this was one of the many building blocks that taught me how to become a leader, increased my self-esteem, and built my confidence. Although each may have been small, these important successes have a cumulative effect over time. You have to cherish the drive to be a leader because you are putting yourself on the line and counting on other people to do what they are supposed to do. It became evident to me during my time at the nursery that the people you are depending on enjoy being given that responsibility as well. We all had a role to play, a job to do, and we all did it together. It was great to experience this concept of teamwork and leadership during those early stages of my life.

During high school, besides working in the nursery, my entrepreneurial endeavors included selling magazines and mowing lawns as additional avenues for making money. I even worked as a salesman in a men's store during my junior and senior years. My philosophy was, *whatever it took*. My positions always revolved around some kind of sales situation. Making some money *and* feeling good about the job that I was doing was so empowering. That kind of positive reinforcement at a young age laid a foundation for me to build upon later in life.

But it begs the question: Without that nursery experience early in my life, would I have gone on to be successful? Maybe. Who knows? There would certainly have been a different story to tell. What I knew was that I loved the job and was successful at it.

Loving what you do almost assures success,
but just because you're successful doesn't mean
that you've always loved what you've done to get there.

Maybe the only job you can get at the moment is flipping hamburgers at McDonald's. You probably won't love it, but that doesn't matter because if you do it right, it will only be temporary. If you focus on being the best hamburger flipper there ever was, before you know it, you could begin to move up the ladder. Eventually you could find yourself managing the entire store, or... even owning it.

Once, while talking to a young person who was having trouble finding his way in life and figuring out what he should be doing, I asked him, "What do you really like to do? What do you enjoy the most?"

He said, "Listening to music."

"Well," I suggested, "take that interest and, as the saying goes, drill down into it. Become the best music listener in the world." I was hitting my stride as I continued: "Find out who recorded it, when, how, and who they sold it to. In other words, find out everything there is to know. And before you know it, you'll be an expert on music and you will be doing something that you truly love."

I told the young man that I wasn't sure how one made a living doing that, but I do know there are people who make their living in the recording and music industry, and if that's really what he enjoys doing, he'll keep pursuing it. If it's truly a passion, you will know more about music than anybody else. I've heard that some DJs have become serious celebrities just playing recorded music. "Somehow," I told him, "you will end up communicating that to others and who knows, maybe you'll become an expert. That's the way people start to find the niche in life that makes them their happiest. They'll put in all the extra work that's necessary to be successful and competent in that world."

Most people think there is nothing they can do with their interest or there's no career path from listening to music or whatever it is they feel passionate about. You can create your future—simply by investing in your interests. Many people have trouble translating their passions into something that's tangible, getting stuck on trying to create some kind of financial model that says, *I can make a living doing this.* My advice is to always start with what you love and the rest will find its way from there. If you're not doing something that you enjoy, the path to success is almost always impossible.

PISSED ON = PISSED OFF

During high school, I perceived myself as an athlete. Well, it was more that I *wanted* to be athletic, although coordination and exceptional athletic prowess were not in my realm of God-given talents. Nevertheless, it was important for me to stay in decent shape. During the spring months, my time was spent with the track and field team and, because of my size and strength, my specialty was throwing discus and shot put. Never particularly great at either one, it didn't bother me when I didn't receive any significant accolades. It provided the workout I was looking for— running, and building my strength. Always a bit heavy, running didn't come easy for me, but it was a way to maintain some physical conditioning for when football season came back around. Although I wasn't spectacular at football either, it was a significant interest of mine. My lack of natural athleticism was countered by my consistent effort and determination.

Of the 50 or so boys on the high school team, I happened to be the only one who was Jewish. I had never shied away from my Judaism before, but it became my first experience in which my faith was used against me in a derogatory manner. It seemed there was a certain amount of anti-Semitism that was a part of the football culture at that time. Double teaming me or doing their best to hit me really hard gave me the impression that some of my teammates were picking on me. It became more apparent when, in some loose conversation, one kid said, "Take that Jew." I'm not sure it was anything truly malicious, it may just have been young kids trying to vent a little bit and, fueled by that, hit me a little bit harder. I'm not really sure what it was all about, but for some reason I didn't take it that personally. Maybe I shouldn't have tolerated it, but it didn't register enough to really bother me. Quite the opposite, in fact. The incident made me even more determined to never quit and to do my best to hit them back harder than they hit me. It never occurred to me to say anything to anyone; including the story in this book is probably the first time I've even acknowledged it. It didn't always feel exclusive to me because several of my teammates used derogatory names based on ethnicity and other cultural differences to expend their testosterone-driven competitive juices.

There were many different types of bullying on the football team. An event that stands out for me happened one day after practice while we were all in the showers. Hot water was running everywhere while we were all washing away the sweat and grime from the practice field, and when just happening to look down at my legs, I couldn't believe my eyes. Had I not glanced down, I most likely wouldn't have noticed (because of the warm water pouring out of the shower heads) that a teammate was urinating on my leg. Although he was looking at me and knew what he was doing, my initial reaction was just to pretend I didn't notice. After thinking about it for a minute, my predominant thought was, *I can't let him get away with pissing on my leg; this has gone too far.*

After pondering my options for retaliation, my decision was to hit him. Knowing that if he didn't see it coming, there wouldn't be a very long fight, I cold-cocked him in the face. Our teammates freaked when they saw him knocked out laying on the shower floor as his blood ran down the drain. They said, "Oh my God, he killed him, he killed him—he's dead." It was quite a scene, but after rinsing off, I simply walked out of the shower. He never pissed on my leg or talked about it again. It was an unpleasant experience, but I'm sure all of us at one point have felt like we were getting pissed on, in one way or another.

I want to point out that it wasn't just me; everyone was vulnerable to this type of abuse. It was part of the culture. If we didn't look like the rest of the boys, have the same religious beliefs, or the same accent, we didn't fit in. Anyone who was a little bit different typically suffered the discomfort of being an outsider. This changes people's behavior because most people are going to do everything they can to fit into their current environment and culture. For example, if a child with a heavy southern accent relocated to New York as a teenager, they would be ridiculed. Conversely, if a child with a New York accent relocated to Alabama, they wouldn't fit in because they would be immediately identified as an outsider.

There was also a racial issue—whether you were Asian, African-American, or any other race—and if you came into a group that was homogeneously consistent, you were the odd one out. Typically what happens is we acculturate, meaning we take on or adapt to the dominate culture, accepting it as our own. This is why you hear about the boy from New York, who relocated to Alabama, who wants to fit in so he begins using typical southern words like *y'all*.

This affects many aspects of children's lives. If the culture they're in dictates that *at 16 years old we drink around here*, they drink because they want to be part of that culture. It can be very hard for young people to choose to be different because it is such a powerful force on our ability to operate as individuals. There are some strong people who can maintain their individuality, but certainly during the impressionable teenage years, the most important thing in the world is to fit in. Everybody wears the same jeans and the same sneakers, and if you're not wearing the right ones, you're considered an outcast, or worse, not cool. This applies to gang culture as well. Boys who need protection and want to fit into that world have to prove themselves by beating someone up. They would probably never think of or do that on their own, but when a gang says that is what they need to do to be part of their culture, they will go and do it. I've found that what goes on within our children's lives has such a powerful impact on what will become of our society as a whole.

Maybe the big questions are: What can we do as individuals to help change a culture that quietly accepts these behaviors and allows them to mold young and impressionable individuals in a negative way? And how can we, as a community, positively impact our teens and young adults so that later in life when they become part of a company like Apple, Google or Starbucks—or Sleep America—they bring positive influences that enhance that culture?

Chapter 3

MUCH HIGHER EDUCATION

"They are free to discover who they are,
and who they are not.
That's something you can only figure out
through experience."

When it came to applying to colleges, it was a competitive time because it was the height of the baby-boomer generation. There was a tremendous influx of kids my age vying to get into all the universities.

"THE WORLD NEEDS PLUMBERS"

My first choice was the University of Buffalo, the best public university in New York state. Initially I was not accepted, but placed on the waiting list. The contingency acceptance annoyed me to no end.

Trying to be supportive, my father said to me, "Not everybody is supposed to go to college." He added: "The world needs plumbers and electricians, and maybe that is your calling."

Completely taken aback, I was speechless. My insides were screaming, *What! Are you crazy? I'm more than capable of going to college—and of course I'm going!*

My father had more to tell me. "Don't worry about it. If it doesn't work out, you'll be okay. We'll still love you and everything will be fine."

It was during that conversation that one of my first life-changing epiphanies occurred. Almost instantaneously, the concerns I had of what my father or mother thought about my decisions vanished. Up to that point, there was always an underlying drive inside of me to make them proud. Along with that came a constant awareness to either avoid confrontation or please them in some way. As we discussed my future and college plans, my father's comments and attitude instantly irked me into maturity. I thought to myself, *I really don't care what they think of me anymore.* It was a sea change.

It was not that I didn't care about them or about their feelings toward me. Rather, it had finally become evident to me that the person *I* needed to be concerned about impressing was myself. There was no longer a question that it was up to me to determine the level of my satisfaction with my decisions because, for the rest of my life, there wasn't anyone that would be closer to me than me. There is a beautiful poem that sums this up perfectly. Written in 1934, it is famously referred to as *The Man in the Mirror*, but the actual title is

The Guy in the Glass
by Peter "Dale" Wimbrow Sr.

When you get all you want and you struggle for pelf,
[an informal word for money]
and the world makes you king for a day,
then go to the mirror and look at yourself
and see what that man has to say.

For it isn't your mother, your father or wife
whose judgment upon you must pass,
but the man, whose verdict counts most in your life
is the one staring back from the glass.

He's the fellow to please,
never mind all the rest.

I believe that one of the keys to success and personal fulfillment is being happy with who you are. Over the years, I've questioned myself—often standing in front of a mirror when I'm at my least attractive, brushing my teeth or rubbing sleep from my eyes—*Are you happy with who you see? Are you saying to yourself—I'm really glad to be you; I'd rather be you than anybody else in the world!* I've posed this same challenge to those I've mentored over the years, encouraging them to let a mirror be their window into their personal vision of themselves.

Even with my (many) flaws, issues, illnesses, and faults, I'm pretty pleased with who I am. And it was that moment, with my father in a conversation about college, that triggered this self-awareness for me. It felt like an instant understanding that each of us *has to* take responsibility for who we are and what we do. And most importantly, that we need to be motivated by self-love and self-approval first and foremost.

With the fact that my father put too little importance, so little weight, on my goal of obtaining a college degree—which was so far from *my* thought process—it became crystal clear that my actions were no longer going to be driven by what he thought of me. Becoming, at that point, the only person I needed to impress from that moment on, I never again worried or judged my decisions based on what he or anyone else thought of me.

If my father had lived to see my accomplishments, I expect they would have been staggering to him. I imagine they would rank far out of the realm of possibilities, based on what he seemed to think of my abilities. Admittedly, every time that thought crosses my mind, a rush of pride exudes for him. That's because, spiritually, I still feel very much connected to him. It is obvious to me that the intention behind his thoughts was not born from cruelty or disappointment; quite the opposite. He was reassuring me of his unwavering love regardless of my profession or accomplishments. That day, that conversation, was the catalyst to owning my power of self-motivation.

And what a gift it was. Because, sadly, many people operate for much of their lives from a place of guilt. They feel that if they don't do what their parents want, they are disappointing them. Some parents even take it so far as to place blame or expect their children to live up to what they want for them. My mom and dad never made me feel guilty, giving me the freedom to think and act independently based on my own desires and aspirations. There is a huge difference between the two approaches and it can have an enormous impact on one's happiness and direction in life. Setting my own standards and course was completely liberating, allowing me the freedom to be driven by my own passions.

ADMISSIONS ANXIETY

After being called up from the waiting list, my college career began at The State University of New York at Buffalo, which at the time was the largest campus in the state university system. Having done well enough in high school, I even received a small Regents scholarship which allowed me to receive a first-class public college education.

The first semester, my first class began at 8am but my next class wasn't until 4:00 in the afternoon. Standing in long lines to secure a schedule that required me to be at school the whole day, five days a week, for five courses was completely unnecessary to me. Thinking *I'm never going to do this again*, it became my mission to figure out how to avoid it the following semester. And although it's not a story I'm particularly proud of, I can report "mission accomplished." Here's the whole—true—story...

My solution began by going into the Admissions and Records Office and looking around the large room of people until I found the least attractive girl there. After approaching her and introducing myself, I went into great detail pleading for her help with a fictitious malady. Explaining to her that my serious psychological problems, involving anxiety and panic attacks, were greatly exacerbated by the act of having to stand in line for hours to register for classes. It was, I told her, almost too much for me to endure. I asked if she could think of an alternative way for me to register for the second semester.

In those days there were no electronic scheduling systems, so when you registered for a class you were handed a paper card called an IBM punch card. If the class could accommodate 40 students, then there were 40 cards printed. After securing a card for your seat in each of your five classes, they would complete your registration by putting them all into a computer, an early mainframe that was the size of a huge room. Very kind and sympathetic to my plight, she assured me we could figure it out. She said, "Why don't you come to me two weeks before next semester's enrollment. All of the cards will be printed by then and I'll pull the cards for the classes you need."

"Could you do that?" I asked.

She said, "Oh sure, no problem."

I'm sure my smile lit up the room when I said, "That would be wonderful, I'd be so grateful."

Two weeks before the second semester, I picked out my classes and she gave me the first registration card to each one. My schedule ended up being the most amazing one possible! It was Monday, Wednesday, and Friday from 8:00 a.m. to 2:00 p.m., going straight from one class to another. Not having to kill eight hours in between classes, and only having classes three days a week, made my life so much better. Many of my classmates were jealous and asked how it was that my schedule was always so perfect. I never told a soul.

To thank her for her time and assistance I gave her flowers and told her what a phenomenal human being she was. The next semester, she received candy. The next, another gift, and this continued throughout my time there. Although it wasn't my proudest moment, it did occur to me over those years that I was doing something nice for her by making her feel special with my gifts, compliments, and sincere appreciation. She had done something for me and made me feel special, making it a reciprocal relationship. I am grateful to her to this day.

MY BROTHERS

College life was pretty interesting, to say the least, especially once I joined the Alpha Epsilon Pi [AEPI] national fraternity. Still large today, The University of Buffalo's chapter, Upsilon Beta, attracted me because it centered on the two key elements of my life—Judaism and a New York upbringing. My pledge class included 50 pledges and about 80 or 90 active brothers. It was a social fraternity where we did some of the crazy antics that fraternity kids do—pranks, kidnapping brothers, and rowdy toga parties. Pledging was great fun and quite a challenging experience for me. We had to do things like wear a beanie [a little cap that made you look very foolish] to signify that you were a pledge. During hazing, the brothers had a poker game every Friday night during which the pledges would have to serve sandwiches and beer, basically acting as their servants for the evening. Many games lasted well into the early morning hours.

The pledging process lasted a whole semester with one person who became the president of the pledge class at the beginning of the year. It was so much work and effort that, halfway through the semester, I was elected the president for the remainder of the term. Being in charge of 50 pledges, who were all going in different directions, was one of the first points in my life when my potential as a leader became noticeable to me. I definitely *don't* recall thinking how cool it was to be president. Quite the opposite, in fact, because it was a burden. Most often my role was being the "responsible one," but make no mistake: my very strict academic philosophy and drive to be productive did not hamper my wish to have fun as well. Never wanting to sacrifice one for the other, I enjoyed it all. Recently, I encountered one of the fraternity brothers from my pledge class and it was interesting to hear his recollection that they all referred to me as the "adult" in the group.

After becoming a brother, I didn't seek out any serious leadership roles within the fraternity, but for two solid years my position was one of the most vital jobs—the Social Chairman. Organizing all of the parties and events was both important and exciting. We were mostly all Jewish, prompting us to treat the better cocktail parties as if they were bar mitzvahs, wearing shirts, ties, and jackets. Having bands and live music was one of our customs. One of the most memorable parties for me was when Peter, Paul & Mary, a popular folk band, performed a concert at our college. We organized a party for the brothers after the concert and invited the band to come. To our surprise (and delight) they graciously came and mingled with us!

There were some wild times as well, like toga parties where we wouldn't wear anything under our togas, and other creative events. Our favorite live band, the Del Royals, played frequently for us, bringing their families along, including their wives and kids. If you remember the movie *Animal House,* when they were singing *Shout,* that's exactly the way it was. As the social chairman, it was my job to make sure the band had enough to drink and had a really good time. Our infamous party drink was called *purple passion*—one part grape juice, one part vodka, and one part gin— which we mixed in plastic garbage cans because there were so many people at the parties. One time the brothers got extremely drunk and took the trombone from the band, dipped it into the garbage can, and drank out of it. I was in charge of paying the fraternity's bills, and I remember having to pay to clean their instruments. They would throw the purple beverage at each other and the sticky grape-juice concoction would get all over the furniture, drapes, and everything in between causing more expense.

If you take what we did 50 years ago to extremes, maybe that's why some fraternities are having some trouble today. I'd be first to acknowledge that, at times, things came close to getting out of hand. But by the grace of

God, we didn't hurt anybody or ourselves in our pursuit of fun. Especially given the fact that the more a person drinks, the more impaired their judgment becomes, often leading to poor choices. With the world we live in today—where everybody has a cellphone camera and are taking and posting pictures everywhere, it makes anything we do instantly available to the world. I am definitely grateful there wasn't a steady stream of pictures memorializing all that we were doing, and things may have been different if there was. You would think it could be a deterrent, living so much in the public eye today, but I'm not sure if it is. Our son JJ went to Arizona State University and was part of a fraternity there. He lived in the fraternity house for a while, and for him it was a memorable experience where he made some good friends and had a great time as well.

Overall, for me, being part of a fraternity was a positive venture. Plenty of my fraternity brothers are still close friends today. Quite a few of them went on to do wonderful things. One good friend, who was a judge in Brooklyn, unfortunately recently passed away. There were also many good friends of mine who weren't necessarily in my fraternity but they became huge successes in their own right.

I think college is all about experimenting because for most kids, it is their first time away from home where...

They are free to discover who they are and who they are not. That's something you can only figure out through experience.

Although my studies came first, there wasn't much I missed. We weren't far from Ithaca, New York, home to Cornell University, so we took short road trips several years in a row to visit our fraternity house there. We always had a great time staying with our brothers and they, in turn, visited our campus. The exposure highlighted the very unique cultures at the different schools. While the people were similar, the cultures at the two universities—a traditional Ivy League school and our large, public university—were quite different.

I Try Not to Miss a Meal

My friends and I did various and bizarre, spur-of-the-moment things as well. One night, we had a yearning for a Nathan's hot dog. Nathan's was big in Brooklyn and, just like that, five or six of us climbed into a car and took turns driving for eight hours from Buffalo to Coney Island in Brooklyn. After engorging ourselves with their famous hotdogs, french fries and orange drinks, we got back in the car and drove back to school. Since the University of Buffalo was only one hundred miles from Toronto Canada, we used to go up there too—when we wanted to eat some great food. There was a restaurant, Town & Country, that had an all-you-can-eat buffet that included lobster for an extremely reasonable price. Quite a few times we went up there, forced ourselves to overeat, and then turned right around and went back home. We surely got our money's worth at the all-you-can-eat buffet.

Loser Wins

One evening, my friends and I decided to go to the racetrack with grand plans of becoming rich. A few of us were looking at the racing form in the newspaper at the horses that would be running that day when we saw one named *Lenny Boy*. My mother said, "I want you to take $2 and bet on Lenny Boy for me."

I said, "This is truly a long shot. This horse will never come in."

"That's all right," she said. "I want to bet on *Lenny Boy*."

Prior to the race, the horses were walked around the track area and, after spotting *Lenny Boy*, it occurred to me not to waste my mom's money.

Appearing ready for hamburgers and the glue factory—rather than a race—I took in this old, ugly horse that seemed like he would have trouble finishing, no less winning anything. But I promised my mom that I'd bet her $2 on him and that's what I did.

To my and everyone else's amazement, *Lenny Boy* won! We couldn't believe it. No one in their right mind who saw him prior to the race would have bet on this horse. Needless to say my mom's $2 turned into $45 because it was such a long shot. On my way home that evening, we stopped at a convenience store to change her winnings into all $1 bills. My mom was already asleep so I taped the 45 dollar bills all over our tiny kitchen, and completed the scene with a handmade sign that read "Lenny Boy Finally Paid Off." When she awoke the next morning, she was so excited. If we had cell phone cameras and Instagram then it would have been a great picture that I'm sure would have "gone viral." I can still recall how hard she laughed and how it made her belly shake, which I teased her about, making her laugh even more! It was one of those moments I've never forgotten.

NOT SO INNOCENT

Although dedicated to both my academics and to having fun, my serious work ethic stayed intact. Certainly there was some diversity within our fraternity; a couple of our classmates had really wealthy parents, but most of us knew that nobody was giving us anything for nothing. There was no sense of entitlement, and we knew we had to work for what we were going to get in life. That's probably why many of us chose careers as doctors and lawyers, because we wanted to excel but we knew we had to do it all by ourselves.

The first summer of college, my job took me 90 miles north of New York City to the Catskill Mountains—an unusual ethnic resort community. Primarily populated by transplants from NYC trying to escape the sweltering city heat, it was filled with families who rented small cottages. Some only visited for a week or weekend to escape the humidity and enjoy the cooler mountain air, but many would spend the entire summer there. In the early '60s, most families didn't own two cars, which meant that husbands drove up at the beginning of the summer, rented these little cottages [or, as they were called, *bungalows*] and left their wives and children there, returning to visit on the weekends throughout the summer. A cluster of these bungalows were called *colonies*. During the day, the kids would go to a day camp while the wives socialized with one another.

Many people called the Catskills the *Borscht Belt* and it was predominately made up of Jewish New Yorkers. It was a very specific demographic—and culture. A large percentage of people spoke in Yiddish because most of them were from Eastern European backgrounds and many of the older folks were immigrants. We're talking 1964 here, so it was not even 20 years after World War II. If you do some research you'll find a collection of interesting stories about that time and place. Today, people go to Vegas for entertainment and release, however, during that time in the '60s New Yorkers went to the Catskill Mountains on the weekends to let off some steam. It was well before the sexual revolution, but the relaxed environment led to quite a bit of premarital sex and hooking up that people take for granted today. All of the major comedians used to perform at the hotels in the towns like Monticello. The big hotels included the Grossinger's, the Concord, and Kutcher's.

My first job in the Catskills was as a busboy at the Laurels Hotel. An interesting aspect of this job was that we developed relationships with the guests because we waited on the same people for three meals a day, seven days a week. It was similar to what might happen on a cruise ship today. Our goal was to work them up to receive a significant tip by the end of the week. Depending on what was going on in your life at the time and how skillful you were at telling your life story, many of the guests might have wanted to be your parent—or at least to take care of you. Most of the waiters and busboys were struggling college students studying to become doctors because in that culture, every Jewish mother or father wanted their children to become doctors. You would hear them saying something like, "I'm a pre-med student, I'm going to medical school, and I really need your help." Maybe 10 percent of the workers were actually going to be doctors, but everybody had the same story because it evoked so much sympathy, compassion, and support.

It was actually quite funny when you step back and look at what was going on there at that time. In many cases there weren't nearly as many single young men coming up to the Catskills as there were single young ladies. This left a significant shortage of men to satisfy all of the attention-starved young women, which led them to turn to the wait staff, who were also young college men. Basically, we were sexually harassed by the guests—forced to drink, dance, and party with them. It was paradoxically difficult because we were working a great deal. We had to be in the kitchen setting up for breakfast at 6:30 a.m. dressed in black pants and a white shirt, socks and shoes. Getting up that early in the morning required some rest because as soon as breakfast was over, we had to start setting up for lunch. We slept 10 to a room in a building that resembled the barracks at a camp. All that the room contained were little cots with two-inch mattresses. That's it. The shower was down the hall. It worked, because we didn't need much beyond a place to sleep and clean up.

It was a grueling schedule. Many times we'd work breakfast, get in a quick nap, get through lunch, rest a little bit or take a swim, and then work the dinner rush—which was the most crazy meal of the day. Afterwards, the girls wanted to go out. And we did our best to oblige—at least for a couple of hours. Then at one or two o'clock in the morning, after we had fallen fast asleep, they were pounding on the door of the sleeping quarters enticing us to come out with them again. Remember, many of them were sexually repressed girls (I say in jest) and this was their chance to cut loose. It was a simple matter of supply and demand—a low supply of young men and a significant demand. Although that may sound like a utopia for young men, we were also trying to work and make some money.

Initially it was loads of fun, but after a month or so I was unable to keep up. Exhausted and feeling myself headed toward self-destruction, it was lucky for me that my cousins, who owned a bakery in the nearby town of Woodridge, asked me to come work for them for the rest of the summer.

LENNY THE BAKER

For that time and my age, it was quite a coup to receive $300 cash a week to drive around to all of the bungalow colonies and sell baked goods off of the truck. The women didn't have cars so they were so happy to have fresh bread, bagels, brownies, and pastries delivered to them.

My cousins Al and Charlotte Schwartz lived in a house up the hill from her father, Abe Mortman who started the bakery. He invited me to stay with him at his house that summer. At just five feet tall and 82 years old, Abe was one of the most beautiful human beings I've ever met. He was such a wonderful example for me of what it looked like to combine *doing what you love* with a *strong work ethic*. Although his wife had passed away several years before, he was still there baking bread every evening until one o'clock in the morning. Using wood-fired ovens—it was old world baking at its finest.

Arriving at the bakery before 6:00 every morning, my first task was to go to some of the smaller hotels that didn't bake their own bread. Primarily we delivered bread—rye, white, and everything in between. After that [which they called a *commercial run*] I would come back and fill the truck up with all sorts of baked goods—brownies, cookies, rye bread, and so forth—and go around to the bungalow colonies to sell my wares off of the truck. Typically the older owner of the bungalow colony would be the first house that I encountered at each property. After tooting my horn, he or she would get on their public address system and announce "Lenny, the baker, is on the premises!" They would repeat this five or six times as I did a little swing around the property parking in the same place each day.

All of the women would come up to the truck and pick out what they wanted. Oddly enough, several of the women made it known that what they wanted was *me*. Many of them were wearing their nightclothes or robes and some exposed themselves in ways that a 19-year-old with raging hormones found pretty exciting. I still smile when I think about it. They would say things to me like, "Why don't you come back tonight without this truck?" Most of the time, because of my naïveté, I had no idea what they were talking about. My reply was usually something like, "What good would that do? I won't have any bread to sell if I don't have my truck." Looking back, I can't quite believe how dumb I seemed. It's hard to fathom that was 50-plus years ago... the summer of 1964.

Even after my *third summer* of working for Mortman's Bakery, I still hadn't figured out what was going on. At one time there was a well-known racehorse named Kelso. One day, a woman reached over and grabbed a bagel and said, "These bagels are harder than Kelso's nuts." It wasn't until years later that it dawned on me: She was saying the bagels weren't fresh. I've asked myself more than a few times: *What had I thought of her comment at the time?*

After finishing up at the bungalows around three or four o'clock in the afternoon, my work day continued as I helped out in the retail bakery. One day an older woman with a very heavy Eastern European accent came into the bakery and said, "I want rye bread, half with seeds and half without seeds." Getting half of a rye bread with seeds, and half without seeds, I wrote on the bags the way she sounded when she ordered—one "mit sids" and on the other "mit ot sids." She looked at it, smiled, and told me that was exactly what she wanted. Recalling that day still makes me smile and I'm reminded that those years held so many amazing experiences. It was such a wonderful time for me.

Making enough money those summers to pay all of my expenses during the school year was wonderful, but just as important, were the lessons I learned about life, people, business, and culture. It wasn't a culturally diverse group, but they were certainly intense. Although they were demographically very similar to one another, it was fun for me to meet all kinds of people. It seems that most people who experienced the Catskills of that era agreed it had a big impact on them as well. This was before Las Vegas really took off, so some of the major comedians of the 20th century—Johnny Carson, George Burns, Jack Benny, and Jackie Mason—were all a part of that scene. They talked about the Catskills and seemed to have experienced exactly the same things as I did. It's a cultural phenomenon that has passed and most of those hotels are closed now. One of the last, Grossinger's, closed in 1986. The Concord Hotel was the largest, with 1,500 rooms and a dining room that sat 3,000 people at one time. It closed in 1998. Today, people are hopping on planes and going to Las Vegas instead, and the really well-off New Yorkers go to the Hamptons on eastern Long Island in the summer.

NO EASY 'A'

The first semester of my junior year, my courses became significantly more difficult. Knowing that it was going to be a challenging schedule with four extremely difficult classes, I chose the fifth one based strictly on its reputation for being an "easy 'A'" with little effort. Dr. Marvin Zimmerman was well-known as the professor who didn't require that you to come to class, and all that you had to do to receive an 'A' was to write a half-decent essay at the end of the semester. A wonderful philosophy for a Professor of Philosophy. It had been my plan to save that class for the first semester of my junior year to bolster my grade point average, assuming my difficult courses would be the offset. The second semester was the time to apply for graduate school, making my grades in those courses the most recent and therefore most important ones of my four-year college career.

For a student who didn't care about good grades or academic achievements in high school, college had been a time of intellectual blossoming for me. Although my grades were very good, it didn't come easily for me. Since the material—marketing, finance, management, math, and psychology—was so interesting to me, it was worth the effort to apply myself. By this point, the war was raging in Vietnam and it was my plan to go to graduate school rather than to war. Lo and behold, I got 'As' in all four of my difficult courses, but Dr. "easy 'A'" Zimmerman gave me a 'B.' Completely baffled, I polled the entire class to see what grades each of the other students received. It appeared that my 'B' was the only one in the class. Figuring that maybe he had to choose someone to give a 'B' to, just so it didn't look like he gave everyone 'A's, I went to him to plead my case.

I said, "Dr. Zimmerman, I only took this course to get an 'A.' You have a history and precedent here, and I did everything that everybody else did. Why did I receive a 'B' when everybody else got an 'A'?"

"Well," he said, "you probably just didn't measure up to everybody else."

I explained my plight and said, "If I get straight 'A's this semester, it would be a great impetus for my application for graduate school, ensuring my admission."

He said, "Young man, if my 'B' is the reason you can't get into grad school, you probably shouldn't be there anyway." Nothing I said convinced him to give me the 'A'. He wouldn't even acknowledge that was the case, although I already knew it. A disappointing but important "lesson learned" for me.

EARLY RETAIL

In the late '60s, college graduates, especially business majors, were in high demand. That was probably why I was offered a full-time job in market research for *Corning Glassworks* the summer prior to my senior year of college. My first business trip with them was to St. Louis, Missouri. There were only 15 of us soon-to-be college seniors who were invited into this market research program. Meeting the other students from all around the country was my first experience of the vastness and competitiveness of a national scale. Until then it had always been somewhat locally competitive.

Corning Glassworks was highly selective with whom they chose, and all 15 of us were proud to be included.

In those days, retail sales data didn't exist for manufacturers. Forty years ago, all a company knew, for sure, was what they'd sold to their distributors. There were no bar codes or SKU data, what's now known as *stock keeping units*. Our job was to help Corning gain market information and transactional data by performing retail inventories in the stores where their products were actually sold. Every month we traveled to multiple retail locations with a long pad that listed 100 of their items [branded Pyrex and Corningware] to check off how many of each item were actually on the shelves. A great perk of the job was that they compensated us for our work hours, travel time, and travel expenses. The objective for Corning was to create an inroad with top students, hoping we would feel some sense of commitment and loyalty to the organization after graduation. Throughout the year, they sent me information about what was going on within the company. It made me feel included and important. They also kept in physical contact by having me report to a regional manager occasionally.

I continued to work for them through graduate school—making them even more anxious for me to come work for them after completing my education. Work for Corning was not nearly as interesting as working in the Catskills and interacting with all of those people, but it was probably more important to my overall business education. Although it was much less personal and the tedium of counting products wasn't fun, my understanding of why I was doing it remained intact. It wasn't terribly important for me, [although I think it was to Corning] but the flexibility and compensation worked out great at the time. It certainly wasn't something to aspire to do long term, but it was a great part-time college job.

SEEKING JOY

Lucky enough to have discovered my passion during college, it is fulfilling for me to help people discover what motivates them. A large part of being able to discover your calling is the ability to tune into yourself and your inner speak. One of my favorite visual examples of inner speak is a scene from the movie *Animal House*. A young man has a dilemma when he takes a girl, who is obviously drunk, up to his room. On one shoulder there is an angel who says, "Leave her alone. Let her go to sleep."

On the other shoulder sits the devil who says, "F@#k her!"

The angel says, "No, you're not going to do that."

For me that's inner speak, the angel and devil who sit on our shoulders throughout our lives telling us what to do—or what not to do. And, in many cases, how to do it. The question is, what is the conversation taking place within each of us? Keep in mind, we have control over the outcome because we oversee both sides of that conversation. The largest factor that influences our inner speak is the attitude that we have toward ourselves because it creates the context of that conversation. If, deep-down inside, we feel good about ourselves, we're going to have positive internal conversations, allowing us to create an internal environment that will inspire us to do the best we can do.

Following *your* passion is critical, because there will be outside speak, too. And it's completely different from your inner speak. The outside conversation, which is advice from people who don't have to live with the results, may say *you should* go to law school, or business school, or do any number of things. If they don't have to live with the consequences, they have nothing at risk. If they have nothing to risk, they shouldn't participate in the decision about what path you should follow.

When deciding what it is that you want to do, have the conversation with yourself, taking advice from *your* heart and *your* mind. Ask yourself, "What is it that I'm really good at? What is it that I really love?" When you can find the intersection of those two important imperatives, you will find your direction.

Chapter 4

LIFE AND DEATH

*"I had learned enough by that point
that even if I didn't know what to do,
I knew that I had to do something."*

My father had rheumatic fever as a child, which apparently damaged his heart. Although he knew his heart was not in the greatest shape, it didn't deter him from living the way he wanted to. His favorite expression when anybody tried to talk to him about his health was, "As the famous Polish nobleman once said, 'If you drink you die, and if you don't drink, you die.'" Frankly, that's the way he lived his life. He drank, smoked, ate the wrong foods, didn't exercise, and died young at just 47 years old. But he lived life on his own terms. He seemed comfortable with that.

NO GOOD-BYE

In the mid 1960s, medication to help reduce high blood pressure was not available, so those afflicted just dealt with the symptoms, and those concerned enough worked on what they could to help themselves. At one point, my father's blood pressure was so high he had double vision. Understanding a bit more today about the ramifications of high blood pressure, his condition was probably not a surprise. Doctor Syde Taheri, a heart surgeon and a good friend of his, told him he was a candidate for bypass surgery, which was still experimental at the time. Unfortunately, he never had the chance to see if it would help, and probably would not have wanted to be a pioneer.

On March 4, 1967, after returning home from a Saturday night dinner out with my mom, he collapsed and died instantly. While it was probably a blessing for him, it was life-changing for the rest of my family. I happened to be with him that night. We were talking, when suddenly he coughed, gagged, fell to the ground, and died. While I gave him mouth-to-mouth resuscitation, my mom called for an ambulance. They arrived a short time later, but he was gone within minutes of falling to the floor.

Up to that point in my life I had never seen a dead body—no less that of my father falling right in front of me and not being able to do anything about it. It was a profoundly traumatic moment for me. My mother and younger sister were hysterical, so it was up to me to be the adult in the room. It wasn't my nature to shirk responsibility, but I had no experience in handling this type of situation. Certainly I had learned enough by that point in my life that even if I didn't know *what* to do, I knew that I had to do *something*. Either you have to step up—or everything falls apart. There's a difference between knowing exactly what to do, and having the tools to solve a problem, figure out a next step, and think clearly enough to navigate through what was truly a disaster.

We followed the ambulance to the hospital and the doctor came out to talk with us. "I'm sorry," he said. "There was nothing we could do."

"What happened?" we asked.

"He had a massive heart attack," the doctor informed us. And time seemed to stop for me that evening, along with his heart.

The next day, I was in a funeral home alongside my uncles choosing a casket for my father. My recurring thought was, *What the hell am I doing here?* It didn't seem real or even possible that I would never see my father again. It is a Jewish tradition to honor the death of a close family member by observing Shiva, a week-long mourning period. In the more orthodox congregations of Judaism, the family of the deceased also went to temple each morning. Even though my father was not terribly religious, my uncles and I attended services each day out of respect. Typically, it entailed sitting on a hard bench so you wouldn't get too comfortable. After arriving at 8:00 in the morning and saying some prayers, the rabbi gave us each a little shot of whiskey. It was cheap and harsh so it was painful to drink, causing my whole body to shake as I swallowed it. That week of mourning my father was one long blur, not from the whiskey, but because it seemed almost unfathomable that this could be happening.

After his funeral, my aunts and uncles returned to their homes, leaving the three of us on our own. It felt unreal that my father wasn't there anymore, as if it was a cruel magic trick where, with the wave a wand, he simply vanished. At age 21 and just two months shy of graduating from college, it didn't seem right or fair to have lost my father. After returning to school the following week, nothing was the same. My perspective on life and my future had completely changed and it felt like I was watching everybody walk around inside this huge bubble where nothing had happened to them. But to me, it felt like I was stumbling through endless piles of rubble in the aftermath of an earthquake... without anyone taking note of my struggles. I thought to myself, *Don't they know what just happened? Don't they understand?*

For the next two months, it seemed like I was watching my fellow classmates on television. In hindsight, I would describe it as an out-of-body experience. It was very strange to be in the midst of so many people, yet feel so far away, alone, and detached.

Of course they didn't understand. They couldn't and I wouldn't have wished it on anyone, but it felt painfully awkward. My whole world had turned upside-down while nobody seemed to notice or care. This was a huge epiphany, teaching me empathy and compassion for what others are going through at any given time. Until I had lived through a heartbreaking experience, it was difficult for me to truly understand that what was really important to me, was irrelevant to most people. It was hard for me to tackle the concept that no one was rushing up and putting their arms around me. The people who were close to me were sensitive and kind, but no one else had a clue about what I'd been through and how it had shook me to my core, the heartache reverberating daily.

As they say, *time is a healer* and eventually life began to feel a bit more normal for me as the days and weeks passed by. Sadly, my mother was never the same. It was painfully evident that the day my father died, parts of her died along with him. Prior to his death, she was completely devoted to him and her children. Being so dependent on him to make decisions and handle the tough issues in life, left her somewhat incompetent when he was gone. Without him she became insecure and nervous, never driving a car again. Although she was a young woman, she never had another relationship or any men in her life. She was so devoted to him that I don't think she even thought about it. I never had that conversation with her, but my guess is if we had ever suggested there was "a really nice man we knew that she should meet," she wouldn't have had anything to do with it.

She leaned on me and I tried to be there for her, but I had a life to live too. My sister took on a caretaker role, much more so than I did. We sensed that there was very little we could do to help her, so we just accepted where she was and let her do as much or little as she was comfortable with. I wouldn't have described her as "unhappy," she just wasn't the mother we knew before my father's passing. Eventually, she moved to New Jersey and lived with her brother for a while, helping him in his business. Fully embracing her role as a grandmother when my sister and I each had our own children, she showered her grandchildren with love and attention. Even though my guess is that she never fully recovered, she was always a beautiful and loving woman and mother.

L'CHAIM

Prior to my father's death, I had met the woman I knew I would marry. She was a girl from the neighborhood who had captured my heart at an early age. Eva and I had finalized our plans to get married in May, on the day before my college graduation. Everyone concurred that if my father had had a voice in it, he would have said, "Go ahead and get married! Do what you need to do, I wish you well." We didn't see any real reason to postpone the wedding—even though it seemed to be so soon after my father's passing. Without a doubt there was a palpable void left by my father's absence, but we celebrated a joyous wedding day nonetheless.

High school sweethearts, Eva and I met when we were teenagers. I was 16 and she was 15. Although we went to different high schools, we met through a local Jewish organization. She was beautiful, smart, dedicated to her studies, and very charming. It was easy for me to fall for her. Although we attended different colleges, we stayed together over those four years. Eva was quiet and worked hard in school, studying biology at the New York State Teachers College in Buffalo. Wanting to share her love for biology, she eventually became a biology teacher. Always the dutiful person, it didn't occur to me to stop and question if Eva was really the right person for me to marry. We had dated for so long, marriage seemed like the inevitable, responsible and desirable next step. At that time and place, the cultural norm was to finish high school, graduate from college, get married, and start a family. That was considered the American Dream, and it all felt very "normal" and comfortable to me.

Along with marrying Eva, came the blessing of her wonderful family. Both of her parents had been incarcerated in concentration camps during World War II. They were taken from their home in Poland and, fortunately, were youthful and very strong so they were considered assets by the Nazis. Although married before the war, they were separated and placed into different concentration camps. Miraculously, they both survived and found each other in what they euphemistically called a *displaced persons camp* after the war. Their story of survival and reconnection was beautiful, but darkened by the tragedy of losing both of their families to the senseless holocaust. It was shortly after their reunion in the displaced person camp in Germany that Eva was born.

Following her birth, the United Jewish Federation offered to bring the family to the United States and help find them a job and place to live. Her father, a skilled tailor, found work easily making men's suits at a large factory in Buffalo, New York. They had such an interesting family dynamic, living very modestly with what seemed like almost zero material desires. The most inspiring part was to watch how they lived each day: grateful to be alive.

Physically, they were tiny—which made me feel like a giant next to them. During visits to their home they marveled at my (and my friends') physical size. But what they lacked in stature, they made up for in spirit and strength. Some of my most profound life lessons were learned just by observing the small nuances in the words they regularly used. Eva's mother would say, "Do you need some bread?" It was about a *need,* rather than a *want.* There were no wants or likes in their vocabulary, just needs. They seemed to have no sense of desire for anything material and were extremely grateful to just have their basic needs met after living through the atrocities they had experienced. In retrospect, it was so apparent to me because it was a completely different way of asking a question. It wasn't because they were immigrants, many people were in the United States from all parts of the world. It was because of the experiences they had endured. I can still hear her saying, "Do you need a coffee?" or "Do you need some more coffee?" My mother, on the other hand, would say, "Oh, let's have another cup of coffee," or "...have some more," telling me what I needed. One environment was brimming with abundance and generosity while the other was one of survival and sustenance. They were two completely different worlds. This was the first time in my life that I saw the vast difference between needs and wants, and began to understand the strong cultural variations.

You couldn't help but admire how hardworking and lovely Eva's parents were, even after all that they had been forced to suffer through. To find the tenacity to survive and accomplish what they did was inspiring. I was thoroughly impressed with them as people and embraced them as my extended family. To a certain extent, that attitude transferred to their daughter. She, too, was very quiet and hardworking. Her needs were simple. There was nothing at all flashy or pretentious about her. The fourth member of their family, her brother Harry, was seven years younger than Eva. I do not exaggerate: He was an absolute genius. And probably one of the smartest people I've ever known.

Because of this family's limited means and exposure, when Harry was ready to go to college his parents planned to send him to the same local university that I had attended. I said, "You know, he's more than capable of doing whatever he wants. He will find it boring." While still in high school, he was already taking and mastering difficult college courses like calculus. His intelligence was not only in math but linguistics and English as well. He had taught himself Japanese—from a book. He was a bright and gifted kid.

When I look back on the maximum score you could receive on the math section of the SATs (800, likewise for the verbal section of the Scholastic Aptitude Test...) it meant that combined, a perfect score was 1600. Harry received a score of 1590, with 800 in math and a 790 on the verbal, which apparently was very unusual at the time. Socially awkward, Harry never really ventured out on his own, so after doing some research and figuring out that MIT was probably the best math school in the country, I contacted the university and personally took him the Massachusetts Institute of Technology (MIT) for an interview with the Director of Admissions.

I said to the Admissions Director, "We're obviously impressed with this young man because he's our family, but you represent MIT so you have a much better perspective on how special he may or may not be." We were interested to learn how he would rank when compared to the other candidates who had applied to MIT. It wasn't a really risky question, but I wanted him to articulate it since he wasn't telling me anything specific.

He said, "Well, this is MIT and we do get several students every year who receive an 800 on the math section, but I can tell you that I've never seen anybody combine it with 790 on the verbal side." He concluded: "So even by our standards, he is pretty special."

I said, "His parents have no financial resources and cannot afford to send him to MIT."

"Finances will not be a problem," the director told us. We'll use a combination of work, scholarships, loans, or whatever we have to do—but we will make sure that a lack of financial resources won't keep him from attending our school."

"That's all we need to hear," I told the Admissions Director as a shook his hand. Mission accomplished.

Indeed, Harry went to MIT and, of course, did amazingly well in his studies of electrical engineering and computer science. After graduation, he went on to Harvard where he earned a Ph.D. in Linguistics. Keep in mind that this was decades before laptops or personal computers and laptops were fixtures in offices, homes, and vehicles. And at one point during Harry's years at school, he worked on building computers. Knowing he had the capacity to invent something really spectacular, I said to him, "Look, you're a brilliant young man. Why don't you just tinker in an environment that suits you best, where you can come up with things that nobody has thought of?" I went on to tell him: "Whatever you come up with, I'll market it and figure out how to sell it. And during that process I'll pay all of your living expenses."

Harry had other ideas. "No, thank you," he told me, "I just want to teach."

Reluctantly I had to say, "Okay. Whatever makes you happy..."

It was evident to me that he possessed the ability to figure out a way to communicate with computers verbally because he understood the scientific study of language. I had no doubt in his talent to translate his language skills into electrical impulses and communicate with computers verbally. In those days, areas like artificial intelligence were unheard of. Although it was exciting to me as I tried to make an entrepreneur out of him, he wasn't interested. He was an academic at heart. One interesting thing he did after realizing that Yiddish was a dying language was to co-write a Yiddish dictionary that you can still purchase today by Harry Bochner & Solon Beinfeld.

MISSION ACCOMPLISHED

One day after Eva and I wed, and just shy of three months since my father's passing, I received my Bachelor's Degree. It was bittersweet. I was ready, excited, and proud to receive my diploma, and filled with a sense of appreciation for my effort to not only graduate, but to do well academically. It was an important milestone, having exceeded my own expectations. Although, I recalled the conversation that changed my philosophy to one of impressing myself instead of my father as my motivation in life, it still would have been a happier day if he had been there to celebrate with me.

Although my academic goals and chosen career path had remained intact over the years, the death of my father changed my perspective. Many of my classmates seemed to have changed even more than I had. When we started college everybody was *preppy,* although that term really didn't exist in those days. Back then we called it *collegiate.* Basically it meant the same thing—short hair, clean-shaven, and a uniform of button-down shirts and khakis. Then things changed dramatically. And the Vietnam War had a hand in that. From when we started college in the fall of 1963 until we finished in the spring of 1967, everybody went through an enormous transformation.

At graduation, most of my classmates hadn't cut their hair or shaved in a couple of years. Many of them were very much against the war, and had discovered marijuana and other drugs. Quite a few friends who had started their college years as clean cut young men and women had transformed into just the opposite. They wore army flak jackets, while my attire was still a London Fog raincoat. I had short hair and was cleanly shaven, [except for a mustache] and carrying an attaché case. Thinking back, I must have looked as strange to them as they appeared to me. We were there together, still friends, but residing in two very distinct cultures.

Watching many of my friends succumb to the pleasures of drugs scared me. So many of them lost their ambition and energy, and experienced huge changes in their attitudes. Not wanting to go down that road or take the risk that I might not be able to control myself, it was a conscious decision on my part not to try drugs. Not because it was *wrong* to do, but because of my fear of what it might do to me. It's not that they went off the deep end; they didn't. But they certainly changed visually *and* their ambition levels and enthusiasm for their careers and futures changed. Most of them recovered from that period. I was unprepared—and unwilling—to take the chance of becoming seduced by drugs, not because I thought my outlook was better or worse, but because it was just my choice in how to deal with it at that time. We were still friends, but we certainly had less in common. There was never any real pressure on me to do drugs, it was more a case of them being very readily available. If you wanted to, you were more than welcome to join in... but nobody said *"You've got to do this."*

Academically, there was a change with many of my friends as well. Most of them started out in pre-law or pre-med with lofty goals, but during those four undergraduate years many of them changed their majors to psychology and philosophy. One of the few who didn't change majors, my heart remained with business. My interests didn't change, they just became more focused on delving deeper into marketing and finance. It was always extremely stimulating for me and so unlike high school when my teacher would report, "Leonard is not achieving to his potential."

High school was just a little too easy because it felt like a regurgitation of whatever the teacher wanted without having to put any effort into it.

Have you ever opened up a new book and felt—and *heard*—the binding crack? Well, I would return my brand new books at the end of the high school year, untouched and unread, but not before cracking the binding on the last day of school just to be clever. My report cards in high school were full of 'A's and 'B's, but those grades were from paying attention in class and being able to recite back as much my teachers wanted me to on tests. Looking back, it was probably nothing more than youthful arrogance, but college was very different. Stimulated and challenged by subjects that were interesting to me, I went way above and beyond what was necessary to achieve good grades. There were very few semesters when my name didn't appear on the Dean's List.

I LOVE TO...

Have you ever asked yourself, *What do I really love to do? What am a good at? How can I best use the skills and talents I've been given?* These are questions that I pondered as a young boy and ones that I see so many people struggle with. Sometimes it's hard to figure out what it is you really like... and how we'd like our lives to unfold.

A key, I've found, is to focus on what piqued your interest to the point that you're bursting with curiosity. For many people, it is one of life's greatest moments. That energy and drive will propel you to dig deeper to discover where your greatest interests lie. A great question to ask yourself if you're having trouble figuring this out is, *Where do I find myself exerting the most energy when I'm not required to?*

Chapter 5

CHASING A CAREER

*"My goal was always
to do something that was gratifying for me."*

My original intent after graduation was to continue my education at Columbia University in New York, but after my father's death, my plans changed. Feeling the need to stay closer to home to help care for my mother, sister, and new wife, I remained at the University of Buffalo. There were several reasons for my interest in pursuing a Master's Degree. I felt certain it would open additional doors for me, and I believed in my ability to go far in life. I had done rather well with obtaining my Bachelor's Degree and I was also adamant that my future would not include going to war, and remaining enrolled in college ensured my continued deferment from the draft and the Army.

Vietnam was raging and I found myself, like many other young people at the time, bewildered by the war. It was very unpopular and few of us understood what we were doing there since, in our minds, it was a civil war. There was a draft, new people were conscripted into the war, forced to go and fight. It was an awful time. My feelings were not very different from most others, and I was adamant in my conviction that I wasn't going to war. People defected to Canada and it was a real concern of mine to avoid the Vietnam War at all costs. You could say that the first strategic plan that I ever wrote was my plan to stay out of the army.

Approaching it as a serious business project, my timeline involved utilizing all of the different deferment options that I separated into plans labeled A, B, C, and D. Eligible to be drafted up to the age of 26, my plans included involving myself in the activities that supported a deferment. If for some reason my deferment was declined, I studied up on the ways to appeal and how long that would take. It seemed pretty likely that if all of my plans and appeals failed, I would be older than 26, therefore, free and clear.

BACK TO 7ᵀᴴ GRADE...

Happy to have entered graduate school for numerous reasons, it was a fantastic experience. My classes were small, affording me close relationships with my professors. Along with my classes, I was simultaneously given the opportunity to teach in a middle school in an underprivileged area. Desperate for teachers, my job included teaching Math as well as English during the two years it took me to complete my MBA. For me, this equated to serving my country in what I felt was a much more positive and productive manner than putting on a uniform and shouldering arms. Rather than fighting in the jungles of Vietnam, my time was spent in an urban poverty-stricken area helping children learn.

The kids seemed to enjoy it as well because we had a wonderful relationship. I'm not sure if it was so enjoyable for me because I knew it wasn't forever and because I allowed my style to be laid-back and relaxed. We laughed, joked, and had a great time together. But, not wanting to just get by with teaching the minimum required curriculum material straight from the books, my approach was to use my time there as an opportunity do some memorable activities with the children. And I did it as much for them as for myself. I was committed to having a really enjoyable experience and it was much more interesting for me to talk about my interests. It was my job to teach them math—fractions and percentages—and how they related to the real world. Usually my lessons were spontaneously devised the night before, like my idea to set up a little company in math class.

The next day I came in and handed a cup of Coca-Cola to each student. After choosing the most disruptive boy in the class to be the president of the company, I said, "Billy has come up with a new idea. He calls it Coca-Cola. Here's Billy's new idea—he's created this drink." Then I began to engage them with questions: "What do you think?"

"We like it. It's really good!" came a chorus of responses.

I said, "Do you think other people will like it? Could you sell it to others?"

"Oh yeah, we could sell it!"

I took it a step farther: "Do you think we can make some money?"

They got excited and involved, saying, "Yeah, we could make money!"

I asked, "Billy, how much do you need to get started?"

His response was immediate: "a million dollars." I wrote $1,000,000 dollars on the chalkboard.

I said, "I'm very excited about this. I'm going to invest $100,000 into Billy's company. Anybody else interested in participating?" They all signed up for different levels. Afterwards, we converted their investments into percentages to demonstrate how much of the company they owned. As the semester went on, I said, "Billy needs some more money because he's run out so we need to add another $500,000. Who's going to come in with that? And how does that relate to what we already have?" Creating different scenarios I said, "You are now stock holders in the company of Coca Cola and Billy's the president who runs this company. At some point in time, if we have earnings and start making money, you're going to get a return on your investment." This is how they learned about calculating percentage returns.

After they began to understand our classroom fantasy company, our next lesson was to have each of them pick a stock on the New York Stock

Exchange. Again, it held my interest because it was actually a part of my life. My father was a stock broker. After getting licensed to sell securities, I had taken over quite a few of his clients. Thanks to my friend in Admissions at UB, my class schedule was just as spectacular as it had been during my undergraduate program, which allowed me the time to teach and work as a stockbroker. Using what came naturally to me when teaching, I said to my math class, "We're going to write down the price that you buy your stock at today. The person that has the largest percentage increase during this semester is going to win a very special prize."

Our first step centered on how to read the stock charts so they could check what their "investments" were doing. After teaching them that percentages were more important than dollar amounts, we discussed how everyone was doing by calculating their percentages during class. The principal, Charles Baumler, began to notice that his morning newspaper was becoming very popular. Billy and some of his classmates would go into his office and say, "Mr. Baumler, can I see your paper?"

He'd say, "Sure... but why?"

"We need to check our stocks," they'd say.

He came to me one day and asked, "What's with the kids and this stock market thing?"

I explained what we were doing and he loved it. It must have seemed strange to him at first to see these seventh- and eighth-grade kids from families that had very little in terms of financial resources, reading the stock market listings every morning. It was such a great experience for me, and it was obvious they enjoyed it as well. We really had fun. It worked well for me because I liked the challenge of entertaining and teaching them at the same time. Teaching English was enjoyable for me as well. One memorable assignment I had them do was to write a love letter.

One day I said, "We're going to write a love letter."

They said, "Not me!"

Pointing to a classmate across the aisle, I said to one student, "You could write it to her."

He said, "Oh, no!" His classmates and I laughed.

I said, "Well, then... whom do you love?"

"My mom."

"Okay," I said, "Why don't you write a love letter to your mom?" It was a great exercise that forced them to write down their innermost feelings and learn how to express themselves. To my surprise, they loved it and most of them volunteered to share their letters. To my delight, some of the kids I taught connected with me later in life to tell me how much they appreciated the time we spent together. Talk about heartwarming and rewarding.

After two years of applying myself to the best of my ability, I did very well and earned my Master's Degree in Business Management and Marketing. Although I was proud of myself for having set and accomplished another milestone, my father's physical absence from my graduation pulled at me. Somehow, though, I could feel him and his joy as we celebrated. With graduation, came the freedom to field offers from many corporations that were extremely interested in business majors with an MBA. Unfortunately when I graduated, the war was still going strong in Vietnam and my school deferment was no longer valid.

ARE YOU KIDDING?

December 1, 1969 was the day of the infamous lottery used to determine the order for reporting for their draft physical for military service in the Vietnam War. No longer a student, I was one of the many unlucky ones called in for a physical in 1970. Some of my high school classmates happened to be there at the same time. I remember one of them saying to me, "I'm just going to go and do this."

"You don't have to do it. There are ways to get out of it," I pointed out.

"No," he said, "I'm just going to go do it and get it over with."

That was the bottom line for me as well, and I told him: "I'm not going to war or having anything to do with this war, but I'm going to go through with my physical."

The first thing they did was take my height and weight. The young man doing the basic measurements was very short so he stood up on a step stool to try and use the height ruler they put on the top of your head as you stood on the scale. For some reason he took the silver arm and slammed it down on my head. Although it felt abusive, I kept quiet because the way he slammed it made it come down and forward, showing my height to be 5'9" instead of 6'3". My weight was 220 pounds.

A hearing test followed. He said, "Raise your right hand when you hear something on the right and raise your left hand when you hear sounds on the left."

I put the headphones on and listened, but I didn't hear anything. I came out said, "I didn't hear a thing. Does that mean I fail?"

He said, "Did you hear the instructions?"

"Yes," I said.

"That's good enough."

At the end of the physical, a doctor not much older than me came in. He said, "Is there anything else that would preclude you from being in the service?"

"Well, I brought a letter from my podiatrist because I have flat feet. I thought maybe that might get me out because I can't march or walk very far," I said trying to make it sound like it was the worst thing in the world.

He said, "Let's see your feet." He looked at my feet and said, "They don't look that bad to me." He looked at my chart, then back at me, and then at my chart again. He looked me in the eye and said, "Why don't you gain a couple of pounds? If you gained some weight you'd be too heavy for your height."

Apparently, the miscalculation in my height made me fall just two pounds short of being too overweight to qualify for the draft. That's when it became apparent he was working with me. He was on my side, because it was obvious that my documented height was inaccurate.

"You know what?" he said. "I'm going to give you a six-month deferment for your feet. After six months they won't bother you because you'll be too old so they won't call you back for another physical. You'll be done with it."

"I 'd like to kiss you," I told him.

He said, "That's not necessary."

That was it. My years of worrying about the draft and dying in Vietnam were finally over.

THE WORST BEST OFFER

Fortunately for me, in the 1960s and early 1970s, having an MBA was very unusual. Most major corporations were competing for MBA graduates from accredited schools. It was in vogue and certainly not typical, so it put me in a great position to entertain and choose from numerous offers. Although my initial motivation was to avoid the draft and a stint in the Army, it afforded me a wonderful education. After interviewing with and receiving offers from some of the top companies in the United States—

IBM, Procter & Gamble, Corning Glassworks, McGraw-Hill Publishing, Ford Motor Company, and Simmons—I had a choice to make. The worst job offer, hands down, was from Simmons.

While considering the offers, I continued to work as a stockbroker. Without giving it my full time and attention, my income was about $25,000 a year. In 1970, $25,000 a year for a 25-year-old meant I was living rather well. On top of that, my wife was working as a teacher and making around $8,000 a year. So, for just the two of us, we were doing pretty well financially. Most of the job offers I received were in the $20,000 to $25,000 a year range. Except for Simmons. That offer was for $9,000 a year. As I've said, it was (by a significant amount) the worst offer I received because they didn't take into account my MBA. They didn't care about it. Unlike all of the other companies that had a developmental management program where they hired you with the intent of management training and, one day, a position as a manager in the company, Simmons didn't have anything like this.

During the interview process with a company, it's typical to continue to go higher and higher up the food chain as you progress. During my last interview at IBM, I had no idea what my interviewer was talking about. He did most of the talking, and I said to myself, *You are so far out of your element that you're going to be very uncomfortable here.* It wasn't a lack of confidence. It was just that the conversation was so far above my head that I knew it would be a very long road to get to where this man was. It felt extremely uncomfortable and I knew it wasn't the right fit for me.

With the other companies, as the interviews elevated through the organization, the people became more and more imposing. At Simmons, it was just the opposite. The higher my interviews went, the less impressive the interviewers, the corporate executives, seemed to me. It felt like a college fraternity rush where they said, "You've got to join us because we play golf, have a good time, and we're the leaders in the industry." They were selling *me*—rather than me selling them on my strengths and skills. It was apparent to me that Simmons was upside down, unlike all of the other companies I interviewed with. Young and arrogant enough at my final interview to believe that I was smarter than he was—and if not smarter, then certainly prepared to work harder than he was—this opportunity seemed to be screaming at me. My thought process was there was an abundance of opportunity at Simmons and maybe they would destroy the company so much that there won't be anything left, but if I handled it right, I would learn a great deal, get more responsibility at a younger age, and be able to move up quickly. My fear of them ruining it before that happened was quieted by the fact that with my education, and experience, there would be something else available if there had to be.

To my sincere delight, I was right. My acceleration through the company was rapid, much faster than it would have been if it were run well. If you are wondering why my choice wasn't to continue a career as a stockbroker, it was because I needed a balance between making money and doing something meaningful and valuable. Making money was never my motivation. My goal was always to do something that was gratifying for me personally. It made sense that if my approach was right, the financial rewards would follow at some point.

Teaching was a great experience because it showed me how good it felt to do something I really enjoyed, while significantly helping others. If it could have provided a decent income, it may have been something I would have pursued long term. It did teach me, along with the other jobs I'd held, that it was important to do something that I felt passionate about. The stock brokerage sales business was very difficult because to me it felt as if you could never truly make people happy. My theory is that if you manage expectations and promise reasonable returns and exceed those expectations, people would be really happy with you. That's not the way it is with securities sales.

For example, I might say to you, "Let's buy this stock at $10 a share." You buy the stock on my advice, and it goes to $20 a share. I'd say, "I think it's time to sell. We've made a nice profit, so let's move on."

A client might say, "Oh, great, absolutely." Then the stock doesn't stop moving and goes from $20 to $30 after you sold it. How does a client feel? Annoyed at me for a missed opportunity? Or pleased with a nice profit? What if the stock you buy at $10 a share goes down to $2, and I suggest you sell. You're certainly not happy, *right?* Let's say the unusual happens: You buy it at $10, sell it at $20, and then it goes down to $2. You would say, "Man, Len Gaby is a genius." But that's not what happens. People think *they* are the genius. They think they've solved the riddle of making money in the stock market, so it's not the person who gave them the advice, it's all about them. And when the best possible outcome isn't achieved, the broker is the one at fault. Consequently, you can never really win. Not that my goal is to win all the time, but I need to have a sense of satisfaction that my work helped my customer, and that I added value to the transaction.

In the investment business, no matter how hard I worked at bettering my understanding about the investments, there were so many variables beyond my control that it never felt comfortable to me. There were so many things that could change and that uncertainty had no appeal for me on a long-term basis. I didn't like the way it made me feel about myself because my goal was to become more competent. The problem was the only thing I was getting more competent at was my ability to sell. Selling more stock was attainable, but making more money through my sales skills without truly helping my clients felt wrong. It felt as if I had to disengage my moral compass and just maximize my income, which didn't sit right with me. I'm not saying it can't be a very reasonable goal for others, based on what works for them. It just wasn't the right fit for the future I envisioned.

With Simmons, my sales skills could be used to sell a tangible product. I reveled in relating what the products could do for a buyer and what made them really wonderful products. At point it was the buyers' prerogative to buy or not buy that was fulfilling for me. As a Sales Manager at Simmons, I was able to present a product and show wholesalers and retailers how to sell it and make money.

Selling was only one part of my job. The other part—which I didn't really understand until I got into the trenches—was managing people. Working with people and helping them be successful was the aspect that I loved the most. As a stockbroker, all you can do is tell people to work harder, make more phone calls, and give them some techniques and tips for improvement. At Simmons, my job included teaching people how to create events and promotions to show their customers they appreciated them. We were doing tangible things to create a more profitable business. My greatest satisfaction came from guiding people's development and helping them define and reach their goals. Not everyone who is good at sales is a good sales manager because success as a manager involves the ability to teach and motivate people. Keeping people excited about what they were doing came pretty naturally to me and it was extremely fulfilling.

As time went on, my position encompassed not only managing people, but the management of a business that included understanding strategy and complex issues and finding innovative solutions. Most importantly, these challenges required the ability to implement solutions within an environment full of intricate limitations and balancing that within a competitive marketplace. What kept me going was the stimulation from what I was doing and the challenges that were in front of me, never really giving a thought about the money I was making. After taking the position with Simmons, it never again occurred to me to concern myself with how much I was making or how much I was going to make—because, for me, that was never the issue. In retrospect, my lack of focus on money gave me the opportunity to make more money. My advice is to do what you love and what you're good at. Typically, if you love something, you will be good at it. In my experience, you'll never put in enough work or effort if you don't love what you are doing. Money is really irrelevant. It's the last thing on the list.

If you think about it though, it makes sense because the market, economy, and the world will reward people who do things exceedingly well. Look at the big picture: If you do something uncommonly well—much better than other people and it's a meaningful thing to do—you're going to get rewarded somehow. Now, if the reward that you want or need is financial, then think about what you're doing and put it in the context of how to get financially rewarded for it. People with higher callings are rewarded in spiritual and less materialistic ways, which is wonderful too. You may wonder why someone would become a priest or give his or her life to their church or to their God. Obviously, they're giving up financial reward for something that is more important to them. People who become teachers have the reward of helping people learn and educating others in the process.

Just as I had learned in college, I wanted it all. It was important for me to do something that felt valuable and fulfilling to me, while sustaining my appetite for the "finer things in life." That was important to me. It has always been in my nature to choose quality over quantity. If something that I want is going to cost a bit more, I would rather do without than settle. At my 60th birthday party, my daughter, Rebecca, said, "My dad always taught me to appreciate the finer things in life. And then he taught me how to appreciate life."

It seems to me that in our quest for *infinite wealth,* we need to focus on what is truly important to each of us. Exerting our energy toward goals and objectives that are not our own or shared, only drains us of our passion. Working toward the goals we set for ourselves energizes us for the journey ahead.

Chapter 6

A DOOR OPENS

*"Something that sets people apart
is their willingness to go above and beyond their call of duty."*

In February 1970, my professional career began as a trainee at Simmons Mattress Company. Although still living in Buffalo, my training took place at a nearby Simmons factory in Elizabeth, New Jersey. I still recall reporting to Norm Hipsley, the Northeast Regional Sales Manager. Simmons didn't have a formal training program so they had me travel with various salespeople to observe how they operated and developed relationships with customers, and to get an overall feel for the dynamics and culture of the company.

Their customers were divided into different categories based on size. The largest accounts in New Jersey were typically department stores like Macy's, Bloomingdales, Abraham & Strauss, and Bamberger's, a division of Macy's. My first trainer, Everett Smith, had at least 30 years of experience with Simmons and was a sales representative for the smaller accounts. A bright and charming man, Everett was extremely involved with his customers and was an ideal example of what a sales representative should be. For the better part of a month, I soaked up his invaluable skills, experience, and charm.

An indelible lesson I learned from him has stuck with me over the years. One of Everett's smaller accounts didn't have the financial resources to advertise on its own because an advertisement in *The Star-Ledger* in New Jersey was an expensive proposition. To overcome this dilemma, Everett put together four non-competing retailers to share one ad. The newspaper covered all of New Jersey, so each store had its own small radius of influence from northern, central, or southern New Jersey. It was quite ingenious to combine four retailers together knowing that the person reading the ad would *only* be attracted to the one in closest proximity and most convenient for them. Collectively, they were able to run a larger, more prominent ad at a quarter of what it would have cost them individually. The bonus was that the cooperative strategy provided each of them with a much broader marketing impact. Although the approach Everett used was not new or original, he used it frequently and successfully.

Everett reminded me of *Colombo*. I'm referring to a television series starring Peter Falk as a homicide detective with the Los Angeles Police Department. I remember thinking of Everett as Colombo—hunched over, wearing a rumpled raincoat, and always extremely humble. It seemed as if almost everything he said was apologetic. He said, "I'm sorry," quite often. One day, we went into one store where the owner had been on vacation and wasn't available to sign up when Everett was running the ad. Everett took it upon himself to sign him up for it, knowing full well that was what he would have wanted. He greeted the owner and said, "Look, I'm probably going to get fired for this but I committed you to an ad without your permission. You were on vacation and I just thought you would not want to miss this opportunity. Please forgive me for overstepping my bounds, but I signed you up and your share of the ad is $500. Simmons will cover $250 of it, but I obligated you for the other $250. Please don't shoot me."

The owner smiled and said, "Everett, you know I always sign up for these ads. I really appreciate you looking out for me while I was away. Thank you. Don't be silly—this is great."

We walked out and Everett was smiling too, happy to have filled his order to cover the ad.

I said to Everett, "That was just amazing. I love the way you handled that."

"Why?" he asked.

"Because I would have handled it in a completely differently."

"How would *you* have handled it?" he asked.

"I would have said to the owner, 'You owe me dinner.' Once I had his attention I'd say 'While you were relaxing on a beach somewhere, I was looking out for your business and I signed up for this ad that you would have missed because you were on vacation. Not only are you signed up for the ad, but you owe me dinner.'"

Everett thought about that for a moment. "That's really interesting."

It is my belief that either approach would have been effective, although they were totally different. Mine came from confidence, maybe even a bit of cockiness, but intended to be taken as it was meant—with a jocular sense of arrogance. Everett's was apologetic and came from a place of humility, which was also extremely effective. If presented properly, my approach most likely would have worked, but watching him offered me the opportunity to witness how one could present something advantageously from both ends of the spectrum.

This was an initial stage in my understanding that there are many ways to get to the end of the road. There are different paths that can lead to success and we all have to carve our own way depending on what is most comfortable for us. Even more importantly, it taught me to respect each person's path. Although his approach hadn't occurred to me, he was very successful. My eyes were opened to the fact that *my* way wasn't the only way and most likely there wasn't only one *right* way to approach any given situation.

FYFE DOLLAR

The Simmons training program evolved for me as I continued to learn from other salesmen and their accounts. Another memorable experience was with Fyfe Dollar, a key account manager who called on department stores in New York City. The first several weeks Fyfe introduced me to his customers and taught me the day-to-day demands of the job—how to enter orders, determine pricing structures, train retail salespeople, as well as all of the different responsibilities we had that related to selling and merchandising our products. Not long after my training with him began, Fyfe found out he needed a hernia operation and that he would be out of work for about six weeks. Since I was nearing the end of my training, the plan was that I would take over his accounts during his absence.

This was an unheard of opportunity for a trainee: to call on major department stores in New York City. Knowing this, I was determined to make the most it. During this period, there was a contest for the month of June called the "June Boom." The idea was to see if we could generate an enormous month of sales for our premium product—Beautyrest Mattresses. Since Fyfe was out for the month of June, with a sales trainee on his accounts, everyone thought the prospect of him meeting his quota and hitting the contest goal was highly unlikely. I took that as a personal challenge. I might point out, at this juncture in the story, that not only was I not highly compensated as a trainee, I wasn't going to get any additional financial reward from the contest, since Fyfe was really the competitor. Technically, it was his territory...so I was just representing him. As you might imagine, the lack of financial incentives didn't deter me. It felt like my first chance to see what I could do under challenging circumstances.

To make a long (but interesting) story short, I achieved his quota for him. With only five months of training, my results were in line with the highest-level sales goal for Simmons. This was a huge lesson for me to take any opening and seize the moment. It's like in sports when the star athlete gets hurt and the coach says to the second-stringer, "I'm putting you in.

Let's see what you can do." The implied message is loud and clear: "We're counting on you to step up and perform." This was my moment in the spotlight. Knowing it was an unusual opportunity, I gave it my all and was successful. The most important reward was the tremendous confidence I gained. Confidence, in everything we do, is part of how we perform. If we can build our own level of confidence and say to ourselves, "That's a challenge and I accept it," then we can rise to the occasion and build on it throughout our lives and careers. Call it an "aha moment" or whatever you'd like, but this was not a casual victory for me because my heart and soul had gone into it. I don't remember how many hours it took. It never occurred to me to count them because, frankly, it didn't matter. All that I knew was that it was imperative for me to help make Fyfe's quota.

How did I do it? I can sum it up in one word: relentless. The key to success was just being relentless. Knowing that my best chance was to make it easy for them, I encouraged the clients by going above and beyond my required duties. In the early '70s, we didn't have the analytics and data processing capabilities that we have today, so I cranked the numbers by hand. The detailed specific data provided them with sound business reasoning as to why it was a good investment to buy more than they might need at the time. It was important to incent them to make the purchase and to build up inventory in their warehouse. Not only did I have to ask for the order, but I worked hard on the analytical side of it to explain to them why it was a sound investment for them. Simply being a likeable or affable person would not have been enough. These were businessmen and women OR professionals who needed a concrete business premise to be interested in having that conversation with me because they would have said, "You're a nice young man, but I don't have room in my warehouse," or "I don't have the financial resources to buy $200,000 worth of Beautyrest today," or whatever the reason may have been. At the time, it was not commonplace to have analytics or calculations broken down because people just didn't have the tools to do so. With the intention of creating a solid business case for their investment, my plan included an explanation of how reduced-price incentives increased their margins and more than offset whatever interest rate they had to pay to buy the additional inventory. I methodically and analytically made the case for why it made good business sense for them to buy six weeks' worth of inventory instead of one.

Was this something taught to me during training? No. It was probably a combination of my education and what I learned while selling investments and securities during graduate school. Having an understanding of return on investment allowed me to present the information in a professional manner, which may have been unusual for a sales trainee and outside the proverbial "box." The combination of my effort on their behalf to supply the hard data to justify the purchase and my continued persistence was a recipe for success. And I took it a step farther. Instead of merely asking for an order, I actually worked up the order for them, offering my suggestions about what to buy based on what they were selling. By creating their order in advance, all they had to do was tweak the numbers a little bit, rather than having to initiate it from scratch. Again, this wasn't something I was taught during training, but just another way that made sense to me—and made it easy for buyers to say "Yes."

Something that sets people apart is their willingness to go above and beyond their call of duty.

Many times, when you're given parameters or guidelines for something people think, "This is all that's really expected, so this is what I will do." Doing your job and doing it well is great, but if you really want to excel it is imperative that you do whatever it takes without waiting for somebody to tell you what to do. These are some of the key building blocks of success for young people. The opportunities that we don't recognize at the moment can become some of the most significant when we reflect on them later in life.

AGGRESSIVE LEARNING

Over the years, as I worked with management teams, I developed a concept I called *aggressive learning*. My explanation of that concept was that, in life, no one is likely to sit down and tell you exactly what to do. If you want to learn, you need to be aggressive about *how* you learn. You need to ask questions and say, "I didn't understand what just happened, *could you explain that to me?*" That is how we can develop an understanding without somebody actually saying, "Now Bob, here's what I did, and how you need to do this..." If you're an aggressive learner, you're going to take notes, ask questions, and seek wisdom. If you ask, somebody will help you. If you just watch passively, at the end of the day you may find yourself wondering *what just happened.* If you are waiting for somebody to tell you what to do and how to do it, to me, that's passive learning. Passive learning isn't going to get you anywhere, but aggressive learning certainly will.

Aggressive learning may sound like an oxymoron because it seems contradictory. Many times we think that if we are learning, we should be passive. The problem with that is, if you wait for somebody to hand you information and knowledge, you may wait forever—and never learn anything. If you're aggressive and fearless in asking what might seem to be dumb questions, you'll learn. If you don't get the answer from the person you're talking to, ask somebody else. If you are tenacious enough, you're going to get an answer that you understand and will most likely learn more than you thought you might along the way.

ALL GROWN UP

Upon completion of training, my first sales territory was in upstate New York. For some reason I thought the sales trainee compensation would increase after receiving my own territory, but it wasn't that much more than the trainee compensation of $9,000 a year. I said to my district manager at the time, "That's really not adequate for me and not what I expected after acquiring my own sales territory."

His response: "I understand, but that's what it is for everybody. We will have a conversation about this in six months, after we see how you're doing."

Life as a sales representative for furniture and retail stores in upstate NY wasn't terribly eventful, but it was a learning experience creating a routine and developing the discipline to visit each store on a regular basis. Calling on 70 accounts each month required an immense amount of driving and local travel. A typical day meant driving an average of 200 miles—and provided me many hours of solitude and time to think. During those long days, it became clear to me that my goal was to develop relationships with people in each of the stores in my territory and become invested in their success. Remember: This was long before the luxury of having personal computers and customer relationship—CRM—software, so it was up to me to organize and manage myself.

Developing my own system to manage all of the accounts, I kept a file for each account in the trunk of my car. Stapled to the inside of each file folder was a piece of lined paper on which I detailed every visit—date, who I met with, what we covered, what I promised, and what follow-up was needed. On the other side of the file folder was another sheet where I had kept notes on all of the people at a particular store and their personal and professional lives. It included the owner, manager, and the salespeople, as well as the names of their wives, children, and even their dogs. If they said, "I just had a baby," that note was always added to my file. Upon returning the following month, I'd review the file before going into the store so I knew exactly what we had talked about during our previous conversations. Walking into the store I'd say, "How's baby Joe doing?" They attributed this to my remarkable memory, which of course wasn't true. There was never a doubt that they appreciated my personal touch.

This, too, was something that wasn't taught to me during training; it just occurred to me after visiting so many stores. It quickly became apparent that customer service and sales was a complex process and the way to be effective was to develop good relationships with people by not only showing interest in their business, but in them as human beings. Unable to remember all of the details about so many people's lives, it seemed necessary to take notes and organize them. It also became quite unmistakable that this extra effort quickly separated me from all the other sales reps that were coming through the door, salespeople who were unable to remember all the pertinent details and who, apparently, did not care as much as I did.

My filing system also kept me organized related to my commitments to each store, including all of their advertising and order information. Anything you ever needed to know about a store, its people, and its business could be found in my file. When it was my time to leave that territory, I bequeathed them to the next sales rep. I told him, "This is the most valuable gift I can give you, much more important than the sales records." When I got quizzical and incredulous looks, I added this kicker: "These files give you the key to every account." Not only was it an act of generosity, but a form of leadership training for them to pass along to their successor.

As I moved up into the hierarchy of the Simmons company, it became my policy to insist that every salesman create files and meticulous records—by showing them how. It created better relationships with our customers, and more continuity as we moved people around from territory to territory because there was one, consistent way to manage and strengthen important business relationships. Although everyone understood the rationale behind this system, I'm sure there were a few who didn't follow through because of the extra work it required. In my opinion, it was definitely worth the added effort because the results were the proof. People were just delighted that you remembered details about their lives and more importantly, their business. It was an early-stage management skill that had eluded me until then.

SIX MONTHS LATER...

My first territory was western New York, although my boss was located in Elizabeth, New Jersey, just outside of New York City. I still have a vivid memory of the look on my astonished boss's face when, six months to the day from our conversation about increasing my pay, I walked into his office.

He looked up from his work and asked, "What are you doing here?"

I replied, "You know, it's time for us to talk about getting some more income for Leonard Gaby."

"Well," he said, "That's a little premature."

I looked him in the eye and said, "You know, yesterday, it may have been premature, but today is another story. Today is exactly six months from the day you promised that we would have this conversation. So here I am." I didn't do it with anger or hostility, but it seemed to disarm him nonetheless.

"Well, I'm not prepared for this conversation," he said. "But I do remember telling you that. I'm just not prepared to do it today."

I was relentless. "I really need for you to deal with it."

He said, "I understand. And I promise I'll get back to you."

After a moment's thought I answered, "That's good enough for me." I wanted to trust him and I did.

Within two months, I was promoted to the eastern side of New York State where I made significantly more money. Making progress felt incredibly good to me. In retrospect, it was not the money that made the difference, but the need to continue to grow within this company. Had I not stood up for myself, I believe there was a good chance they would have forgotten me, only making a move when it was convenient for their needs, not mine.

SELECTIVE NEGLIGENCE

Along with my promotion to territorial manager came an increase in pay, a move to Albany, New York, and the additional responsibility of running a small, 12,000 square-foot warehouse. In addition to my sales responsibilities, it was my job to manage this warehouse full of merchandise as well as the personnel—a warehouse manager, truck drivers, and a clerical person. I recognized fairly early in the experience that the warehouse was a seductive trap. Each day I was faced with a choice: either get in my car and drive a hundred miles to see a retail customer or opt to be an executive and sit in my office in the warehouse and work. It was much more convenient to sit in the office and many people choose that route. This made them pseudo-executives with meticulous warehouses where everything was in its place. Although many of them exceled at the logistics of managing their warehouses, their sales suffered.

Realizing I didn't want to stay in Albany for very long, my choices and point of view on the situation were different. My analysis was that if I ran a great warehouse, they were going to keep me there forever. If my sales were spectacular, they were most likely going to promote me because they'd see my capacity to do bigger and better things. Management would send reports and inventory analysis requests, as well as numerous other administrative tasks to me to take care of. If I was out on a road calling on customers, it was impossible for me to accomplish everything. My first priority was my customers and my sales efforts, so the warehouse assignments were neglected, intentionally.

This was where my term *selective negligence* was born. Somebody would call me and say, "Hey, you didn't get that report out."

I'd say, "You know, you're absolutely right, I did not get you that report. I've developed this priority system that I call selective negligence. It was my choice to ignore some of the warehouse duties because I believe that calling on my customers is more important. You're convincing me that I probably shouldn't have ignored this. It's going out of the neglected pile into the active pile, and I'm going to get to it. I want you to know that it wasn't an accident or an inadvertent oversight. It was literally a conscious decision to ignore it."

It was an aggressive posture to take in expressing my stance that my customers were more important than warehouse tasks. It appeared to me that they would never hold me back because I didn't get the report in, but they would if my sales weren't up to par. One way or another, it was obvious to me that the culture they were supporting was not the culture that was needed. It was clear to me that it should be a requirement to get up off of your ass and sell something, and the inventory management would, necessarily, take second position. Not that it wasn't important to have accurate administrative records and so forth, but to have me take an entire inventory of the warehouse every three months wasn't intelligent priority and time management. It required me to stay completely off the road or come in on weekends to count everything in the building. That wasn't my idea of being productive as a salesperson because sales did not improve by taking inventory in the warehouse.

CYA

During those years at Simmons, it was definitely a *CYA* [cover your ass] culture. It was your boss saying, "Get me the report. I just want you to make sure that I have these things done and that my superior knows that I'm doing my job." People were motivated by and making decisions based on covering their ass, not because they were good for the business. They were insulating themselves from criticism and any kind of retribution. It was a mentality that drove most people to make sure they weren't found to be at fault for anything—not worry about doing anything worthy of praise. It was the complete opposite of creating a culture of excellence, which dictates that you take risks, put yourself out there, and try new things even if they may not work and or if you make a mistake in the process. If you're so afraid of making a mistake because somebody is going to punish you for it, you create a culture where people won't assert themselves. They believe it's better not to try than to try and fail. Success was defined as "staying out of trouble," instead of breaking barriers to create more opportunities for the company... because that wasn't valued.

UNCOMPETITIVE!

This wasn't something unique to Simmons. I think many once-large and successful companies suffered from the same problem. Typically, in those cases, it was a result of not having any competition. For years, Simmons dominated the market in spite of their heavily laden bureaucracy and centralized management. Until a small company named Sealy had a growth spurt and came into the picture. What made them different? They were entrepreneurs. With a network of factories owned by entrepreneurs, they built Sealy products through a licensing agreement. During this time they became successful for numerous reasons. They had a lower-cost product than Simmons did, providing better margins, which they used to invest in advertising. These factors enabled them to build their brand around their Sealy Posturepedic mattress.

Interestingly enough, they had a factory in Albany. And I competed against them all the time. The difference with their management was that when factory orders didn't come in as expected, they went out and got orders. The owner/entrepreneur model made things happen. On the other hand, if I went into an account and they said, "Well, we have an idea. Here's what we need..." I didn't have the authority to respond to it the way the Sealy entrepreneur did. I had to ask my boss, who had to ask his boss, who had to ask his boss. By the time my answer came back, my customer was no longer interested. Unfortunately, at no point in the Simmons chain of command did anybody really care about the profitability of the business. Instead, all they thought about was their little world and not getting into trouble. The organizational structure of the company was designed for failure, creating a culture of low expectations and poor performance. Here I was in a little warehouse in Albany, NY being drained by bureaucratic demands on the warehouse, while the Sealy factory in Albany was kicking my ass week after week because they had somebody who owned the business, could make decisions, and was aggressive in the marketplace. They were applying guerilla warfare, while I was retreating back to my warehouse and protecting myself so that I didn't get criticized. This was not a formula for success.

It was a great opportunity for me to observe Sealy and how they were operating, because it helped me to eventually implement much needed changes within Simmons years later. It was at this point when it became obvious to me that we needed to drive the decision making down lower into the organization. The further we could drive it down, the more successful we would be. In order to do that, we had to start trusting people. When you have a large bureaucracy, it's built because you don't trust people to make decisions and to understand what's in the best interest of the company. Typical thinking is that salespeople are just there to sell so they must not be concerned about profitability. It's a how-can-I-trust-them mentality or *a fait accompli,* which basically means, I know what's going to end up happening because he doesn't know how to make a profit, therefore, I can't trust him. Nobody ever said, "Well, what if I teach him how to make a profit? What if I explained to him how the factories worked, could he learn enough to make good business decisions, ones that I can trust?"

INTREPRENEURSHIP

At Simmons, it felt like the culture was so negative it was as if I had three flights of stairs to climb before even getting to the ground level. Instead of throwing in the towel when Sealy came into the picture, it was motivation for me to create something different at Simmons by utilizing Sealy as a model for success. They were entrepreneurs, sure, but we had a big company, so my way of translating that within Simmons was to create a new way of looking at business. I even made up a word for it: *intrepreneur.*

What is an intrepreneur? It is an entrepreneur within a large organization. A person who lives and works in a large organization but thinks like an entrepreneur. In order to be an intrepreneur you have to take ownership, have pride, and become passionate. How do you create ownership in an organization when you don't literally have ownership? That was the task at hand and what I knew we had to create.

Where did it start for me? My motivation was simply to do the best job I possibly could. How? By fulfilling my promises to my customers by selling them high-quality merchandise at the best possible price, delivering it on time, and then showing them how to market and sell it profitably. If it required me to get involved with the factory then that was what I did. It was imperative for me to live up to the credibility that I was trying to develop. While holding any of my various positions with Simmons, my objective was to do it as if it was the job I would have for the rest of my life. Personal integrity and a commitment to excellence was what motivated me. For me, success begins with a personal commitment to the task at hand. If you don't take these things personally, you don't care. If you don't care, then... *guess what?* You will never be successful. Even if I never went beyond the job I had at that moment, which would have been fine, I would have strived to be the best I could be.

HERMAN THE GERMAN

One thing you may face when taking pride in yourself and your position is the disapproval and envy of others. Keep in mind that what they say about you usually has more to do with how they feel about themselves than anything else. My success didn't come without backlash from colleagues. A memorable one was named Herman Kling, a senior salesperson. The reason he stands out in my memory is because of how I chose to deal with the situation. Herman was German and although he didn't have an accent, he certainly exuded the strong and stoic personality traits for which Germans are known and how we hear or see them portrayed in movies. With his short-cropped hair and we'll say less-than-friendly demeanor, he didn't do much to dispel any preconceived notions that might be based upon his nationality or attitude. He always wore short-sleeved shirts that were so tight they appeared to be two sizes too small. I used to wonder if he was going to burst at the seams, because he looked like he was stuffed into his clothes. Not only was he extraordinarily intimidating, the way he looked at me made it clear to me that my being Jewish didn't sit very well with him. Although he never said anything specifically, I knew it was a sincere point of irritation for him. This probably only exacerbated his disdain for me and my success at such early stages in my career.

Herman made numerous comments to other people about me, which eventually made their way back to me. One comment was particularly interesting, so I decided to confront him about it. Although it was most unusual, Herman had his own private office. From what I understood, it was because he was calling on a national account. Upon entering his office, I found him sitting behind his desk looking tense. His teeth were clenched and so were his fists as he looked at me with contempt.

I dove right in. "Herman," I said, "Somebody told me that you said something about me and I'd like to know if it's true."

"Yeah?" he said.

"I heard that you said that Len Gaby can walk on water without getting his shoes wet."

"Yeah, I did say that," he admitted. "So what?"

I said, "That's the first honest thing you have said about me."

He didn't respond but he appeared to clench his teeth even more tightly. Our encounter didn't stop him from talking about me, but eventually he seemed to disappear into the woodwork. It is my belief that we can't go through life disregarding the feelings of others, or without an awareness of the impact we have on them. On the other hand, everyone represents a transient relationship, compared to the relationship we have with ourselves. Even our parents, children, spouse, and co-workers are in our lives for only a limited period of time. The relationship we have with ourselves is, literally, for a lifetime. For our entire lives, who else will be closer to each of us than ourselves?

I know it sounds almost trite to express that, but I think it's an overlooked relationship, and one that people don't concern themselves with often enough. The expression, "To thine own self be true," is critical. While it matters to me what others think of me—and I'm cognizant of it—I'm much more concerned about what *I* think of me. My standards and assessments are always much more important to me than theirs. This concept is the essence of our own personal culture, which is really the most important one of all. What are our standards? What is our sense of service to others? What responsibility do we have in this world? Are we sensitive to our environment, to our relationships, and how we treat others? In my opinion, this is much more important than how others treat us.

Chapter 7

THE FAST LANE

"If you don't learn something new every day, you're probably not paying attention."

O ne evening in November of 1972, I returned from a long, day trip to Syracuse where the weather was cold and snowy. After watching some of Monday night football, I went to bed exhausted. Shortly after falling asleep, Eva got up and went to the bathroom adjacent to our master bedroom. When she came back to bed, I said, "That wasn't even worth getting up for," because I hadn't heard the toilet flush or the water run.

She said, "Oh, yes. It was."

"What do you mean?" I asked.

"My water broke. I think it's time..."

I said, "Oh my God!" In my stupor, I tried to turn on the light by pushing the button on the clock radio, which only turned on the music. After what seemed like minutes—but was probably just seconds, the light went on—and we were grateful that one of our closest friends was her obstetrician. I called him and he said, "Go to the hospital and when she's sufficiently dilated they'll call me and I'll come and deliver the baby." We went to the hospital and were up all night, but her labor never progressed.

At 8:00 in the morning, the doctor came in and said, "Well that's enough labor, we're going to induce her."

OH, MAN!

In the delivery room, probably from the combination of excitement and lack of sleep, I felt lightheaded. Although remaining upright, there were a few moments when it occurred to me I might topple over. In 1972, there was no such thing as an ultrasound so we didn't know if we were having a boy or a girl. After delivering the baby, the doctor said, "Well, look at the balls on this one." And that's how I learned we had a son. We named him Jonathan Stuart. It was a special day that I still remember so clearly that it feels like just yesterday. It is hard to believe that Jonathan is in his 40s and a father now himself.

THE POWER OF CONTROL

Six months after Jonathan was born, my next position took me to NYC as a key account salesman for Simmons. After receiving this promotion, we moved from Albany, New York to Westfield, New Jersey where we rented a house for our newly expanded family. My new responsibilities involved managing major accounts in New York City. The most memorable and interesting account for me during that time was the Klein Sleep Shop, owned by a couple named Herb and Gloria Klein. Beginning with one humble store in the Bronx, they eventually expanded into multiple stores throughout Manhattan. It wasn't luck; they were really excellent in their execution. Recognizing early on that Herb Klein was an exceptionally bright man, I was drawn to him, soaking up all of the wisdom and knowledge possible. He wasn't perfect, but who is? One could say he may have even been a bit nefarious, not always choosing to follow the high road, but that too was a learning experience. He never did anything illegal, that I know of, but his highly aggressive negotiating style always led with a confrontational, what's-in-it-for-me approach. Nevertheless, it was a superior educational experience for me on how to (and how not to) negotiate, run a business, and treat people. It also included unparalleled training in merchandising, marketing, and advertising.

While setting up our working parameters, Herb said to me, "You manage the orders and the flow of the merchandise. Here are your sample slots, reorder as you need to to keep us in business, and make sure you keep us supplied with solid inventory." Although it didn't occur to me at the time, it was a brilliant strategy on his part. Acknowledging my commitment and personal integrity, Herb trusted that if I saw the next order coming in too soon or not soon enough, I'd go to the factory and slow it down or speed it up. It was his management of the relationship he had with me, rather than the management of the business, that truly inspired me.

We became extremely close and he had such trust in me because he knew that I would never do anything to intentionally hurt our relationship or his business. Because he counted on me, he gave me the power to do my best for him by providing me the opportunity to sell my goods on his sales floor. In return, he expected me to take care of all the details. I took that obligation very seriously and together, we were notably successful.

This relationship not only afforded me the opportunity to be the sole supplier who had access to all of his records—allowing me to see exactly what was selling and what wasn't—but it allowed me to place orders without ever having to ask for his approval. This responsibility was priceless, teaching me flow and supply chain management as well as providing an understanding of the raw materials needed to produce the goods. This first-hand experience of becoming embedded in his world allowed me to learn his business backwards and forwards on a level that wouldn't have happened without the shared trust we had for one another. Our collaboration was so extraordinarily positive that it taught me an invaluable business lesson: if you and your client agree on ground rules and then work to accomplish clear goals, both of you can achieve your objective. It became clear to me during this time that if I helped his business become more successful, I would prosper as well. It was more than just a business experience, it was a life lesson that taught me when you work together, you can have a proverbial *win-win*.

As our relationship grew, my role eventually morphed into somewhat of a gatekeeper to his office. When other people who admired Herb wanted to approach him, they would come to me. Harry Acker, who at that point had one furniture store in Brooklyn, wanted to meet Herb because he viewed him as an industry guru. Harry said to me, "I want to talk to Herb Klein, can you get me in to see him?" After arranging a meeting for him, Harry was extremely appreciative. Klein Sleep doesn't exist anymore but Harry Acker built a company much bigger than Herb Klein's ever was. It's called Sleepy's: The Mattress Professionals and today he has over 700 stores in the New York, Philadelphia, and Boston areas.

Another memorable experience during that time was a collaboration with Herb Klein's son, David, a very bright and creative young man in his own right. We were selling a hide-a-bed sofa covered in a dyed-corduroy fabric. It was available in eight different vibrant colors because of the vat dyeing process, another learning experience of mine dealing with the textile processes of dyeing and weaving fabrics. One day, an idea struck me and I said to David, "We need to take a picture of this sofa for advertising because we don't have any yet. I think we should stack them all to showcase the rainbow of colors available." It also occurred to me to place the ad in *New York Magazine* to cater to the affluent urban crowd. It was a perfect fit for New Yorkers because not only was it an attractive sofa that could double as a bed where space was limited, but it was a great deal. For only $700 you could own a bright yellow [or any color of the rainbow] traditional tuxedo sofa that held a comfortable Beautyrest queen-size mattress. The ad was very compelling and it represented a great consumer value. David loved the idea and pondered where to take the picture. Deciding to play up the flavor of New York, he found a decrepit old navy dock in Brooklyn that captured the Statue of Liberty as the backdrop to the rainbow of sofas. Together we created one of the most effective ads we'd ever seen. Not only was it a wonderful experience that allowed me to understand what types of advertising excite consumers, but we were wildly successful with it.

WAIT A MINUTE...

Although my career continued to be stimulating and fulfilling, my life wasn't free from challenges. Unfortunately, in my late 20s I was diagnosed with ulcerative colitis or what they call *inflammatory bowel disease.* With this type of autoimmune disease, the body attacks itself causing inflammation of the bowel. This led to years of extreme discomfort and embarrassment as I suffered through bouts of cramps and diarrhea. At the time, my doctors were unable to determine a specific cause, but they did say that certain groups tended to have a genetic predisposition to the disease and that it was somewhat more prevalent in Sephardic Jews. The doctors told me that it had nothing to do with what I was eating, doing, or feeling... and that it was just something beyond my control. There were a few medications available, although nothing like the ones we have today, but even with them it was a difficult experience that came and went over the years. Today, and for the last 30 years, it has remained in remission, for which I am very grateful.

THE ROLEX

In spite of my struggles with this illness, my career blossomed and with it came opportunities to change my view of the world. My father had been a bright and erudite man who always seemed to be aware of what was going on in the world before it became *big* news. One of the many things that fascinated him was Rolex watches. It wasn't the status or cost that he marveled at, but the hand workmanship that went into each and every piece. He loved the engineering and precision that created a product with such impeccable integrity and it was something he found captivating long before anybody had even heard of Rolex watches. I have no recollection that he ever felt any real longing to own one, and he was so frugal that

I don't think he ever considered it. Even so, it didn't stop him from admiring them, and I believe, aspiring to own one.

About five years after joining Simmons, I was doing well financially and a friend of mine was going to Switzerland on business. I said, "If you get a chance to buy a Rolex watch, just the most basic stainless steel model, I'd really appreciate it." Buying it there would save me some money and I'd reimburse him when he got back. Sure enough, he brought me back a Rolex watch, which cost $600 there, although in the United States the price tag would have been closer to $2,000. Even the cost of this basic model, acquired overseas, was quite a bit of money to me, but it was definitely worth it because I wore it with great pride for many, many years.

Even after all of those years, the watch was never really mine; it was always my father's watch. Every time I looked at it, I felt a connection to him. As if it was yesterday, I still recall having spiritual conversations about the watch with him. I'd say, "Dad, this watch is great and it keeps great time, and it didn't take any food off the table. My family is still eating well and I haven't sacrificed anything important to get it." I wasn't sure he was getting my point, so I continued: "You see, you can have a high quality watch, enjoy it and appreciate it, and the rest of the world is not going to fall apart." It was quite private and personal to me, offering a very spiritual and reassuring connection to my dad by having a reminder of him on my wrist all the time. Until now, I haven't shared this story with many people.

Many years later, when my son, Jonathan, graduated from college, the watch was a gift to him. I said, "Jonathan, this is really not my watch, it is your grandfather's. You never met him because he died before you were born, but I see him in you sometimes..." I told him about my relationship with the watch and with my father. I said, "I want you to have it and treat it like it was your grandfather's watch. It's your connection to him and to me." Indeed, he was very proud and grateful. Not only did that watch bring me years of a tangible connection to my father, but, that day, we created a family heirloom that I hope will be passed along and cherished for generations to come.

The watch had been a metaphor for me to say to my dad that *You can have the things that are important to you without so much as a blip on the radar screen of life for the rest of the world.* My dad's perspective was quite different: This is something that's beautiful and I may lust for it, but it's unattainable. My message was to show him that it *was* attainable. We can experience the moments and objects we love, without causing upsets in our life, if we handle it well. It's great to aspire to do or have something, but it's really frustrating not to be able to accomplish it. For me, it goes back to this question—If you have a goal and you want it badly enough, *what do you do to get to it?* It may sound arrogant, but whatever I've set my mind to do, I've been able to accomplish. If I wasn't able to accomplish it, I decided that it wasn't a goal that I wanted in the first place. It's a way of keeping my ego intact to say—*I've accomplished all of my goals* rather than saying—*I've accomplished some things and I've failed at some other things.*

> *I have failed at many things,*
> *but I've never really been discouraged about it*
> *because I decided to just modify my goal.*

This is another example of the inner-speak that can help sustain our confidence. Others may call it rationalization and, in fact, it may be. For me, however, it works extremely well.

TAKING INVENTORY

In 1976, I received a promotion to my first management position for Simmons as a District Sales Manager. At just 31 years old, my responsibilities included managing 12 people, who were all older than me, in the Washington D.C. area, as well as overseeing a 150,000-square-foot warehouse and all of its distribution systems, merchandise, and people. It was quite a challenge, making my management of the 10,000-foot warehouse seem like a simple cakewalk. But that didn't deter me; quite the opposite in fact. The new and significant magnitude of my responsibility was a rush— even though commuting back and forth between our home in Westfield, New Jersey and my office in Laurel, Maryland kept me immensely busy.

The new position came with its own challenges, but to me they were merely opportunities to stretch myself. One such instance came about because my predecessor had been negligent with custom-labeled products for Levitz, one of our national accounts. They were such a large account and so important to Simmons that we built and warehoused private-label merchandise for them—Beautyrest for Levitz. After my arrival and review of our inventory, I noticed that we had more than 2,000 pieces of discontinued Levitz merchandise sitting in the warehouse. Knowing it was impossible to sell it to anyone except the six major Levitz stores we serviced from this distribution center, I decided it was imperative for me to meet the general manager in charge of the Levitz stores in the area. I called, introduced myself, and asked for an appointment. He said, "I'd love to meet you, but I'm busy travelling around visiting the stores." He paused a moment before adding: "We're doing what we call a *caravan*, taking all of our management team to do in-depth visits. We look at everything— the merchandise, backroom, warehouse and distribution, sales training, housekeeping, and even building maintenance. It's intensive—and we spend several days in each store." As I was taking this all in, he added: I'm going to be in Baltimore tomorrow and we will finish up around 6:00 P.M. If you'd like to meet us for crabs and beer, you're welcome to join us."

"Okay," I said. "I'll see you tomorrow at 6:00. I need to talk to you about something."

He said, "Great. We'll have dinner and a beer."

We hit it off nicely and I still recall how delicious the soft shell crabs were. After a while he said, "What is it that you wanted to talk about?"

I said, "Well, I've got a tough situation here. We have over 2000 pieces of merchandise with your name on it—and it's all discontinued. It's really not your fault that we produced it and you didn't order it, but it's my problem now. Before bringing in new merchandise, I need to get rid of what we have sitting there. I'd be happy to make you a deal, but I would need your help."

He went into a bit of a tirade and said, "That's what I'm finding out. These stores I'm visiting have way too much inventory and we don't have enough room. We don't have the financial resources right now to carry the extra inventory. Maybe some other time." If I thought there was room for discussion, he put that to rest adding: "Sorry, but I can't help you."

I thought about that for a minute and offered a half-hearted response. "I understand, I'll find another solution," I told him.

After a minute he said, "Well, tell me what the deal was."

"I understand you're in a tough spot. I'll wait and figure something else out."

He repeated his request: "Just tell me what the deal is. I'd like to know what you had in mind."

I stood my ground. "No," I said. "I'm not going to do that because I don't want to force something on you under duress. You told me what your situation is and I respect that. I want to start off on a good note with you and have a good relationship. I'm looking at the long term, not the short term."

After I kept putting him off, he got to the point of almost screaming at me, *"What the hell is the deal?"*

"Well, I'll tell you the deal, but I don't want you to buy it. I don't want you to get seduced by it."

Well, he kept asking and every time he asked, the price went up in my head. By the time I finally told him what my offer was, he was begging to buy it. Because he had already said no to me, I had refused to tell him what my offer was. After it was all said and done, he sent 300 pieces to each store and paid me 20 percent more than I would have originally sold it for. When he told me he didn't want it without hearing my offer, I took that offer off the table. By choosing not to push him and then, basically, taking the offer away, it made him salivate. It was one of the most gratifying sales experiences I've ever had and on top of it, I made a good friend.

It was one of those wonderful moments in life when you truly understand something. It taught me that, in sales, sometimes you have to act like you don't need the order. If you're confident and secure in yourself, people want to do business with you. He really wanted to do business with me after I took the offer away. For me, it became a technique I used more than a few times—taking away something that somebody didn't know they wanted.

DADDY'S GIRL

That same year, 1976, was the year our beautiful daughter Rebecca came into our lives. While at my office in Laurel Maryland, Eva went into labor earlier than expected. It was 2:00 in the morning when my phone rang and my cousin told me they were on the way to the hospital. I said, "I can't get a plane now, so I'm going to drive my rental car. I'm leaving right away!" After a four-hour drive, I arrived at the hospital immediately following the delivery. It was a joyous occasion to meet my wonderful daughter for the first time. Rebecca has always been a bright light in my life. Although welcoming her into the world feels like it was only yesterday, Rebecca just got married last year and it was an honor and thrill to walk her down the aisle. I couldn't be more proud of her.

THE CORNER OFFICE

Shortly after Rebecca's birth and after just one year in Maryland, my next promotion was to Regional Sales Manager for all of metropolitan New York, the most complex and challenging sales management job in the country. New York City was home to 10 different department stores like Macy's, Bloomingdales, and Abraham Strauss—several of which were enormous accounts. My sales management experience in Maryland and the Washington DC area, [including Maryland, Virginia and Delaware] as well as my warehouse experience, prepared me for this new position. Well... somewhat.

Ecstatic just to be working in New York City, my corner office at 33rd Street and Park Avenue was icing on the cake. Although it was an older building, it had great character. I loved the office and I loved working in New York City. It was a challenging position, but that appealed to me as well. Challenges made life exciting and intense. Some people don't like the pressure of sharks circling and biting, in the midst of competition and aggression, but for me it was thrilling to be knee deep in the stress that goes hand-in-hand with aggressive sales and business maneuvering. The chips, per se, were so big that most of the time it felt like I was operating on an adrenaline high. Every day there were new problems to solve, whether from the stores themselves, the sales reps I was responsible for, or any number of issues that could pop up. The old expression "If you can make it there, you can make it anywhere," was truly relevant in this case. Although it felt tough at times, it was a superior learning experience. When you are challenged by the best, it either toughens you up and you become successful, or you fall apart. Because of my love for my job *and* my ability to handle it, I thrived.

One gift of mine that manifested during my time in this position was my almost photographic memory when it came to recalling numbers and statistics. It benefited me well on many occasions. One particular instance with a sales rep helped me to thwart his attempt to "pull-one-over" on me because of talent. At the time Simmons offered about 40 different styles of sofa beds. During a sales meeting, I shared that one of the styles was discontinued. I said, "We're dropping this model."

One of the reps started whining about it. He said, "This is really an important style for my territory and my customers love it. I have lots of orders for them placed."

"How many of those sofa beds did you sell last month?" I asked him.

"I have no idea."

"Well, I do," I told him. "You sold three."

"Really?"

"Yes. Really." I told him not to worry about the one discontinued product. He had 39 other ones to sell.

Everybody wants to test you when you are in a position of authority—customers as well as the people you are managing. You need to be up to the task, but sometimes strategic avoidance has its place. In those days, all of the large department stores advertised in the Sunday edition of the *New York Times* or *Daily News*. We had to manage a promotion calendar to make sure none of the eight competing stores were in the paper on the same day because they didn't want to compete for the Simmons' customers. I used to say to people, "If I had two major ads that inadvertently ran together on a Sunday, on Monday I would hide by saying, 'I'm going to Times Square to watch a porno movie.'" This was before the days of cellphones, and I'd hide from the angry calls until Tuesday, giving the store managers a chance to cool off a little bit.

WHAT'S THE AGENDA... REALLY?

Every quarter, Frank Rosenberry, the CEO and President of Simmons, would visit me in my New York City office. It was dizzying to watch as he paced incessantly, rapid-firing questions at me as I sat at my desk. "What's going on here? What is this company doing?" It was akin to a 45-minute interrogation about what was going on in the mattress business. After this happened a few times, it occurred to me that he planned visits with me on his way to a board meeting—and this was how he caught himself up on what was going on. It wasn't up to me to make a judgment about his methods or style, but it made me smile knowing that he picked the right person to find out what was going on.

This experience taught me that either I just happened to be in the right place at the right time, or I was in the right place at the right time *and,* from his perspective, had a pretty good handle on what was going on in the world of mattresses. He appeared nervous because he moved around constantly. He would ask me a question, and as I'd look up to give him an answer I'd find that he was already somewhere else in the room. After getting more comfortable with him, I said. "Frank, either you need to sit down and talk to me or I'm going to get up and walk around with you because I can't keep up."

Thankfully, he just sat down. You could see the tension building in him because he was under so much pressure. He would talk to me about competition, and how to sell specific solutions to problems. It gave me a birds-eye view into his perspective and what he was facing. It also helped me to see and think about the company on a much more global, bigger picture than the view through the eyes of a regional sales manager. This experience provided me with a more strategic viewpoint. When finally presented with the opportunity to do something about the broader problems, I had already been thinking about solutions.

It is my sincere belief that these experiences indicate an important quality that I was not aware of at the time. It seems that I was a voracious, aggressive learner.

Someone once suggested to me that all experiences
are learning experiences. No matter the outcome or result,
we always learn and grow as we experience life. And constant
growth enriches our lives constantly. I intend to remain alert
and aware of what's going on, so I can continue to grow.
The reciprocal of this is non-growth or stagnation, which
takes an enormous toll on our mental and physical health.

If you don't learn something new every day,
you're probably not paying attention.

Chapter 8

BACK TO BASICS

*"I never had a plan; I just made a commitment
to do what I was doing... really well."*

*I*n 1978, Gulf and Western Industries, a huge conglomerate, bought
Simmons. After having invested in the company for a while by
purchasing shares on the New York Stock Exchange, they decided to
acquire the balance of the equity. They did this for two reasons: they
didn't agree with the way it was being run and they were not holding a
profit in their investment.

It wasn't long before they became aware of the problems we were
facing. One of the first things they did was to recruit Bob Magnusson as
President and CEO. The company, now based in Atlanta, summoned all
12 Regional Sales Managers for a meeting with Bob. As a way to educate
himself quickly about what was going on within Simmons and where the
opportunities for improvement were, he gave each manager a specific topic
on which to present to the group. Some of us reported on the company
itself, others were tasked with overviewing the industry.

Afterwards, while standing in line for lunch in the company cafeteria,
Bob approached me and said, "I would like you to consider moving to
Atlanta to become the Vice President of Merchandising." It was extremely
awkward for me, as such a significant career move was not only important

for me, but for the company as well. While I had not anticipated such an opportunity, it would have been my guess it would've come in private, at least, if at all.

My first thought was related to the enormous cultural change of moving from the hustle and bustle of New York City to the South. I said to Bob, half-kidding, "Talk about culture shock! I'm a New Yorker. As far as I know Atlanta is in the south and I probably wouldn't fit in too well there. Besides I don't know anything about those types of things."

He said, "You'll fit in just fine and what you don't know, you'll figure out."

"We'll have to talk about it," I said, not wanting to give him an answer immediately—in the cafeteria!—and without careful consideration. As far as what my presentation was about, my memory fails me. What I do know is that it was always easy and comfortable for me to communicate well under pressure in front of large groups. I'm sure it was a combination of my confidence and knowledge of what was going on within the company that helped me accomplish that.

Those few minutes in that lunch line set my imagination on fire. We often think that when we're on a career path the next step is clear and logical. In other words, if you do a good job, you're likely to get this next opportunity. At that point, I had no concept of that. It hadn't even occurred to me what the next step might be. In fact, I didn't even know there was a potential next step. Prior to that conversation with Bob, the specifics of my future with Simmons had been beyond my comprehension. And that got me excited because now there was an opportunity for me to do something significant within the company. Many people have asked me, "Did you have a plan?" The answer is, *Absolutely not*.

I never had a plan;
I just had a commitment
to do what I was doing ... really well.

Apparently Bob was anxious to start building a team and finding people he could count on. It didn't occur to me until later that the purpose of the presentations was for Bob to choose the people he wanted to help him make sweeping changes throughout the company. We were auditioning, although we hadn't understood that at the time. This is another good lesson: In many cases you don't know what the agenda really is—so always be sharp. I've often said, *"You just need to be dressed [prepared] and ready to play."*

If you're dressed and ready to play,
you never know what can happen.

It is important for me to mention that it is my belief that some of my success and the opportunities that came my way have to do with luck, good fortune, and good timing. Many people work hard and don't have the opportunities that were presented to me. It may have been due, in part, to my original strategy in choosing Simmons because that was where the opportunities seemed to be. Maybe that was the brilliant choice, having the courage to go for it even when there appeared to be more high-profile, rational—and conventional—choices.

RE-REINVENTING SIMMONS

Accepting Bob's offer, my family and I moved to Atlanta, Georgia. Along with my promotion came an enormous amount of responsibility. At that time, the mattress division made up 80 percent of the company volume and *110 percent of the profit* because, as a division, we made more than the entire company. We actually made up for the divisions that *cost* us money. For about eight years, we were dedicated to fixing many of the problems that stifled and plagued the company—from quality and service issues, to how unresponsive we were in the marketplace. After making real progress on those fronts, we grew into a substantial and more profitable business. It was exciting to play a significant role in that success.

My position challenged me to help change the culture and the perception of Simmons as a company and a brand. At one time Simmons was a respected name, offering high-quality, premium products. But, over time, the industry had seen the brand deteriorate. Although the well-known brand *name* remained well positioned in consumers' minds, the *brand itself* had issues to deal with. To the industry, Simmons was a large company that was very difficult to deal with and represented poor quality, poor service, and poor execution as well as uncompetitive products.

Originally, the technology in our mattresses was what set us apart from our competitors. Offering individually pocketed coils [that were not connected to one another] was our point of differentiation. When produced properly, it was superior technology, but over the years the management became set in its ways, the company became less competitive and began cutting corners to lower costs. If they could save a dollar or two on each mattress by using inferior quality components, it quickly added up when multiplied by millions of units. Inevitably, we began to have performance problems, the most significant of which was with the material used for the pockets that held the coils. The pockets were a non-woven component that were closed by a form of ultrasonic welding. The process implemented a tuning fork at very high frequencies coupled with pressure so that a weld of material was created. DuPont made this material called Tyvek®. It had not been tested for use as a mattress so they were unaware of the problems that would arise.

When someone slept on a mattress made with Tyvek, the body heat created a chemical reaction that caused the foam in the mattress to deteriorate the exterior fabric. Over time, it broke down completely. The coils, which were eight inches tall but held in a five-inch pocket, were always under pressure so when the material broke, the coil exploded leaving you with a mattress that looked like it was pregnant. The more the mattresses were handled, the more frequently the material would break open. Understandably, the retailers were unhappy with us because the customers were unhappy with them. This caused Simmons huge financial, image, and brand problems; that was the reality we were faced with. We methodically began changing the material—and how we built the product. But, most of all, we had to change the culture that allowed these types of issues to be acceptable in the first place.

Bob Magnusson was brought in to lead this turnaround. As the prior CEO of Stearns & Foster, a company known for its high-quality mattresses, Bob brought credibility to Simmons' deteriorating reputation. One of the first things he made clear to me was that it was my responsibility to get this fixed. It was my job to lead this organization in creating products that exceeded our customers' expectations, as well as the high-quality levels of our competitors. Our standards had to exceed what was the norm in our industry, so our mantra became, We *do not have the luxury of being **as good as** our competitors, we have to **be better**.*

BUILDING BRAND

Over several years we actually accomplished that by improving the quality of our products and making sure they were free from defects. One of the first things we did was change both the materials and the construction processes. We added inner tufting, a cord tied to a button on the top and bottom of the mattress. When pulled tight, it ensured that the materials couldn't shift. By adding this design feature in multiple places before the mattress was covered, the upgraded materials would not move or deteriorate over time. The result was a very stable, secure, and comfortable mattress. By using high-quality materials and taking the extra steps [steps unheard of at the time] to create a superior product, we demonstrated to our customers that we had gone the extra mile to deliver a mattress that surpassed any others in the industry.

One of the other things we did was to position Simmons' Beautyrest as the leading luxury brand in the marketplace. One way we did this was by creating a mattress with a surface filled with pure, white goose down. There are different levels of quality when it comes to goose down, so we made sure we used the very best. In blowing 30 pounds of pure white goose down into the quilted top, we tripled the cost of the mattress. At this time, in the late 1970s and early '80s, a good queen mattress set would have retailed for about $1,000. This goose-down-topped beauty retailed for $3,000. The interesting phenomenon was that it changed the perception of Simmons as a company. Now, we were not only a *quality* brand, but a *luxury* brand as well. While we didn't sell massive amounts of these down-filled mattresses, we created a great amount of excitement and interest from it.

I'm sure many people thought, *Why would somebody spend $3,000 for a mattress?* Consumers understood that goose down was comfortable and very expensive, but featuring this mattress in Bloomingdale's, Macy's, and other fine department and furniture stores around the country had a positive effect on our *traditional* mattress sales. Although we didn't sell many of the luxury ones, it certainly made the $1,000 mattress look reasonable. While somebody may have said, "I can't justify a frivolous purchase for that $3,000 mattress, but I sure can afford a $1,000 mattress." We had succeeded in positioning a $1,000 mattress as both reasonable and affordable. Additionally, this strategy paid significant dividends since we also sold the most expensive mattress available at the time.

As far as tackling employee morale, we knew that while the leaders in an organization set the standards, they weren't the ones who actually did the work. Everybody saw that, as a company, we were being recognized for delivering high-quality products and in turn, we found through unannounced audits that the people working in the factories naturally began taking much greater pride in their work. We made heroes of those who were producing exceptional products. As a company, we began to take credit for the superior merchandise we were now delivering.

JUST IN TIME

Besides focusing on changing the quality of the product, we also needed to vastly improve the quality of service to our customers. We measured our success by our ability to take an order from a customer and ship it complete, making sure it arrived by the date it was promised. Originally, we relied on fulfilling our orders by pulling from finished stock located in warehouses around the United States. As you may imagine, when we got an order for 120 pieces of product, it was unusual for us to just happen to have all 120 pieces, exactly as ordered, just sitting in a warehouse. If we had, there would be no issues with taking the order, pulling the merchandise from inventory, staging it to be shipped, and putting it on the truck to be delivered within two days.

The problem with pulling from existing inventory was the tremendous investment it took to make and hold large amounts of finished stock in our warehouses. This approach required an investment in all of the raw materials used to build the mattresses *and* the labor to build, package, and store—without any guarantees those specific items would be sold. Not to mention that when it came time to draw an order from inventory, there was additional labor needed to fulfill the order. It's a lot different than handling widgets or wing nuts—mattresses are very large physical units that require manpower and equipment able to handle them.

The collective wisdom at the time was that we should move from fulfilling orders from finished stock to beginning the manufacturing process *after* the order was received. Switching to a build-to-order business model required an enormous change in culture. When the order was placed, it was paramount that the factory had the raw materials on hand, the production capacity available, and the appropriate labor necessary to build the product within a short timeframe. Along with this transition came more challenges. This approach required daily discipline on the manufacturing side of the business. There was no room for *almost* reaching our daily goals. If our customers ordered 800 pieces, that is what we had to produce and 790 pieces wouldn't be acceptable. If we didn't get the 800 pieces finished during the day shift, we needed to approve overtime until we completed every mattress we needed to ship that day. This required a massive change in thinking because, up to that point, it had been acceptable to produce 700 pieces when a customer order was for 800. On top of that: No one wanted the additional costs of overtime pay.

Another aspect that demanded changes had to do with the raw materials used to build the mattresses. Keep in mind that when we went to purchase the raw materials, it was conceivable that they might not be available. If this was the case, we had the ability to substitute with something of equal or better quality, but in reality the quality of the replacement materials was not always as good. It was a long and arduous task to get the factories to the point where they produced the exact specified materials on a consistent and reliable basis.

The biggest challenge throughout the process of transitioning to a build-to-order business was changing the habits and attitudes within our organization *and* with the outside suppliers. Although we had good intentions, the fact was that we weren't completing the orders in an efficient and effective manner within the prescribed timeframes. Trying to determine where the breakdowns were occurring, we had to figure out if the manufacturing personnel were not performing because they didn't care or because they didn't have the means to do their jobs. It was crucial for us to know if we had provided them with sufficient tools, technology, information, and equipment to get the job done. For example, if we were using fabric as one of our raw materials, *were our inventory numbers accurate? Were we giving them timely information and making what was arriving visible to them? Were we creating reliable supply chain relationships so if our supplier said they were going to send us 1,000 yards of this fabric on Tuesday, that was what happened?* It was important for the raw materials to reach us precisely on time. We called it *just-in-time manufacturing.* We didn't want it a day earlier or a day later, it needed to be there exactly when we needed it. Making that happen was a problem that many of our suppliers were struggling with as well.

American manufacturing had clearly fallen behind the world in many ways. In my opinion, not only did we create a different culture, but we created the tools and the technology to support it. What a transition. Our experience wasn't unique because the entire industry was going through similar challenges. The advent of computer programs and software to manage these processes was extremely helpful because it allowed us to accurately track what we had on hand, what was coming in, and what the lead times were so that everything came together.

On an overnight business flight from Atlanta to London, I happened to sit next to an IBM engineer who was in charge of just-in-time manufacturing for IBM. Fortunately, he engaged me in conversation, providing a glimpse of the inner workings of a brilliant mind for a free, five-hour consulting session. I asked him how they were able to successfully produce products in a timely fashion using the just-in-time manufacturing model at IBM. His answer in short was that they had all of the raw materials that they needed on hand, but they also sequestered all of the raw materials they believed they didn't need, just in case something went wrong. It was called *safe inventory.* They kept it in a cage with a lock and every time they needed to invade this inventory to get whatever they needed at the last minute, they documented and promptly replaced it. Additionally, they continually monitored their suppliers' performance. If they noticed that a supplier was not meeting their delivery dates, causing them problems and the inability to meet their deadlines, they would sit down and let that supplier know that they couldn't accept missed deadlines anymore. Either they would have to improve or IBM would have to find another supplier.

WE CAN DO BETTER

By eliminating millions of dollars of finished-stock inventory, we were able to dramatically improve the quality of service we provided to our customers. This allowed us to surpass our competition by delivering exceptional products in an extremely timely fashion. Once we had accomplished this mission, it was difficult for me to figure out why we weren't getting accolades for this dramatic turn around. It seemed that out-performing our competition became a non-event for many of our customers.

Our service representatives weren't chasing orders anymore since everything was running smoothly with the implementation of our latest strategies. With the extra time they had on their hands, we had them call our customers for feedback about the quality of our deliveries. They would say, "Mr. Jones, you received a truckload of merchandise yesterday from the Simmons Company Dallas factory. We just wanted to make sure that everything went well. Could you answer a few questions?" If he agreed, we'd do some market research: *Was the driver on time and courteous? Did he have all the merchandise that you ordered? Was it organized properly? Was the manifest that you received clear and accurate?*

We asked all of these questions, even though we already knew the answers. We wanted them to understand they were getting top-tier service and just by bringing it to their attention—by asking them to evaluate our performance—they began to appreciate it more. It was an interesting phenomenon, so we continued to do this with every truck that went out. During those follow-up calls, we started to talk about how important it was to us to provide exemplary service.

Again, by simply speaking up about it, sweeping changes occurred for the internal culture of our own organization as well. After we started to share the feedback with the employees, giving them credit for what they were accomplishing, morale improved, attitudes changed, and a sense of we-can-do-this filled the air. People started taking more pride in the way they handled themselves and conducted their business.

Western Culture

My move to Atlanta also came with experiences that demonstrated cultural differences by region and how strongly we often feel tied to them. Mathis Brothers, a large and successful furniture chain in Oklahoma City, was an account of ours. During one of my visits, I found myself having trouble trying to connect with Frank, the head of the mattress department. Transplanted from New York, it was interesting for me to meet people from the deep South and discover our similarities and differences. But being pretty adaptable and having picked up on some of the culture nuances didn't seem to help me much with engaging Frank in conversation.

While sitting in Frank's office one day, and pondering how to better connect with him, he put his feet up on his desk. Lo and behold, he was wearing the most gaudy, outrageous cowboy boots I'd ever seen. It seemed like he was placing the black and red python boots in front of me like a little kid would when they wanted you to notice something without having to say it. I had to comment, so I said, "Frank, those are the most amazing cowboy boots I've ever seen." Not wanting to compliment him, because to me they were anything but attractive, I certainly wanted to take his cue and notice how special they were.

He said, "You see these cowboy boots. I got a pair of cowboy boots for every day of the month without wearing the same pair twice."

"That's fantastic, Frank! You really have that many cowboy boots?"

"I got more than 30 pairs of cowboy boots, all just as beautiful as these."

I said, "Man, that's your thing. I can't imagine personally being that involved in cowboy boots, but I'm really happy for you. You obviously found something that gets you excited."

"You see those boots," he said, pointing at them. "Those are thousand-dollar cowboy boots."

Keep in mind that this is the late 1970s... so I said, "I can't imagine spending a thousand dollars for a pair of boots. Wow!"

He said, "Shit, I didn't spend a thousand dollars, I bought them on sale for $500."

Being a retailer himself, Frank was in the business of taking liberties with the truth with his customers everyday by telling them the sofa they are looking at is worth $2,000, but he would sell it to them for $1,000. [Even though he probably only paid $500 for it.] Yet he seemed to truly believe that he was wearing thousand-dollar boots *and* that he was an extremely smart shopper because he only paid $500 for them.

Seeing Frank fall victim to his own ruse was an important lesson for me in retailing and marketing. It was significantly eye-opening for several reasons. First, I learned that people want to believe what they want to believe. The second lesson was: Not only within his culture because of the importance of cowboy boots to him. If you can convince someone that what you're telling them is real, they'll feel really proud of it. It was just one of those poignant moments when you learn something you weren't expecting to.

Chapter 9

SEEKING BALANCE

*"We all operate differently,
so the more you communicate your feelings
the less room there is for misunderstanding and conflict."*

hen you are a young adult and in the midst of a busy life, it is easy to take time spent with loved ones for granted. Looking back, it's often the little things that stand out as some of the dearest memories we hold. One of those occasions took place on summer vacation on the south coast of Maine with Eva, my mother, and my children. Jonathan was about five years old and Rebecca just a toddler when we decided to take a week off and rent a house on the beach in a town called Kennebunkport. I still recall being able to see George Bush Sr.'s summer home from where we stayed. Although our rental house was old and a bit neglected, the location couldn't have been more perfect. The kids thoroughly enjoyed being able to run right out onto the beach. They were so intent on playing in the water that they didn't seem to mind that it was extraordinarily cold— around 55 degrees, despite the fact that it was mid-summer. I'm sure they were numb, but it didn't deter them enough to stay away.

FOR THE LOVE OF LOBSTER

It was a wholesome and enjoyable time that still makes me smile as I recall how my kids were free to indulge in whatever captured their interest. Surprisingly, Jonathan developed a keen interest in what was called a *lobster pound*. Although I'm not sure why they called it a pound, they were these places with large kettles of boiling water, where they cooked live, fresh-caught lobster. You'd take your plate of food and walk outside and eat at picnic tables on the beach. It was simple yet spectacular, and lobster didn't get any more delicious than that. To top it off, the cost was extremely reasonable, a fraction of what you would have paid in a supermarket or restaurant in other parts of the country. A whole lobster was only $6.

The best part was watching Jonathan eat his lobster with a joy and attention you wouldn't expect from a young boy. We had fun teaching him the technique to get the meat out of the knuckles and claws. He loved pulling it and dipping it in butter. My mother was a huge lobster fan as well, so it was a real treat for all of us. That week was such a fabulous experience for all of us that we went back several summers in a row, and going to the pound to eat fresh lobster became a ritual for us.

A HALLOWEEN HORROR TALE

A few years later, in the early 1980s, work continued to be extremely hectic for me at Simmons. Gratefully, the kids seemed to settle nicely into a fantastic community in Atlanta, Georgia where we were fortunate to have moved into a lovely home in a family-friendly area. Work monopolized much of my time, but the moments I spent with my children are some of my favorite memories. One great moment was on Halloween, when Rebecca was about four years old. She was an adorable little girl and she loved Halloween, but this one proved to be tough for her.

The community we lived in was situated in hilly terrain and the driveways to many of the homes were quite steep. It was typical, on Halloween, for the kids to avoid the long and winding driveways by cutting across the yards rather than walking down a long hill and then up the next driveway. In Atlanta at the end of October, the evenings were cool and dew would form on the grass. Rebecca and I were out collecting candy and having a great time. Determined and independent, Rebecca wanted to carry her own bag but, being so small, she was dragging it on the ground behind her. After about 30 minutes, I said, "Let's take a look and see how you're doing." We picked up the bag, and looked down into it, excited to take a look at all the sweet treats she'd gathered. To our dismay, her brow,n paper bag had a huge hole in the bottom, wet and ragged, and all of the candy she had received was gone.

Rebecca was so distraught, her disappointment was unmistakable as she began to cry. Within minutes she was absolutely beside herself. Halloween was *all* about the candy! I'm sure that to whomever found it, it must have looked like a costume-clad Hansel and Gretel had left a little trail of candy behind them. The horrified look on her face and her priceless reaction was so endearing to me, but it was quite a traumatic incident for her. When we arrived at the next house, we explained what had happened and our neighbors gave her a plastic bag—and some extra candy to make up for what she had lost. Happiness reclaimed.

Very much like me, Rebecca loves food. And that fact became evident that Halloween. A few years later, returning from a business trip in Europe, I called from my layover in New York.

"I'm coming home and I can't wait to see you," I told her. "And I have a surprise for you..." I teased.

"What is it?" she anxiously asked.

"I can't tell you, it's a surprise."

Undaunted, she pressed for clues: "Is it something to wear?"

"No, it's much better than that," I promised.

"Is it food?"

My Rebecca. That apple didn't fall far from the tree...

OFF BALANCE

Looking back, it is plain to see that, at the time, my work consumed me. Month after month, the mental and physical challenges of my job were my top priority. As they say, "hindsight is 20/20," but what I didn't realize at the time was that it was my choice to place work ahead of my family. At the time, my belief was that it was what needed to be done. Most likely it was my attempt to convince myself that I was doing it for my family, and for all the right reasons.

Learning to find a balance between career and family is a difficult challenge that many people struggle with. It is a personal matter and decision. Based on my experience, my best advice is that being aware of an *imbalance* is the most important thing. If you are conscious of the fact that there is an issue, you can deal with it. If you don't think there is an issue because you're doing what you "know is right to do," that's when you can have a problem. When it was happening, I didn't recognize it as a problem. My miscalculation or where my regrets lie is that I didn't understand that it was my *choice* to be constantly involved in my work at the expense of my family.

It wasn't until much later that I realized my business success came at a huge price. Part of the guilt comes not as a result of complaints about my absence, but quite the opposite. Nobody ever said anything to me. Eva never complained or caused tension. My children were always a joy and excited to share their time and interests. If I had talked about it with them, my guess is that Rebecca, the most expressive, may have vocalized her disappointment—or, more likely, sadness—with the lack of time we spent together during her younger years. I can say definitively that it wasn't for lack of caring or love for my family. Simply put, it seemed natural at that time to be doing what I was doing. Working. If I had been smart enough at the time to recognize that my choices involved sacrificing precious time that would cause me regrets later on in life, my choices may have been different. It goes without saying that we all have some regrets in our lives.

Exactly what I would have done differently, I don't know. It's hard to look back and reimagine a life. Maybe some of my choices would have included bringing them on business trips with me or engaging them more in other creative ways.

Changing the past isn't an option, but expressing the lessons learned and sharing how we feel with our loved ones is paramount. Never having the luxury of experiencing those types of conversations with my dad, I've made it a priority to tell my children how much I love them. I can say with confidence that they don't have any doubts about my feelings for them. My father's death instilled the sense of urgency I feel, the need to make sure that there is nothing left unsaid. At any moment it could all be over, which gives me the motivation to continue to express how much my loved ones mean to me. I'm sure at times I may talk or say too much, but it gives me comfort to know that no matter when my time is up, there will be no doubt about my feelings.

During my first marriage, when my children were young, it was beyond my understanding how crucial it was to be explicit about what you're thinking and feeling. Since then it has become clearer to me how important it is to vocalize those thoughts instead of assuming somebody understands how you feel. Many people think, "You should know how I feel." They think we should understand that their feelings have been hurt, or whatever it is that may be bothering them. That's really tough on the other person, because, quite frankly, they don't *know* how you feel. John Gray sums it up well in his book *Men Are from Mars, Women Are from Venus*:

"We all operate differently, and the more you communicate your feelings the less room there is for misunderstanding and conflict. Unfortunately, these were things that eluded me until much later in life."

FRENCH TALK

Not only did work continue to take up the majority of my time, for a few years I was traveling internationally constantly. Always ready for a challenge, I jumped at the opportunity to head up all of Simmons European operations in 1981. The largest company Simmons owned in Europe was located in France. The biggest problem company we had was located in Belgium, where they also speak French. So one of the first things I did when Bob Magnusson asked me to prepare for international business was to get some foreign languages under my belt. Having studied Latin and French in high school, which came pretty naturally to me, I was motivated to put intense effort into learning French so that I could communicate without the hindrance of a language barrier.

Fortunately, the leaders of each of the companies spoke English reasonably well, which shouldn't have come as a surprise since most international business was conducted in English. One day, while on the phone with the president of the French company, I shared my plans to come in and visit with him. He said, "This is really a perfect opportunity because in two months we're having our national sales meeting in Paris." He asked if it would be possible for me to join them and speak to his organization. We agreed it would be a great opportunity for me to share what was going on in the United States and to provide them with an overview of Simmons as a global company. He summed up the plan by saying, "We think this could offer our employees some sense of belonging to the larger organization."

I said, "That's a great idea. I'd love to do that." After hanging up the phone, it struck me that the people who would be attending the sales meeting spoke French. Even with my efforts to practice their language, I certainly wasn't in a position to deliver a 30-minute speech—in French— to more than two hundred people. I immediately called him back and explained that while speaking publicly was a passion of mine, getting up in front of a large audience to speak for more than 30 *seconds* in French would probably be disastrous, and that I felt it would be rude to speak in English.

He said, "I recall you telling me that you are taking a course at Berlitz so you must be learning how to speak French. Why not use this opportunity to become fluent enough to speak predominately in French?"

Always someone who was up for a challenge, I said, "You're right, I'll give it a try."

It was a much more difficult undertaking than I had imagined, but my commitment had already been made. So, sure enough, two months later in Paris, I spoke in French at the national sales meeting for about 25 minutes. Most surprising was the cultural epiphany that occurred for me when it became obvious that that speech was the most well-received presentation I had ever delivered. It was by far the most rewarding speaking experience ever. Certainly not because of the content of the presentation, but because I spoke in French the entire time. When I made the commitment, it hadn't dawned on me how important it was to do that. The gratitude from those who attended —their respect and appreciation that I had made the effort to communicate in their native language—was overwhelming. Although it had been a struggle and my French certainly wasn't perfect, they really appreciated my attempt, which was evident when they kept raving about how special and valued they felt.

Another huge cultural difference was how forward and aggressive the French women were. I was 36 at the time, a fairly young man, and it was unbelievable to me that after my presentation several woman offered me a romantic encounter. I was unaccustomed to women approaching men and with casual offers like this. It certainly wasn't the norm in the United States, so it made me blush. I smartly declined.

La Tour Eiffel

During that first business trip to Paris, I will never forget looking out of my hotel room window at the Eiffel Tower. It was stunning, and a spectacular sight to see in person. I had seen pictures all my life, but never the real thing. It seemed like a great idea to share this experience with my wife Eva back in Atlanta so I called her and said, "Eva, I can't believe this, I'm staring at the Eiffel Tower and I wish you were here with me."

She was dealing with the demands of raising our young children and, within seconds I knew I had caught her at a bad time. "That's wonderful," she said, with little-to-no interest. "I've got to give the kids dinner."

Obviously, my empathy for her position was lacking, but at that moment it became clear to me that we were not only physically in two different places, we weren't connecting emotionally or mentally anymore either. Although there was a sense that this had been building up over time, there was no denying our lack of stimulation, shared experiences, and interests. Even after 16 years of marriage, I still thought she was a wonderful, gentle, and bright person, but my life was changing so much. Attributing my discontent to myself, it never crossed my mind that the reason we were having these problems was because of her. It felt like my evolution was not necessarily good or bad, it just was.

That moment in Paris was when it occurred to me that this was not a good long-term relationship for either of us. Shortly after returning home and realizing that we shouldn't settle for the marriage we had, we started talking about our options. At first, it wasn't a mutual decision to divorce, because she was always confused as to what was going on with me. It was so difficult because of the great respect and admiration I felt for her, as well as the fact that I genuinely liked her as a person. One day, during a conversation with my mother about our plans to divorce, I told her, "Eva and I have never had a fight."

"Now I understand," she said to me.

It had never crossed my mind until that point that if I didn't care enough to have a fight or serious disagreement, I just didn't care enough. It also helped my mom because, up until then, she didn't understand what the problem was. During and after the divorce, there was no anger or hostility between us, just sadness. Maybe it was guilt for breaking up our family or my sense of duty and responsibility, but through it all my goal was to try to do everything possible to be fair to Eva. When you are leaving a relationship that is *not* toxic or bad, per se, it can feel selfish. I don't know whether it is or not, but it's certainly putting yourself and your well-being ahead of the needs of others whom you care about. That's what caused me to have such a tough time. Somewhere along the line it became my norm to feel a strong sense of responsibility. It was important for me to be a person people could count on and that people could trust. It still affects me today, which is why I find it almost necessary to do something that's not expected or required of me, to go beyond the expected.

That time was certainly an upheaval for all of us. In hindsight, I've realized that one of the things that was a bit different about my story of divorce is that most people from my generation just stuck with it and hung in there—no matter what. There was a natural progression of growing up and starting a family. You went to high school and had a girlfriend. Afterwards, you went to college, had a girlfriend, and went steady. In a fraternity, you got pinned. After that you became engaged and then married. You found a good job and then you had children. These were kind of life steps that were very traditional and expected in our culture. It was done almost automatically and often without a lot of conscious thought. Instinctively. In that environment it is difficult to go back and ask yourself, *Did I really do the right thing? Is this really what I need or want to be doing?* When you start asking yourself those questions, it can be like opening Pandora's Box. It becomes very challenging and that was where I found myself... a guy who had always done what was expected of me. Until that point...

In the long run, it turned out to be a good decision for everyone. Eva went on to happily remarry and she and her family are doing very well. Her new husband commented once that I was the best ex-husband anyone could imagine because of my tendency to do things that weren't required of me. One of the greatest lessons I learned after that divorce was my need to stop feeling guilty about things. The initial sense of guilt was tough and it took a while, but eventually it became clear to me that my needs and goals were important too. It wasn't okay to *always* think just of myself, but discovering that I needed to think of myself as well was a very powerful lesson. For many years, it was always my first inclination to put the needs of others in front of my own. I believed that was what you were supposed to do. My divorce from Eva was the first time in my life when I put my needs first.

Chapter 10

TWENTY-FIVE ROUND TRIPS ON THE ATLANTA-BRUSSELS SHUTTLE

*"It was because we believed fully in what we could do
that we made things happen that others
would never believe were possible."*

After we had reestablished ourselves domestically as a company that offered high-quality products *and* outstanding service, our CEO at Simmons, Bob Magnusson, came to me and said, "We have a substantial business internationally that I know nothing about. I feel very uncomfortable not understanding that aspect of the company so I would like you to go figure it out and see what's going on." Bob told me he needed to understand the history of that market and how to operate overseas—and make money there.

Over the next two and a half years, this assignment required me to fly to the major cities in Western Europe. I would spend two to three weeks in a city, fly home to Atlanta for a week, and then go back again to another European city. Although I had no way of knowing it at the time, this would become one of the highlights of my business career, teaching me firsthand the cultural differences that can either divide people or bring them together.

Simmons had wholly-owned subsidiaries in France, Britain, Belgium, Italy and a few other countries as well as licensed subsidiaries in Germany and Spain. Each of the wholly-owned subsidiaries ran their own mattress businesses. Although they were only a few hundred miles apart from one another, they each had their own factories, product lines, and sales organizations. It was shocking to me that the people who ran those businesses had never talked to one another or tried to understand what the other was doing. On a foundation of thousands of years of history, these European communities were full of people who didn't trust each other simply because they were from different countries and cultures.

WHEN 8 A.M. DOESN'T NECESSARILY MEAN 8 A.M.

One of the initiatives that helped me to alter the way these companies operated was to introduce the concept of networking. Having so many subsidiary companies in Europe, it occurred to me that it was important to have the general managers meet and share with one another what they were doing and, more importantly, why. Surely, sharing some of their best practices would provide ideas to improve every company's performance. It was inconceivable to me that they had never met, nor spoken to each other, when the distance between them from London to Paris was a mere 250 miles.

These men were 55 years of age and older. I was 37 and considerably their junior, even though my position made me the person they directly reported to. My challenge was to overcome the cultural shock of an older man reporting to a younger one—and an American no less. This required me to tread very lightly with all of them by trying to win their respect through my deeds and actions rather than my position. One of my first requests was to ask them to join me for a meeting. In that meeting I wanted each man to describe his company, who their customers were, and what type of advertising and promotions they used in their local mattress market. Figuring it wouldn't be that difficult of a task because they were all actively doing it, they all agreed without hesitation. My thoughts were,

Who knows? At the very least, they could get to know one another and they might even learn something.

We met at a small auberge, a country inn outside of Paris and had dinner together the night before our meeting. The agenda was to begin the meeting the following morning at 8:00 a.m. in a small conference room at the inn. And while the meeting agenda was formally structured from a business perspective, it was obvious to me that it was going to be informal when it came to attire. The next morning I was stunned when the arrival times for these gentleman spanned every variation of 8:00 a.m. that you could possibly imagine. The man from France, possibly because he was the host, arrived several minutes early. The man from Germany arrived precisely at 8:00 a.m. The man from the United Kingdom arrived a few minutes after 8:00 a.m. And the man from Italy strolled in 20 minutes later, while the man from Belgium said he hadn't been able to find the room which was why he was the last to arrive. Each of them had a different attitude about what was appropriate or politically correct when it came to arriving on time to a scheduled business meeting. This was another cultural epiphany for me: different people from different cultures each had a different sense of what 8:00 a.m.—or punctuality—meant.

After hearing their different explanations as to why they were late, it became evident this was just an extension of their culture. The Italian was so relaxed that it was hard to get upset with him because that was just the way he was. As for my part, I hadn't prepared them by saying, "Now I know you all have a different understanding of what 8:00 a.m. means, but I literally mean 8:00 a.m. sharp." This type of instructive conversation didn't occur to me until after the fact, because within *my* personal culture, I would be 20 minutes early rather than two minutes late. They all had their own unique points of view. This made me aware of the importance of being crystal clear from that point forward about what my expectations were. It became important for me to explain that regardless of their previous experience with arrival time, when they were coming to a meeting called by me, I fully expected them to be there on time out of respect for the other people in the meeting. Thankfully, we didn't have that problem again.

NIH

One of the biggest goals for this meeting was to try to get these men, these top managers, to understand one another. I felt that, at the very least, they might learn from each other's experiences. There is an acronym—NIH—which never really made sense to me until after speaking with them all. Suddenly it was crystal clear: NIH stands for *Not Invented Here*. Most of these businessmen were not accustomed to utilizing anything that wasn't invented in *their* business. In other words, their perspective was that a good idea that somebody else thought of was only for their own use, no one else's. They believed they needed to invent their own systems and approaches. Many of them eventually came around and implemented some of the things they learned from the others, but it definitely took some cajoling on my part to get them to believe it was okay to incorporate someone else's ideas. Once that happened, they were much more comfortable implementing change. As they embraced some of these concepts, the ideas became their own, and before long they felt they had invented them.

Another factor that may have attributed was a cross-cultural aversion to change no matter where you were in the world. I found this to be especially true in those societies imbued with a long history of traditional culture and values like the Western Europeans. There is a strong underlying thread of *that's-the-way-we-do-it-here,* making change much more difficult. At the time, many aspects of how businesses were run were very different than the United States. In Western Europe, labor, which we considered to be a variable cost, was actually a fixed cost. This meant that once somebody started to work for a company in Europe, they basically became part of the assets of the company. They had a job for life, which made it quite difficult for a company to modify their work force to match business demands. While I was in Belgium in the 1980s, they had wage and price controls in place because inflation was creeping up. This meant that the laborers or workforce could not receive pay increases *and* manufacturers were unable to raise the price of their goods. As you can imagine, the laborers were extremely unhappy about that. Virtually all workers were unionized so they belonged to strong labor parties.

At one point during these wage- and price-control times, the workers in Belgium decided they were going to have a national strike. Everyone who worked for a union was not going to show up to work on a specific day. This happened on a Tuesday, which, I recall thinking, seemed extremely odd to me since a Monday or Friday made more sense. After digging into it, I found out they chose Tuesday because they were already working four-day weeks. They didn't work on Mondays because there wasn't enough work to keep them busy for five full days each week. So Tuesday became the logical day to strike. It still seemed counterproductive to me because instead of trying to understand what needed to be done to stimulate their economy, their choice was to protest by working three instead of four days that week. This was a glaring cultural difference and lesson for me about how different countries approached difficult situations.

In Germany, another interesting example of an ineffective business strategy was brought to my attention. It was fascinating to learn that the Labor Party's solution to the 10 percent unemployment rate was to cut the work week from 40 hours to 36 hours. Somehow, they thought that by reducing the hours in the work week by 10 percent, it would automatically put the 10 percent that were unemployed back to work. The problem was, of course, that everybody would still get paid what they normally made for 40 hours. Nobody considered the fact that everything would cost 10 percent more, because they were applying 10 percent more labor to everything. But for some reason the Germans thought this was a logical plan. In the United States, we would have never come up with that kind of solution because we understand that we all need to be productive. At the very least, it was another cultural difference that kept life interesting.

Another aspect of my job in Europe was reviewing the budgets for each of the companies. In the UK, it became obvious to me that they *always* budgeted a 2 percent increase in sales. In looking back five or six years, it realized that it never changed. It was odd to me that every year they budgeted for exactly the same 2 percent increase. In reality, they ended up with 1.8 percent or 2.2 percent increases and so on, but somewhere very close to the 2 percent they had budgeted. The culture there was focused on always trying to make their budget. After sitting down with the team and inquiring about the consistent 2-percent budgeting, they were unable to supply me with adequate reasoning. Some of their answers were, "We always budget 2 percent because we think that's realistic and we can work to that end." To underscore their point the added: "It's not realistic to budget any more or any less."

This led me to pose the question, "What would it take to see a 10 percent increase in your business?"

"That's impossible," I was told.

"How do you know that it's impossible?"

My UK associates used history as their guide in saying, "We've never done it. We've never had a 10 percent increase."

"What would the conditions have to be create a 10 percent increase in your business?" I asked.

They wouldn't even address the question and responded adamantly that, "There's nothing that could happen that would get us a 10 percent increase."

It was at that point when it occurred to me that unless *they* believed it was possible to increase their sales significantly... it was definitely not going to happen. Even if I imposed a 10 percent goal, without a plan in place to achieve it and buy-in from the stakeholders it would never happen.

Unless you believe something is possible,
it will not happen.

Indeed they were right: without their belief in achieving a 10% sales increase it wouldn't happen. Not willing, yet, to throw in the towel, I began making suggestions for ways to achieve a 10 percent increase. Most were totally unrealistic ideas, but my goal was to begin to stimulate their thought processes and get them thinking about how this might happen. One of my ideas was based on the custom in Western Europe when everything pretty much shuts down for the month of August—because everybody goes on holiday

My pitch was "What if we gave a seven-day trip to the French Riviera to every one of your retail customers that increased in their volume with us 20 percent or more. Would that work?"

"Absolutely not," came the reply—without a moment's hesitation.

"Why wouldn't that work?" I asked.

"Because they will still have to pay the taxes on the value of the trip."

I was undaunted. "Let's pay the tax, too," I said.

"It still wouldn't work," they insisted, but they couldn't explain why.

The conversation ended right where it started: There was no way they were going to have anything other than a 2 percent increase *and* they thought I should be grateful they were projecting an increase at all. It was clear they were so entrenched in their tradition and culture that they could not conceive of breaking out of it. It was futile to even try to convince them otherwise. I chalked this up to my UK education and reminded myself that this was an important part of my mission... to understand their business.

DON'T FENCE ME IN

The Belgian subsidiary of Simmons was the one in real trouble. That was the bad news. The good news was that it provided us with the opportunity to get creative, experiment and try to do things a little differently. They had a factory that was about 150,000 square feet in size, but the reality was their business only required 30,000 square feet of space. Manufacturing was confined to a small area, and the bulk of this cavernous factory wasn't in use. Their main problem was two-fold: they didn't have enough business *and* they had a fixed-labor component. To keep the workers busy, they would have them build inventory in anticipation of orders. The risk in that is when you start building finished-stock inventory you seldom build what the customer actually wants so you end up with product that you need to discount or give away. After pointing this out, they agreed to no longer build finished-stock inventory.

To my dismay, when I returned to the factory two weeks later, there were another 50 pieces of finished-stock inventory—valued at more than a $100,000. It was upsetting to me, to say the least, because they had agreed to no longer operate this way. With the help of some colleagues back in the states, we devised a way to constrain their desire to build inventory by making the factory smaller. If they didn't have anywhere to put the finished product, it would deter them from building them to begin with. To achieve this, we had a company build a chain-link fence around the manufacturing workspace in the factory. It was locked at all times—and the only key was on my key ring. They literally could not access the rest of the building without my key. That was one of the most interesting inventory control systems we ever used: a chain-link fence. With this in place, all they could do was build-to-order and ship immediately.

It took a while to change their point of view regarding labor. Initially they saw labor as a fixed cost so if they had people standing around who were being paid anyway, they may as well have them build some inventory. The bigger picture we were trying to show them was that if they built inventory for which there were no customers, they would end up having to create some kind of a pricing incentive to sell the product. Therefore, the margins they were anticipating would deteriorate. It finally dawned on them that if the only purpose of their business was to keep people working and busy by building inventory (for which there might or might not be buyers...) their whole profit motive became irrelevant. This was not the goal of an American parent company, because in the United States the workers were vested in the profitability of the company.

We were able to make some inroads, at least with their ability to understand and comprehend other ways to accomplish their goals. I should point out that the mattress business in the UK was quite different because the mattresses they produced were high-end and very expensive. Peeking into those factories, it appeared to me as though they were doing occupational therapy in the psych ward of a hospital. Everywhere men were hand-sewing and hand-stitching mattresses. Making them one at a time made it an immensely labor intensive process. As a proud supplier of mattresses to the Royal Family, those orders made up the bulk of their business along with their account with Harrods, a department store known for carrying some of the most expensive and exclusive items in the world.

Throughout Europe, many of the countries had their own philosophies and cultural differences. The business practices in France differed from those in the UK and were more similar to the United States, especially in viewing their labor costs and the need for flexibility. With multiple factories all over France, many of our U.S. marketing and sales techniques were applicable to them.

Scheduling and urgencies found me again in Brussels dealing with the team to turn that situation around. From Brussels, only about 45 minutes away was the city of Antwerp. I heard one day that the European Tennis Championships were to be played in Antwerp that evening.

"Would you be interested in going to that big tennis tournament tonight in Antwerp?" I asked the general manager of the Belgium company.

"I'd love to go, but it's been sold out for months so it's impossible to get tickets," he said.

"I didn't ask if it's possible to get tickets or not, I just asked if you were *interested* in going?"

"Of course, I'd love to go. But it's totally impossible."

Next I approached the sales manager and, repeating myself, asked "Would you be interested in going to that tennis tournament tonight?"

His response was the same as the general manager: "We can't get tickets. It's impossible because it's all sold out."

Again, I reiterated, "I'm not concerned about whether it's possible or not, I'm just wondering whether you'd be able and interested in going."

"Of course I would," he said.

Later that evening, as we were sipping French champagne courtside in the VIP section at the Championship, I said to them, "Don't ever tell me that something is impossible if you really want to do it." They were stunned that I was able to secure tickets to an event they believed was an impossible to attend. During my years of traveling back and forth to Europe, the 2 percent increase story that I spoke about earlier really sums up the cultural differences that existed between capitalism in America and capitalism in Western Europe. We believed *everything* was possible, while they believed *nothing was possible*. In a way, we both were right.

In many ways, this was the essence of our society and our business culture in America. Of course we combined that "everything is possible" mindset with the tenacity to make sure that it actually happened. There was a huge difference in philosophy and mindset, and there still is today.

From my perspective,
it is because we believed we could,
that we achieved so much.

My main objective during my time in Europe was to learn about how those businesses were operating. And while I accomplished that goal, I have to be frank in saying that I don't know that my being in Europe, on behalf of Simmons and its interests there, made a vast difference. Especially when it came to bottom-line results. One could make the argument that you never really know how your actions influence people until after you're gone. My presence for that short time certainly exposed some of those businessmen to a different way of thinking, but in my opinion, even if I'd spent another five years there, it still may have accomplished very little. One significant thing that I did facilitate, however, was the sale of the Belgium company. My report to the top brass at Simmons stated: *You need to sell this company and get whatever you can for it. It's not a healthy business and it's not going to turn around any time soon.* Eventually, Simmons sold the other business subsidiaries in Europe as well.

For me, the personal *and* professional takeaway from this experience was that it really is difficult for people to change their thinking and the ways in which they operate. One of the concepts that has contributed to the success in the American business sector is the almost blind enthusiasm which, at times, gets us through challenges that we didn't really completely

understand. There's a lot to be said about zeal and unbridled enthusiasm...
and faking it until you make it.

---

*It was because we believed fully
in what we could do
that we made things happen—things that others
would never believe were possible.*

This is a vision that has been quite different from the rest of the world
for a very long time. Western Europe is probably as similar to the United
States as any place in the world right now. Eastern Europe and Asia are a
much darker experience, although Asian economies are becoming much
more capitalistic today since they've come to realize that *capitalism* is not
such a dirty word. Even in Russia today, the people are seeing success as
a fruit of capitalism. In my opinion, it is truly the best way to drive an
economy. There are probably more efficient ways to support the masses,
but capitalism works well in keeping free markets alive and driving healthy
competitive. Overall, my time in Europe definitely renewed *my* faith in
capitalism and American style of positive thinking.

ON TO BIGGER CHALLENGES

One cold night in 1983, the phone rang in my hotel room in Brussels. It
was 3:15 a.m. and Bob Magnusson was on the line. After realizing he woke
me up, he apologized but continued speaking. It was 9 p.m. in Atlanta but
he sounded as if he was in the middle of his work day. He went straight to
the point in asking: "Are you ready to come home?"

"I'm ready," I told him.

"I really miss you and I need your help here," he said. It was one of the nicest things he had ever said to me.

I replied, "I will finish up what I'm doing here and get back as quickly as possible."

Bob wasn't really clear about the specifics, but whatever they were, it was okay with me. I was ready to get back to the states. As it turned out, he wanted me to come back and run the mattress division as the Chief Operating Officer. Once again, I found myself with a promotion and, again, the news was delivered by Bob in a completely informal and unexpected way. It was obviously his style—and I certainly didn't mind. It's not as though he lacked the understanding of formality, he just seemed to know he had the freedom to be relaxed and casual with me. He probably thought, *I have to get him back here and get this thing started so I'm just going to call him now.* Bob was an emotional guy and when he felt something, he went with it. If he had planned the phone call to me, he probably would have called at a more appropriate time. None of that really mattered because, as in the past, it hadn't occurred to me to anticipate a promotion, or a significant change.

I didn't dwell on the past or fantasize about the future, my mindset was regularly in the present moment. My thought process was: *This is what I have in front of me, here are the challenges, here is what is expected of me, and I'm going to figure out how to get that done—and more.*

My focus was consistently on performing the job at hand to the very best of my ability.

Bob and I had a wonderful albeit unusual relationship. I had an enormous amount of respect for his intellect and his other exemplary qualities, one of which was an incredible sense of persistence. If things got tough, he dug in harder. Not only was he very strong, he was relentless. This was critical, I realized, since it was an important quality on his mission to turn Simmons around. Bob was extremely passionate, but at times he just didn't have the right skills to get the job done. Which is where I came in.

Together we were a formidable team, as I believe our skill sets complimented, rather than duplicated each another. At this point, we felt we were doing very well. Simmons was healthy and profitable. But unbeknownst to us, it was nothing close to what we would soon achieve.

Chapter 11

REINVENTING SIMMONS

"Life is short.
There are no guarantees or warrantees,
so always grab as much as you can,
while you can, and go for it."

EMOTIONAL INTELLIGENCE

Not long after returning from Europe, I learned that my new position as COO involved expanding our business by adding a significant number of retail outlets. Until that point, a considerable part of our business at Simmons was with Sears, Roebuck & Co. Because they were our largest account and incredibly important to our bottom line, we usually found ourselves caving into whatever they demanded. We found that they were very difficult to do business with. We decided to try and mitigate that by approaching Montgomery Ward, another powerful retail account that could provide us with far-reaching national distribution. Although Montgomery Ward targeted a customer demographic that was a bit lower, they still had the capability to move a great deal of Simmons' merchandise.

My plan was to spend some quality time at their home base in Chicago and get to know the senior people within their organization. Dan Levy, the Executive Vice-President, was the man running the show and with whom I spent most of my time. He was in charge of what they called *hard goods,* which were home appliances, furniture, electronics and so forth. Dan was an interesting guy—demonstrative, flamboyant and loud—but as I got to know him, I came to enjoy his company and respect his skills. After a series of meetings and discussions of our mutual wants and needs, we agreed to do business and a partnership was born.

Dan wanted to have an introductory meeting in which we'd bring together the key players from both our organizations to begin building relationships and working on logistics. Six of us from Simmons flew to Chicago to meet with about 20 of Montgomery Ward's people. In their conference room, at the head of an exceptionally long table, Dan called the meeting to order. Although we had already settled on terms, he backtracked and began talking about his requirements for a deal. Keep in mind, there would have been no reason to have that many people in a meeting to discuss whether or not we were going to do business together. It occurred to me that Dan was using the meeting as an opportunity to show his people how really powerful he was, and how important Montgomery Ward was.

After thanking us for coming and complimenting our organization, he said, "Montgomery Ward really wants to do business with Simmons, but if we can't have a $99 Beautyrest at full margin, we really don't have a deal here." What he was telling us and his team was that he wanted a $99 Beautyrest twin-sized mattress with at least a 50% retail margin. This meant his cost would be $50—although *our* manufacturing cost was closer to $100. Obviously, it was a totally unreasonable and unrealistic demand. It may have been that he was asking for something outrageous to try to leverage his position and put on some pressure *and* make a statement to his team. He knew how much we wanted to do business with Ward's and, obviously, he saw an opening.

Had just the two of us been in a room together, I would have responded in a very curt way telling him it was a ridiculous idea, and he knew it. Looking around the table at the 20 people from his organization, it was evident to me that I couldn't respond that way. Although my perception was that he was putting on a show for them, it wouldn't have been a smart move to embarrass him. Responding with the first retort that came to mind probably wasn't a prudent business move. Instead my choice was to rephrase his request into something that we could both agree on. I said, "Dan, what I hear is that you really want to start this new partnership off with a huge event that is really exciting and absolutely blows the roof off. We're prepared to figure out how to do that."

Taking my cue, he immediately acquiesced to my rephrasing. The tension he built was relieved and everybody went to work on getting things started. He was okay with what we developed because what he had really wanted was a merchandising opportunity and a deal worthy of a big promotion. Instead of saying to us, "What we really need to do is start off with a fabulous promotion. How can we do something really exceptional?" he chose the more aggressive posture of identifying a specific price point and demanding that he receive it. My approach was successful because of my understanding that price wasn't his objective.

Again, it is with gratitude that I look back on my ability to be able to see the bigger picture in tense situations when they arose. It was my first instinct to say *That's ridiculous!*, as it would have been for most people. However, all that would have accomplished was embarrassing him and, most likely, ruining our deal. As it turned out, over the years as a customer, they bought over $30 million of our products and represented a huge piece of business for us.

I knew that Dan knew his request wasn't realistic. So the question I asked myself was, *How do I get out of this situation without embarrassing him and losing the whole deal?* If I had responded in what most would consider a *normal way* in a different environment, we would have lost the deal. He was communicating with a picture— the dollar sign—to express his desire to begin the promotion in a phenomenal way. Aren't we all guilty of doing that at times? We ask for things that have nothing to do with what we truly want. If it had just been Dan and me, my response to his $99 request may have been some expletive followed by, "What? Are you out of your mind? You know that's not going to happen." But, in front of his own team of 20 people, I had to give him an exit—and a graceful one at that.

I've learned that nobody's perfect. Myself included. I've never been as successful in my personal life as I've been in the business world because it has always been much easier for me to maintain my *emotional intelligence* in business environments. It was customary for businessmen to be taught to be aggressive and treat every situation as a win-lose scenario. One could consider it bullying. Fortunately, a little self-control and an ability to detach myself from the situation, if that's what was required, allowed me to remain level-headed and focused. Visualization was a large part of my strategy in this area. In most cases like this, it felt as if people were trying to find the smallest corner in the room and put me in it—and restrict my ability to get out of it. My way around this was to visualize that we were in a perfectly circular room, without any corners, like the oval office. Maybe that's why the President has an oval office. The thought seems simple, but for me it was very powerful. Over the years, I've used quite a few visualizations like this one and they have been quite helpful for me. Another one of my favorites is to observe what is taking place as if I'm literally watching television. As a spectator of something that I'm not a part of, it makes me feel like I'm not a factor in the conversation. This helps me detach from feeling connected to the drama or whatever is happening. When you become detached, you reduce the emotional tension. And when you reduce your emotional tension, you can see the situation more clearly and evenly and then respectfully respond so that everyone involved has an opportunity to walk away happy. Apparently, this doesn't come as naturally to most people as it does for me.

NET... WORKING

In the early 1980s, we reported to senior management at Gulf and Western, the owner of Simmons. We were a publicly-traded company and they acquired Simmons stock on NYSE. Run by an Austrian-born immigrant named Charles Bluhdorn, it was one of the first big conglomerates. Gulf and Western owned many divergent companies such as Kaiser Roth Hosiery, which made socks and L'Eggs pantyhose, Consolidated Cigar Company, premium-brand cigars, Paramount Pictures, and even some auto parts companies.

The meetings were great networking opportunities because the top two executives from each of his companies would typically attend, allowing me to meet people like Barry Diller, who ran Paramount, and Michael Eisner, who was at Paramount at that time and later became the CEO of Disney. It was extremely stimulating to be around these visionary corporate leaders and hear about the challenges they faced. It offered me a unique opportunity to learn a great deal from a very impressive group of executives.

A GIFT?

Eventually, Gulf and Western chose to sell Simmons to Wickes Companies, which owned numerous businesses all centered around the home furnishings industry. The CEO, Sandy Sigoloff, was tough as nails and proudly accepted his nickname, Ming the Merciless. One important meeting was held over a long weekend in Palm Springs, California with senior executives from every company Wickes owned. Bob Magnusson and I both went and were impressed to find our suites adorned with fragrant flowers and delicious fresh fruit. It was absolutely first-class and we received exemplary service at the La Costa Resort. Although we had many hours of meetings and heard presentations from all of the different companies, there was plenty of time for golf, tennis, and other activities.

At the end of the weekend during our final meeting, Mr. Sigoloff (aka Ming) gathered everyone together and shared how he anticipated a great year ahead for all of us. As we entered the room, we saw that each person had a gift box sitting on the table in front of them. He asked everybody to open the boxes at the same time, revealing that each box contained the same gift: an elaborate knife-like letter opener. He said, "This letter opener is my gift to you. I want you to use it at the end of this year to open your bonus check." He let that sink in before adding, "You are going to have a great year and receive a substantial bonus at the end of the year because you've met your goals."

Another pause, then he continued: "But, if for some odd or unusual reason, you do not get a bonus check, I want you to take that letter opener, turn it around, and drive it into your heart."

Now that's a visual we didn't soon forget. And a hell of a closing note, extreme and memorable. After 30 years, I still clearly remember the gift and precisely what he said. That sums up the kind of pressure we were under—either succeed or die. Fortunately, we did well, although I do not recall being motivated by such rhetoric.

LAND OF THE SILOS

During this era, we completely changed the way we did business at Simmons. It was a period that became the most important and significant chapter of my career there. When I originally joined the company, it was organized based on functional disciplines. In manufacturing, starting from the bottom of that group, was the factory worker, who reported to a supervisor, who reported to a plant manager, who reported to the vice president of manufacturing, who reported to the president of the company. We had what is known in business today as a *silo* or a vertical integration of a discipline.

In the finance division, at the bottom there was an accountant, who reported to the comptroller in that factory, who reported to the vice president of finance, who reported to the chief financial officer, who reported to the president. In the sales division, we had the salespeople, who reported to a sales manager, who reported to the vice president of sales, who reported to the president. In marketing, we had another group, another silo, and so on.

After years of learning the ropes and then becoming a leader in the sales organization, it was my opinion that the company was extremely unresponsive to the opportunities within the marketplace. For example, as a sales manager, when a customer asked me for something—maybe he wanted faster delivery times—I didn't have the authority to make that decision. My first step was to talk to the vice president of sales, who in turn would have to talk to the president, who would have to go talk to the manufacturing vice president, who would then have to go to the plant manager. It had to go all the way up, across, and back down.

Previously, I've mentioned that customers used to say to me, "By the time you get me an answer, I've forgotten the question—and have certainly lost all interest." We were *not* agile, nimble, or responsive. So, with the blessing of the CEO, my plan was to change the structure of how the business operated by creating what I called *business teams*, with each of the 16 factories becoming a cohesive and self-contained team.

In each factory there was a manufacturing person, a financial person, and a salesperson, which incorporated the key management functions. The strongest of the three became the general manager for that factory. Instead of the plant manager reporting to the vice president of manufacturing, he reported to the general manager of that plant. This allowed each team to make its own decisions. Every team received parameters within which they would operate and guidelines for building their own profit and loss statement. And they were responsible for making those numbers. Each year, we would review how they had performed and discuss their plan for the following year. After approving their plan, we gave them the authority and the tools they needed to execute it. When a team met their goals, they would get a substantial bonus, and if they exceeded them, they earned an extraordinary bonus.

In the beginning, it was difficult. Most of the executives weren't accustomed to making executive decisions because, in the previous business model, they weren't involved in the strategy conversations or the decision-making process. We had to teach them how to be complete businesspeople. My term, *intrepreneur,* also applied in this situation because although you're a businessperson within a large organization, you are still an entrepreneur. The results were amazing! Not only did the company's performance improve dramatically, but the top management's satisfaction went through the roof as well. Once they developed team chemistry, they weren't criticizing or pointing fingers at each other anymore. Instead, they worked together in their own factories to solve problems and capitalize on opportunities, increasing their bottom line, and—at the same time—the total profitability of the company. They set their own pricing, advertising policies, manufacturing requirements and capabilities, and even wrote their own service agreements with their customers. Before this, the only person who had been really concerned about the profitability of the total business was the man at the top. Afterwards, everyone had a significant vested interest, and they exercised that interest intently.

After this, my job evolved again as I became a confidant and a consultant to help the teams meet their goals. It was beautiful, like a work of art, to watch their teamwork and enthusiasm grow. There were some risks involved in doing things this new way, but in my opinion the rewards clearly outweighed those risks. The challenge was to teach and guide the new leaders to make better decisions without making those decisions for them. It became evident that giving them the responsibility to make their own decisions allowed them to feel accountable, and this meant they took everything a bit more seriously.

From my personal experience...

If you want a successful business,
you need successful people.

Treat people like winners, and they become winners. The impact of empowering people and allowing them the freedom to meet their own goals can be transformative. When things go wrong, and they don't feel like an important part of the organization, they really don't care. When they are making the decisions and are held responsible for results, they care—especially when it impacts their compensation. I've found that most people genuinely love the opportunity to excel. I also recall that we had great times and quite a bit of fun, which is also an important aspect of employee success and satisfaction.

FIFTY SHADES OF WHITE

One of my many responsibilities at Simmons during this time was to lead a committee focused on the mattress merchandising process. The group also selected the new fabrics to incorporate into our line each year. The visual presentation of the mattresses on the retail floor relied on the fashion statement created by the *ticking*, as it's called in the industry. There was a great amount of skill, from years of experience, brought to bear when it came to choosing the colors and textures that would most appeal to the customer. Those of us with extensive backgrounds in this area viewed ourselves as *mavens*—a Jewish term used to refer to experts or connoisseurs of particular subject.

One year in particular, as we were sorting through the fabrics and creating our "yes," "no," and "maybe" piles, it occurred to me that the customers we were choosing these fabrics for were women, since they were the ones who, ultimately, chose the mattress they wanted. That fact brought to light one glaring problem: There wasn't one woman on our nine-person committee. I wondered who *we* were to be deciding what women did or didn't like. They were the ones whose opinions mattered. At that point, I decided there had to be a better way to approach our fabric selection process, which led me to find a research company who could offer some insights on our dilemma.

To make a very long story short, we had the firm perform extensive research through shopping mall intercepts with our target audience—women between the ages of 25 and 55. To our surprise, a clear winner emerged. It wasn't even close. One color in particular was chosen so many times—above anything else that was presented—that the odds of creating such a high level of attraction were one in a million. It was phenomenal! Hands down, the most attractive color to women was pure, bright white. Some may refer to it as *wedding white* or *antiseptic white*, but there was nothing brighter or whiter than this particular fabric. We were ecstatic to have found something that tested so incredibly well. There was just one problem. It wasn't a color we would ever use. Why? Because it would have been nearly impossible to have this bright white fabric run through our old factories on greasy conveyor belts and handled by a dozen workers, and not have a dirty mattress by the time it was ready to ship.

Gathering the manufacturing team together, I shared what we had found. I said, "We did research testing and these are the results. You have to decide what we're going to do with this information." I paused, for dramatic effect, before continuing. "If we want to ignore the results, we can do that and continue doing what we have been doing. Or, we can realize that if we use this bright white fabric, we're going to have huge success based on the facts from our research." Another pregnant pause on my part before delivering the kicker: "However," I said, "to make it happen we are going to have to clean up the factories. Everyone has to be prepared for that, because we can't use pristine white materials without changing the way we operate in our factories."

Surprisingly, they became inspired by that whole concept, willing to make changes at the factories, clean up the conveyor belts, and create new standards for the workers. Teams of marketing and manufacturing associates went to work in each of our 16 U.S. factories to overcome this significant challenge. The White Project, as we called it, provided a much-needed common goal for everyone to rally around to produce a product that was the clear choice by our customers.

It also changed how we selected fabrics for our products. It no longer mattered what any of us wanted or what we thought, it was our customers who chose the product line. The unexpected benefits that accompanied this change were that there were no more deviations, extra fabrics, or appeasing buyers. Our market research dictated that this was the line the consumer wanted and this was what we were going to offer. Not only did this product research change how we as a company did business, but it impacted the entire industry. It was a new approach to marketing, one that even caught the attention of and influenced the fashion-forward apparel business. It was a pivotal and exciting facet of business growth during my leadership years at Simmons.

HEALTH HURDLES

My career was going well and I found myself challenged and fulfilled, but my personal life and health didn't follow suit. Eva and I had finalized our divorce about three years after my return from Europe. It wasn't a smooth transition because shortly after the divorce, I rebounded into an unhealthy relationship. I tried to find a few lessons from that experience and learned one important truth: How people initially appear on the surface is not necessarily what lies beneath. After meeting a bright, intelligent, and vivacious woman, who aggressively pursued me, I felt special, needed, and all the things we long to feel. It was just what my ego craved at that time, but it didn't turn out to be a good long-term relationship.

Complicating things further, just a few months after Bette and I married, I became very ill with a condition called *obstructive jaundice*. The doctors thought that I had developed a tumor that was blocking my bile duct, but they couldn't operate or do much other than relieve the jaundice because it would have poisoned my system. It was a very unusual condition and most of the physicians involved hadn't seen it before. In a very cutting-edge surgery (at the time) that used some x-ray technology, they connected a tube to my liver to drain the bile from my body. Bile is like a sludge, so if it doesn't flow freely, it creates little calcium stones. These stones were getting caught in my bile ducts, requiring the doctors to dilate my ducts to try to remove the stones and allow the bile to flow. It was an extremely painful and frightening experience.

The doctors continued studying my condition and eventually performed an exploratory surgery to see what was really going on. It wasn't cancer, but they diagnosed me with a condition called *schlerosing cholangitis*, swelling and destruction of the bile ducts inside and outside of the liver, which had a high incidence in people previously diagnosed with ulcerative colitis. It appeared that my colon problem had triggered problems with my liver. The main bile duct from my liver to my gall bladder had atrophied so there was no bile flowing through it, prompting them to perform a liver bypass to connect my bile duct directly to my small intestine. Well, it worked, and from 1986 until today that's the way I've been functioning. I thank God for providing me with exceedingly competent doctors who did the research to discover and implement a viable solution. If it had not been taken care of, it certainly would've killed me and this book would be much shorter.

One of the blessings that I think God has bestowed upon us, at least for me, is that immensely unpleasant and painful experiences fade over time, but really wonderful experiences tend to become more vivid. My recollections of the intense pain during those horrible moments are nearly wiped out of my memory, thank goodness. For me, going through those trying times made me more aware, awake, and appreciative. This can be a gift, a way of helping us see things that others can't because we appreciate life much more. Another silver lining is that it keeps you particularly humble. You realize your own frailty and mortality and that, at any moment, life could be over.

Life is short.
There are no guarantees or warrantees,
so always grab as much as you can,
while you can, and go for it.

I don't have many regrets, and I am very grateful for that. It may sound trite, but each day we have is a blessing. I cherish each and every one of them.

Chapter 12

WORDS MATTER

"I learned that if you can keep your head,
you'll have a chance to resolve problems.
If you lose your head,
there's no chance at all."

At Simmons in the mid-'80s, we sought a business relationship with Heilig-Meyers Furniture, a company that had a very unique small-town strategy. With about 200 general stores in very small towns throughout the southeast—from North and South Carolina and Virginia to Georgia—they served dozens of small and rural communities. Each of the stores had a credit manager who had a long tenure with the company and had used those years to build relationships with just about everybody in town. This was long before the era of easy access to Visa and MasterCard, and the way people secured credit was through their local merchants. When you went into these local stores, you would sit across the desk from the credit manager who'd ask you, "Are you going to pay me every week?"

You'd look him in the eye and say, "Damn right, I am. I'll be here to pay you ten dollars a week for the next two years." That was the nature of the business in many small communities and the culture that evolved. The store charged high interest rates, and their real profits came from the credit operation, not the furniture they sold. These were lower-end stores that we would not have typically pursued as customers, but if we didn't have retail outlets in these small communities, we had no chance to sell our products to these people. Heilig-Meyers was a highly desirable account because it allowed us access to markets where we would never have gotten distribution otherwise. It was my personal goal to sell to this account, which ended up becoming one of the most memorable selling experiences of my life.

Through cultivating a relationship with Heilig-Meyers, I discovered the art of being a traditional, Southern gentleman. Spending most of my time getting to know Sidney Meyers, the chairman, my inquiries with him continued on how we could make this business partnership happen. Although at first he kept putting me off and telling me about all the things they needed, he was always incredibly gracious and charming. He always called me by my full name, Leonard. He'd say, "Leonard, you're just a fine young man. We would love to do business with you, however, we're so loyal to the suppliers that we already have. That makes it very difficult for us to make any kind of change."

I'd say, "I understand, but I'm going to figure out what it is that you haven't thought of, that one thing that you need, and I'm going to supply it to you." I knew that our products would enhance the image of his stores because we were a respected brand name, and would add value as well. As you might imagine by now, giving up was not an option. I knew that the right idea at the right time could change everything for both companies. Twice a year, in April and October, the international furniture industry hosts a market in High Point, North Carolina. One year, just two days before one of these markets, I was talking to Sidney on the phone. He asked, "Leonard, are you going to be in High Point?"

Although I had no plans to be there, I said, "Of course I'll be in High Point. What are you thinking?"

"We have all of our area managers in town the day before the market and I thought maybe we could introduce them to you," he said. "Maybe have a drink so you could get to know them a little bit? If they get to know you, they may feel a little more comfortable with this process. Could you bring some fabric down and show it to them to get them interested?"

Without hesitating, I said, "Mr. Meyers that would be a great opportunity, I would love that."

"We're staying at the Greensboro Holiday Inn."

I said, "Interestingly enough, I'm staying at the Greensboro Holiday Inn as well." There was no reservation for me there and probably none to be had, but I didn't tell him that. My first inclination was to take the date and figure out how to make it happen later. It was even too late for me to get a plane ticket, leaving me no other choice than to drive there. Even without a reservation, somehow I would find a way to meet with him and his managers the following evening.

We had no cell phones in those days, so before leaving Atlanta I called the Greensboro Holiday Inn. It was larger than you might think, with hundreds of motel rooms. I asked the front desk manager, "Who is the general manager of the hotel?" He gave me a name and then I asked, "What does he look like?" After thanking him for his help I hung up. A minute later I called back and said, "May I speak to Mr. Jones?" He picked up the phone and I said to him, "Bill, I have a very unreasonable request for you, but you've always come through in the past and I need your help."

He said, "What do you need now?" He didn't know enough to say, "Who is this?" or "I don't remember you..." because I was acting so friendly toward him.

I said, "I need a room just for tonight. I will only be there tonight and then I'll leave." The market hadn't started yet, so there was a chance there might be a room.

"We're completely sold out," he said. "I don't have anything."

"Will you double-check for me? Let me call you back in an hour to see if you can find something."

"Absolutely," he agreed. "I'll do that."

I hit the road again, stopping at a pay phone an hour later to call him again. I said, "Bill."

He said, "Len." [Now he knows me.] "I still don't have anything."

This goes on three or four more times. Finally, I called him again and he said, "Len, I've got a solution for you, but I need your word that it's only for one night."

I said, "You have my absolute word this is one night and one night only. I will be out of your hair tomorrow."

He said, "We have the prestigious presidential suite that's not being used tonight. I can give you that for tonight, but you have to get out of there early tomorrow because I have some big shot coming down."

I said, "That is the most amazing thing you could do for me." I finally got to the hotel and found the man that fits his description. I shook his hand and said, "Bill."

"Len."

I said, "You're my hero. You've renewed my faith in God."

I called Sidney Meyers in his room and said, "I'm on the 15th floor, come on up whenever you like."

He said, "We'll be there about 6:30."

Room service delivered food and drinks for everybody in the presidential suite. The place was just amazing and Heilig-Meyers guys had a good time drinking, eating, and looking at fabrics. These were small-town merchants, very unpretentious, so the suite at the Holiday Inn was a big deal. Sidney said, "Leonard, you sure have impressed the boys. This will really make a huge difference."

I said, "That's great. We aim to please and we'll always take great care of you and your people."

A short time later, Sidney Meyers said to me, "Leonard, you're a fine young man and you have done everything we could possibly have asked for, but we still can't bring ourselves to make this change." Which meant... What can you do for me that I haven't even asked for? There's something in your arsenal of tools that you can do for me that I don't know enough to ask for. You figure out what it is you can offer me to help me get over my reluctance to do business.

It was brilliant. They took me to school. I don't even remember exactly what it was we gave him—in addition to what we were already offering— but we figured something out.

What an experience.

Needless to say, we secured the Heilig-Meyers account. If that hadn't happened the way it did, I don't know that it would have happened at all. It was never the solution I imagined, but politely harassing that motel manager so much that by the end of the day he gave me what I needed. It was an amazing addition to our business and hugely profitable because up to that point Simmons had very little presence in those smaller communities. The account provided us with incremental sales on top of everything else that we were doing. It was also wonderful from a logistics standpoint, because they had centralized warehouses that allowed us to deliver to their main warehouses but gave us distribution to hundreds of small communities all across the southeast.

PLATINUM POWER

After a few years, we became a valued supplier to Heilig-Meyers. Every year they ran a mattress promotion they called the "Platinum Pillow Top," which was a great lesson for me in culture and focus. For a full month, everybody in the organization sold this one mattress. Even the truck drivers and warehouse employees could sell to their friends and neighbors, but they all had to focus on this one mattress in particular. Of course I wanted to supply it even though it wouldn't have a Simmons label on it. From a manufacturing standpoint, it was tremendously efficient to produce only that one mattress set. In those days, Heilig-Meyers sold 100,000 sets during this one-month promotion. No mattress promotion anywhere in the country compared to it.

The pricing was very tight because their specifications had to be adhered to with integrity. After completing the accounting and economic analysis, I determined that removing a quarter-inch of foam from the quilted top would allow me to make a small profit on the deal. Although they probably never would have known, I wanted to be upfront and honest about our modification to their specifications. My approach was to submit samples, demonstrating three sets and allowing them to see two that were made exactly the way they wanted, and one that was made with a quarter-inch less foam.

I assured them, of course, that if they could tell the difference—if they could identify the mattress with a quarter-inch less foam—we would include the quarter-inch of foam at the price we'd agreed upon. If, however, they couldn't, we would like to take the quarter-inch out of the mattress so we would have the chance to make some money.

It turned out that they couldn't tell the difference, but they hemmed and hawed and said they didn't like reducing the quality of the product. Holding firm to my position that if they couldn't tell the difference, it didn't add or detract anything from the product, didn't help. My boss, Bob Magnusson, who was there for the presentation, said to me, "I don't think your customer is going to be happy without the quarter-inch of foam, and I know you want your customer to be happy."

I told him that I agreed. "I want them to be happy too, but I also want to save the cost of the quarter-inch of foam from these mattresses." Without hesitation, we agreed to add the foam back in and we obtained the promotional order. Explaining to my boss, I said, "If I didn't make a fuss over the quarter-inch of foam and ask them to accept it, they would have asked for a lower price because they were so good at negotiating." By the time I had whined and bled over the quarter-inch of foam, they knew that there was nothing left to ask for. My plan was to go through the sampling to get to the point where they felt they had the upper hand.

It was one of the most challenging sales of my career, but the beauty of it was that they always acted like gentlemen—never threatening, carrying a big stick, or playing big brother by trying to dominate the relationship. I found it so impressive that they could be respectful, generous, and thoughtful in the way they did business. In New York, I had experienced a completely different culture, so the real lesson for me was learning to think like these Southern gentlemen—How could I get what I want and maintain a great professional relationship, while being admired and respected along the way? It also became clear that dealing with gentlemen in North Carolina required a completely unique approach, much different than dealing with businessmen in New York City, Chicago, or Los Angeles.

Those were very exciting and important times for Simmons and me, and although my career began as a college graduate, I was worked over by the best of them. These experiences became my real education—learning all of the various ways to get what I needed and wanted—and eventually allowed me to start my own business.

ANGER MANAGEMENT

Rhodes Furniture, another large and memorable account, had dropped us as suppliers shortly after Bob Magnusson had taken over as CEO at Simmons. Their leader, Irwin Lowenstein, was volatile as well, and together Bob and Irwin were an extremely challenging duo. We eventually won back the account and embarked together on a new promotion with them. One day, Irwin Lowenstein called Bob Magnusson and said to him, "Your company screwed up again, you're not delivering our orders. You haven't delivered anything for this huge promotion and we're going to drop the line again."

Bob Magnusson called me in and closed the door before screaming at me. Wild with anger he said, "You've screwed up again! Your people have let us down. I want you to find out who screwed this up and fire him today!" Not seeing the reaction he expected from me, he said, "The thing that bothers me the most is that you're not as upset about this as I am."

I said, "Well, if you want me to be upset and if that would be helpful to you, I'm ready. If you want me to jump out that window, I will hold your hand and go if that's what serves you best. On the other hand, if you want me to figure out what's going on here and get it resolved, I'll do that. You decide how I can best serve you."

That pissed him off even more. "Get out of here!" he shouted.

After doing some research, I found out that we had indeed shipped nearly every order. The problem was within *their* warehouse. Rhodes' computer was not recognizing that they had received anything, so they didn't know they already had our merchandise. Knowing they received thousands of pieces from us and that the problem had not been on our end, I called Irwin Lowenstein. I said, "Irwin, I want to apologize, you are absolutely right. We shipped 2,988 pieces of merchandise to you, but we did miss 12 of them and I want to sincerely apologize for that."

"What are you talking about?" he asked.

"You received your merchandise. I don't believe your computer is *recognizing* that you received it, but it's all in your warehouse. We did miss 12 pieces of the 3,000 that we should have shipped and I want to personally apologize for that."

"Your boss is pretty upset."

"Yes," I said, "he's climbing the walls."

"I think I owe him a round of golf."

"You owe him more than that."

"Alright, alright..." he said. "I'll call him."

And that was the end of it. Clearly they were both too emotional to stop and try to find out what was actually going on. You have a CEO of a big company crazed with anger, emotion, and hostility. In a calm and collected manner, the number two man figures out what's going on and resolves the problem. My thoughts at that time were that my job was to protect my boss from himself.

During this period in my life, my thinking was very clear, but I do believe there was divine intervention at play. God gave me the gift to respond appropriately by helping me to step outside of the anger directed toward me, see an opportunity, and take the steps needed to make it happen. It allowed me to be a catalyst for resolution. Gratefully, this gift provides me with the opportunity to look back at situations like this with respect for myself. Maybe that is a big part of why some of these scenarios seem so interesting to me. Not because I'm that smart, but because I learned that if you can keep your head, you'll have a chance to resolve problems. If you lose your head, there's no chance at all.

Another time, I was in Bob's office with the door closed and he was yelling at me about some change that he wanted to make. I sat and listened patiently while he screamed at me. "This is what you're going to do. This is when you're going to do it. This is exactly what you're going to do. Do you fucking understand?" he shouted as he pounded his fist into his desk.

I said, "I got it and I'm going to get it done in a way that doesn't convey that this is your idea. I'm going to make people believe that I think this is a great idea. But I want you to know, between you and me, and it'll never ever leave this room or my lips: I think it's a bad idea. I have a responsibility to tell you that. You are the only person that will ever know that I feel this way because I'll get it done."

Unbelievably, his response was, "If you don't believe in it, then we're not going to do it." I kid you not.

My first thought was: *Thank you God for giving me the right words.*

Thinking back on my response, what I wanted to say was, "What a stupid idea. I'm not doing that. That's ridiculous!" But what would he have done? His temper would have flared further out of control and he would've grown more angry and hostile. Then he would have shouted louder and maybe even said that he would find somebody else who *would* do what he wanted. The other option was for me to be intimidated into following through on what I believed to be a bad decision and just do what he was telling me to do. Without choosing either, I acquiesced to his power and his control by saying "I'll do it. I'll get it done." And not only would I do it, I'd do it the right way. But respectfully, in the privacy of his office, I needed to tell him what I really thought. And do you know what? He didn't even ask me *why* I didn't think it was a good idea. There wasn't even a debate. He completely gave up because, I believe, of my ability to handle it the right way.

The other managers in the company that he bullied would probably have said, "Yes, sir, I'll get it done." In my private conversations with him, I told him that he intimidated people into making bad decisions, and that wasn't a good thing. While he was a brilliant man, I learned a great deal from him on how to run a business—and how *not* to run a business.

IT'S ALL IN THE PRESENTATION

Since Bob and I were both analytical, we wanted to base our decisions on sound data. One of our research projects came back with inconclusive results and we didn't get the answers we needed. During my presentation to him I said, "I need your advice."

"What do you mean?" he asked.

"I need your suggestion on how to present this to *you*," I said. "If I tell you that the results were inconclusive but that we need to make a decision anyway, I'm concerned that you might say, 'Bullshit, we need to redo the research, hold off on the decision.' If I tell you that the results were inconclusive and we should redo the research before we make a decision, I'm afraid you're going to agree. I need to get some advice on how to convey to you that the results are inconclusive *but that* we still need to make a decision."

He said to me, "You always get your way anyway."

"Ah..." I said, "As long as we understand that then we can have the conversation."

We had these on-again, off-again encounters and confrontations. After we knew each other rather well, I said to him, "I need your brilliant mind to help me solve a problem because you're the only person who can help me. When I tell you what the problem is, you're going to get upset. If you get upset and start screaming at me, you're not going to help me and I truly need your assistance. Can you handle that role?"

"Of course I can handle that," he said impatiently. After telling him the problem, he started screaming.

"Wait a minute," I told him. "You promised you wouldn't do that."

"You're right, I did."

I said, "Now help me get out of this situation instead of telling me how bad it is or how stupid I am for being in it." Getting to know him well over the years allowed me to approach him in ways that others could not. I told him once that my problem was that I didn't have Leonard Gaby working for me and helping me like he did. If you know that you're effective in what you do and you're helping somebody else achieve their goals— which is all well and good, mind you—you would like to have someone doing the same for you. I'm sure you'd agree.

"JEW YOU DOWN?"

The ability to remain calm, cool, and collected while responding in a manner that enables you to achieve what you want, not only applies to bosses but to any difficult person you may encounter. One day, while coaching at a market in front of a hundred of our salespeople, a young salesman asks me, "What do you do when a customer tries to Jew you down on a price?" Everybody knew that I was Jewish; it certainly wasn't a secret. The room filled with the loudest, most nervous laughter you could ever imagine. It was a terrifying moment for me. I was standing there in front of the group, so I couldn't avoid the question or pretend I didn't hear it. Wanting to respond in a way that didn't let him off of the hook for making such an inappropriate statement, I knew my response needed to be effective but get my point across as well. The skies opened up, God shined his light upon me and gave me the response, and thankfully the laughter gave me the time to get it.

I said, "Jeff, I don't think that is what you really meant to say. What I believe you meant to say is 'What do we do when customers try to negotiate with us on price.' And, I think you are fully aware that some of us are better at it than others." God himself spoke through me, and apart from that I have no idea where that answer came from. Given the circumstances, I doubt if I could have come up with something better. Without flushing him down the toilet or berating him, I got my point across with a smile. It was a memorable moment.

No matter how irrationally, volatile, or rudely someone acts, you and you alone are responsible for how you respond. You have the ability to escalate an already livid boss, or diffuse the situation by remaining level-headed and respectful. You have the power in any situation to make it work for you. By putting in the extra effort required to step aside from your ego and look at any situation from a larger perspective, you give yourself an opportunity to have a much more constructive impact.

A Culture of Winners

Communicating effectively and respectively are extremely important skills, but don't forget that creativity and plain old fun go a long way as well. Having reached an all-time high level of success as an organization at Simmons, it was my wish to create a contest to help everybody feel as though they had a real opportunity to be a winner. In the past, since we had 16 different regions, the contests became extremely competitive and only afforded the top person to win something special. Encompassing the winner and loser mentality by nature, if there were 15 people in a group and only one could win, it implied that everybody else lost. It was important to me to create a culture of winners. To accomplish this, everyone in the organization was given a goal, and literally anyone who reached his or her goal could join us on a fabulous trip to Hong Kong. They were even allowed to bring their spouse or significant other along as well.

After employing our financial experts to help me verify the mathematics of it all, we determined that if everybody did, in fact, reach their goal, we would have such an enormously successful year that we could easily afford to pay for these trips. While presenting this to Bob, I said, "I want to give everyone the opportunity to be a winner. If they reach their goal, they *all* go to Hong Kong with us."

To my surprise, he didn't miss a beat in supporting this. "That's great, I love it."

Knowing we had to keep a certain pace to make this happen, halfway through the contest I sent a gift to each person who was behind where they needed to be to win. It was a pair of knee pads like the ones basketball players wore and they were accompanied by a handwritten note from me that read, *"Don't be afraid to ask for the order."* Why knee pads? Because sometimes you need to get down on your knees and literally beg for an order. My note didn't say, *"Don't be afraid to beg for the order,"* it said, "Don't be afraid to *ask* for the order," letting the knee pads say the rest. Most of them put two and two together eventually, but it was funny to hear people say, "I got knee pads. *Did you get knee pads? Why did we get knee pads?*"

When the contest was over, more than half of our 160 salespeople went to Hong Kong with us. It was an incredibly exciting trip and we spared no expense. One evening we all had dinner on the Victoria Harbor Ferry, a ship that served dinner in the harbor. Another evening we had an outdoor cocktail party on the rooftop lounge overlooking Victoria Harbor where I arranged to have a piano player for an hour. Well, the party had started and there was no piano player to be found. My first reaction was to get upset. Bob said to me, "What's the matter? You look agitated."

I said, "I had a piano player coming here to play some nice music and he's not here."

"Do you realize you're the only person in the world who knows the piano player's not here?"

"Yeah, you're right," I conceded.

"Nobody cares. It's okay. It would've been nice, but don't worry about it."

As a gift for all the winners, we took them to a tailor who made each of them a custom suit with their name embroidered inside. The tailor shop went all out, throwing a party for us with lunch and drinks while everyone picked out the fabric they wanted for their suits. It was something tangible they could take home with them, a reminder of goals set and achieved and their adventures in Hong Kong. It was fortunate for Simmons that a custom-made suit in Hong Kong was cheaper than buying one off of the rack in the United States. The beauty of that gift was the great source of pride the recipient received from it. When the trip ended, they had more photos than we could count and some amazing memories, but it was important to me that they had something that endured from the trip, something that gave them bragging rights. It was fantastic to have all these people return as winners, dressed impeccably in a custom-made suit. Not only did they feel great, but they looked incredibly professional.

This contest did so much for our morale and Simmons' bottom line that we did it more than once, traveling to St. Martin in the Caribbean and other exotic locations as well.

Part of winning or experiencing success comes down to determination. That's a personality trait in those who are committed to getting the job done. Determination involves understanding that everybody has constant inner dialogue that is extremely powerful. If you're saying things to yourself like, *I'm a failure,* or *I didn't accomplish anything, so I'm a loser,* you probably won't accomplish what you were seeking. This applies not only on an intrapersonal level, but interpersonally as well. I learned that if you treat people like winners, you get winners. If you are constantly telling somebody they're a loser, then that's what you're going to get. During my years of managing people, I've always tried to treat them like winners. I'm sure I might have slipped up along the way, but that has always been my intention. No one really taught me to treat myself like a winner, but I always felt that I was going to win. If for some reason it looked like I wasn't going to win, I kept my confidence by choosing to change the goal. Then it became a conscious decision not to achieve that goal, making it okay. This relieved my having to deal with losing or failing. While some may consider it playing mind games with yourself, it worked for me… and still does.

Chapter 13

IT AIN'T ALWAYS EASY

*"It was a defining moment to have worked so hard
and climbed so high, yet not be comfortable with
where I was, what I was doing, or who I'd become."*

My mother was living near my sister Susan in Glendale, California in 1987 when a spot was discovered on her lung. It was lung cancer and obviously the result of many years of smoking. Shortly after she began chemotherapy and radiation treatments, I went to visit her. At a loss as to what gift to bring, I finally chose a beautiful photo of my children, Jonathan and Rebecca, that she could place on a table near her bed. Unable to purchase a frame in Atlanta before my flight, I asked my sister where I could find one once I landed in California. She suggested the local Nordstrom store.

SETTING THE BAR

After finding my way to the display of picture frames with the help of an immensely pleasant sales associate, I decided on a simple brass one for $19.95. Surprisingly, she was able to get me to share my feelings about what I needed and why, while graciously helping me to select the perfect frame. Afterwards, she showed me to the counter, suggesting we put the photo in the frame and gift wrap it as well. She gently guided me along and, sure enough, within a few minutes she presented me with a beautifully wrapped box, looked me in the eye, and said "Your mother will love this gift. Your children are beautiful." That touching moment occurred almost 30 years ago, yet it still brings tears to my eyes and appreciation to my heart. It amazes me that a sales associate would extend themselves so compassionately for the simplest of purchases because someone was going through a difficult time.

On a separate occasion, in the midst of a large sale at Nordstrom, an associate not only asked me if I was looking for anything specific, but she took the time to go through an entire table of sweaters to help me find the size I needed. Although the store was extremely busy, she put in the extra effort to help me. My experiences are a testament to their dedication to providing attentive and caring customer service. Nordstrom is a spectacular example of how creating a positive culture can shape and impact a business from the top-down, inside-out.

As luck would have it, I had the honor of sharing my mother's picture frame story with Jim Nordstrom himself when we were both participating in a panel discussion for the Women's Apparel Association many years later. Intrigued by the research project I spearheaded about women's preferences on mattress fabrics, they invited me to New York to be a part of their conference even though my expertise was in the home furnishings industry. Afterwards, Mr. Nordstrom and I had a chance to visit. Retelling my encounter with the lovely associate who helped me find the perfect picture frame for my mother made him smile and he said, "We hear these kinds of stories quite often. Gratefully, we have associates who go the extra mile."

It was impressive to me that not only did he often hear stories similar to mine, but he and his family created an organization where that type of behavior was valued and celebrated. Sadly, I find it to be atypical with most businesses that take the position that it would be a waste of time to talk to someone who is making a small $20 purchase.

There is a now infamous story about the "return policy" at the original Nordstrom store in Seattle and it's worth recounting here. As the story goes, a petite elderly woman comes in and complains about a set of tires she believed she had purchased there. The store clerk explained to her that the store has never sold tires, but she insisted she bought them at that location. Evidently, at one time the building had been a store that sold tires, leaving her with the impression that she purchased the tires from Nordstrom. As the story goes, that although it was impossible for her to have purchased the tires from Nordstrom, they gave her a store credit for them anyway. I asked Jim Nordstrom if this was a true story and he said, "I hope not." True or not, it made for a great story supporting Nordstrom's exemplary customer service.

CIRCLE OF LIFE

As it turned out, the lovely sales associate at Nordstrom was right: my mother loved the framed photo of her grandchildren. During our visit I saw that the doctors had drawn a circle on her chest to indicate where they were targeting her tumor for radiation therapy. My eyes kept going back to it during our last conversation. I'm not sure how many times I said it, but I recall repeating over and over how much I loved her and cared for her. Then I said, "Mom, I just don't want you to suffer. You're too wonderful of a person to suffer for even a moment."

She said to me, "I don't want *you* to suffer either because of this." Worrying about others first and herself later was typical of her sweet and caring nature. We are very much alike in that we both found it difficult to be a burden to others. Grateful that she didn't suffer long, but devastated to lose her at just 67 years of age, my mom passed a short time after my visit. It felt like a blessing to have been able to say goodbye to her. Losing her reminded me to make sure not to leave things unsaid. It was also a reinforcement to be honest and direct with people so that they don't have to try to figure out my feelings. This has gotten me in trouble at times because some people don't really want to hear your truths, their truths, or your perceptions. I've learned that sometimes it is best to keep some things to yourself. When it is evident to me that they may not want to know my take, I've learned to try to wait for them to ask first. However, I believe one of the reasons I don't have many regrets is because my experiences taught me to speak up when you can. Maybe that's why having a 60th birthday party for myself was so meaningful to me. Being around friends while I'm still alive and not leaving anything unsaid is important because we just don't know when it will be our time. So my suggestion is celebrate life—and have a party for yourself and tell the people you care about how much they mean to you.

S-CORP REWARDS

Unfortunately, the sadness surrounding my mother's death in the late 1980s wasn't the only darkness I walked through during that time. And although it wasn't easy, that time—like other times of sadness and challenge—taught me more about myself.

Sandy Sigoloff, the Wickes Company CEO, had just sold Simmons to Wesray Capital, a private equity firm, in what is known as a *leveraged buyout*. Basically, it means the assets within the company are used as collateral toward the debt that is needed to buy the company. By creating what's called a Subchapter S Corporation [*S Corp* for short] they did that quite successfully. What happens is the profits of the company flow through to each of the partners that own it in direct proportion to their stake in the company. The benefits of operating as an S corporation are the entity protections that come from being incorporated, but also the tax advantage of avoiding double taxation on the profits. Therefore, those profits are passed directly to the shareholders. The challenge involved with an S corporation, at that time, was that you could only have 35 partners and for a typical public company, that wasn't practical since there were usually quite a few more than 35.

As a management team, we were given 20 percent of the total deal and the private equity partners received the other 80 percent. Although we received the minority share, we were still able to benefit from the success of Simmons, which was terrific. Expanding in an industry that had very little growth meant we were building a larger market share. What little debt we began with was relieved by selling off real estate. For example, we sold a factory in Dallas, Texas to a real estate company and then leased it back. Rather than owning the real estate, we leased it, providing us with plenty of cash to pay down the existing debt incurred to buy the company. Within a period of about 18 months, there was no debt on the books. We were exceedingly successful and all of the difficulties and challenges that we dealt with in the early 1980s were behind us.

TAKING STOCK OF OWNERSHIP

After owning the company for less than two years, Wesray came to us and said, "We're selling the company." But that was only a part of the story. They also told us, "We're going to sell it to the employees."

We had many questions: "Have you talked with the employees? Are they interested in buying the company?"

They admitted they hadn't and said, "We're going to do what we call a leveraged ESOP." An ESOP is an Employee Stock Ownership Plan, and it means that the company is bought on behalf of the employees. As the manager of the entire mattress division, they came to me and said, "We need a business plan from you as to what your sales and profits are going to be for the next five years." I worked on that for quite a while before giving them my projections. They came back to me and with their assessment of the plan: it wasn't good enough.

"Well," I told them, "that's what it is. It is what it is."

They challenged me and said, "What if everything goes perfectly? What if everything falls into place and you do extremely well, would you do more than this?"

"Yes," I admitted, and realized that what they were really asking for was a best case scenario projection. "I will do that, but I will also give you a worst-case scenario. In other words, I'll balance the best-case with the worst-case and you will have what's in the middle, which is actually what I think is going to happen."

After supplying them with *all* of the projections, they started to do *their* calculations with the numbers, eventually going with the best-case scenario and completely forgetting about the other two projections—middle- and worst-case. To top it off, I was expected to support and justify this best-case scenario. Remember, I'm part of the management team that owns the company *and* part of the management team going to buy the company. In selling my share of the company, and in a position to significantly enrich myself by making a large amount of money. As a manager of the business, it's also important for me to figure out how to run this business *after* the transaction happens. This was a clear conflict of interest, causing me to feel extremely torn throughout the entire process. It was frustrating that there was nothing I could do to change what was about to happen.

In retrospect, it was pretty naïve of me to believe the banks were going to finance this transaction without asking, "Is this a pie in the sky projection? What do you actually believe is going to happen?" Inconceivable, though, nobody asked. To my surprise, when presenting this best-case projection to representatives from 60 different banks in New York City, they all asked a massive number of questions but never asked hardball questions, only softball ones, or really challenged what we were doing. They ended up oversubscribing for the debt by offering $200 million, which was far too much money for the company.

In less than two years, Wesray Capital made $200 million on this transaction alone. Prior to the sale of Simmons, they had concluded a similar deal for Avis Rent-A Car, buying and selling it for a profit of over $600 million. There were two principals in that organization who benefited the most from the sale: William E. Simon [the *Wes* of Wesray] who was the Secretary of the Treasury under President Richard Nixon, and Ray Chambers [the *ray* of Wesray] who was an equity partner.

Unbelievably, the banks subscribed for all this debt based on collecting their interest from the free cash flow that Simmons threw off. In simple terms, let's say after depreciation the company had $20 million of free cash flow. They were borrowing $200 million, so if the interest rate was 10 percent, [which it wasn't but just to make it simple] the $20 million that the company threw off would pay the $20 million in debt service owed to the bank. Since it appeared that the interest owed to the bank could be paid, they were considered to be doing fine.

Simmons was now leveraged to the maximum amount that the free cash flow allowed, and nobody seemed to care how it would operate going forward. Not a month, six months, or a year down the road, but the very day the transaction closed, the company was technically non-compliant with the loan covenants. Wesray Capital walked away from a transaction where the company, based on the loan documents they had just signed, was unable to pay its debts. The transaction started the trouble and it just continued to get worse and worse. The sellers of the company, myself included, ended up giving some of the money that we had received back to the bank because we couldn't deny the sale price was too rich.

On top of that we, as the management team, had the added responsibility of actually running the over-leveraged company. This one transaction changed everything—all my feelings about Simmons and my part in it. Prior to this, it was easy for me to be proud of my choices and actions, but for the first time in my life, I was not proud of myself.

It was a defining moment
to have worked so hard and climbed so high,
yet not like where I was,
what I was doing, or who I had become.

Until that point, my goal had always been to put the best interests of
the company first. In the process, my needs, goals, and aspirations were
also achieved because they were totally in-line with the benefits that the
company would reap. There had never been any disconnect between the
two—until that point. On the very day the transaction closed, I made
a commitment to myself to leave Simmons. At the same time, I knew I
couldn't leave immediately, because running away didn't feel right either.
During my final 18 months with Simmons, trying to figure out what my
next step was going to be was always on my mind. Sadly, the environment
at Simmons during that last year was filled with hostility. Many of the
employees were now burdened with significant debt but weren't seeing any
personal benefit. Rightly so, they were full of questions and some even
began asking, "Who is the trustee that is representing the interests of the
employees?"

Having always prided myself on being an ethical businessperson, it
made me feel absolutely horrible. Although the deal had not involved any
of my personal actions, it wasn't possible for me to totally wash my hands
of it. I couldn't say, "I wasn't part of this at all," because to some degree
I was, which was regrettable. It felt like being stuck between a rock and
a hard place. In hindsight, I don't know that there was anything I could
have, personally, done differently. I could have chosen to leave *before* the
transaction occurred, but that didn't seem to be have been an option at
the time. Afterwards, my goal shifted to trying to do the right thing by
staying on and helping to get things settled and set us on a proper course.

In the long run, the stock ownership plan did well, so the employees made out well over the years. More recently, the company has gone through a bankruptcy, in part because they sold and leveraged the company so many times. Knowing that it wasn't the end of these financial transactions, it was my choice to leave Simmons in early 1991.

RETAIL 101

A customer from Simmons that I came to admire and know well, Melvyn Wolff, owned Star Furniture in Houston. It was a well-run and profitable business, so when he offered me the opportunity to move to Houston and become the President of his company, I decided to go for it. In fact, it was my intention to buy Star Furniture, and Melvyn knew it. Once I was settled in Houston, Melvyn said, "Let's make sure that you really like this business, because you are coming to the retail side. You know the manufacturing side, but that's a different ball game." It seemed smart to spend some time learning and running the business prior to buying it. And it definitely turned out to be much more complex than I had initially anticipated, so it took quite a bit of time and effort on my part to feel comfortable with everything. Eventually it made sense to me, I felt I was good at it and looked forward to the day that Star Furniture was mine.

The company's impeccable warehouse was enormous. In excess of 600,000 square feet—40 feet high with seven different levels—it was necessary to use heavy-duty equipment to move the furniture on and off the steel storage racks. Every piece of furniture was traceable by barcode at a three-dimensional location, even though like stock was not grouped together and in random locations. The inventory was precise and real-time, in the warehouse *and* throughout the six stores in the organization. Unlike the early lack of warehouse functionality at Simmons, which was a real weakness, Star Furniture executed at a superb level. It taught me that you might have excellent computer systems, but if you don't execute well, then you just have a great system with bad follow through. It's not enough just to have the capacity to keep track of inventory, you also need to have the discipline to do it.

In my opinion, another aspect that led to Star Furniture's success was the in-house repair shop located right inside the warehouse. After the piece of furniture was retrieved from its location, it was taken out of its box and inspected before being placed on a delivery truck. If any damage was found, it was sent to the repair shop. Although this was something any larger retailer could do instead of sending it back to the supplier, it was somewhat unusual at that time. Not only did this save time and money but Star Furniture was able to charge what we called *shop time charges* to the supplier based on how long it took to repair the damage. All of the vendor suppliers found this preferable to the costly option of returning it to the factory of origin for repair.

The entire organization was a gleaming demonstration of what a culture of excellence looked like. It came from the top down, beginning with Melvyn Wolf, and exuded from the inside out. You could see it each day and throughout every aspect of the operation. Melvyn established these disciplines many years before my arrival and expected everybody to adhere to them. I was totally impressed with his ability to be consistent and extremely disciplined in the operational side of his business. It was evident that is why it worked so well. Not only was he involved in every detail, but he worked seven days a week for at least 10 to 12 hours a day. Running the operation was a great deal of work, but he was meticulous about it.

The inventory numbers were also extremely important to him. Buyers and merchants spent a massive amount of time on the mathematical equations of balancing the inventory based on estimated purchasing patterns. For example, if you were talking about bedroom furniture, typical customers would buy a certain combination or grouping including the bed, headboard, a nightstand, a particular dresser, and so forth. Retailers sell only one nightstand with most bedroom set purchases, so it didn't make sense to order two for every bed that you acquired. On top of that, there were special orders, creating complex formulas for managing inventory. Star Furniture did it all extremely well.

On the flip side, many of those who worked at Star described Melvin as a micromanager. Although his attention to detail definitely benefited his company, it taught me how invaluable it was to empower people throughout an organization. At one point during my time there, a reporter from *Furniture Today*, one of the industry trade newspapers, came to interview us. They asked for both of our perspectives, Melvyn as the owner and CEO, and me as the number two man, the President. The young man, Clint Engle, asked a very interesting question. He said, "How do you make decisions?"

Melvyn proceeded to explain that he looked at an issue and decided where he wanted it to go. He expressed that he basically controlled the conversation by convincing people that what *he* wanted to do was the right way to do it. It was important to him, however, to make them feel like it was *their* decision. He knew he was manipulating them, but Melvyn thought it was great that they were happy with the outcome that they believed was the result their choice. It was a remarkable moment and a huge epiphany for me as I listened to him articulate his philosophy. Clint then turned to me and asked the same question.

I said, "This business is growing rapidly and it appears to me that the best decision I should make is to make as few decisions as possible." I let that sink in before continuing. "What I believe *I* should do is decide who has what job and what the parameters are around that position, and then let them make the decisions in areas where they are the most knowledgeable. I view my role as someone who picks the best people and then nurtures them so they make great choices."

It was then that I realized just how different our points of view were.

I recall the time Melvyn and I agreed to hire an assistant buyer, but there was a question about where we were going to locate her office. We were having a lengthy conversation about this when Melvyn finally said, "Why don't you just take care of this and decide where her office will be."

"Okay, I'll do that."

Later that same day, he came to me and asked, "Well, what did you decide?"

"We're going to put her over there," I said, pointing to an office down the hall.

His response was, "Oh, don't do that. This is where she should be." He pointed to a different office

"If you wanted to make the decision about what office she was going to have, why didn't you just do that instead of telling me to and then deciding that you don't like the choice I made?" I asked him.

It felt like he was playing games with me, which I didn't appreciate. That's not a productive way to work together. Where our new hire's office was wasn't as important to me but, obviously, if he had strong feelings about it he should have just made the decision and said, "Let's put her over here." Although we had a few interactions like this, Melvyn was always a gentleman. He was extremely bright and articulate, but he was a man accustomed to making all the decisions and that was the way he liked it. Learning about Star Furniture and the retail side, in general, was very beneficial and educational for me.

Overall, my time at Star Furniture went well and we implemented a number of strategies that positively impacted not only the business efficiencies but Star's profits as well. Over my four years there, Star Furniture's business volume almost doubled and the profits TRIPLED. Although I cannot take full credit for that, I know that with my help the business did flourish during my time there.

Unfortunately, it hadn't occurred to me to create a contract with a stipulation that stated that my purchase price for the business would be based on what it was worth when I started working at Star. During my four years as president of the company, the overall volume of the business went from $50 million to over $90 million, which was great for Melvyn, but at that point—and based upon current value—I could no longer afford to buy the business.

DELEGATE… OR DIE

Although it was unfortunate to have learned such a tough lesson, my time at Star Furniture not only taught me a great deal about retail, but reinforced my beliefs about the most productive ways to manage a business. Near the end of my time as President of Star, Melvyn decided to bring in an outside group of advisors to help him with his struggle about what to do with the business. Since he was getting older and had no succession plan, he didn't want to die and leave the burden on his wife to sell the business in a fire sale. One day the advisory group interviewed me and we were discussing Melvyn's need to micromanage the business.

They said, "We've developed an expression that describes Melvyn."

I said, "What's that?

"There's no decision too small for him to make," they said with a smile,

These were obviously bright businessmen who were respected and sought-after advisors, so their assessment of Melvyn stuck with me for all these years. And it occurred to me that nothing they said came as a great surprise, because I'd seen it for myself from the beginning.

When I first joined Star Furniture, Melvyn had a staff meeting with more than 30 people in management positions from throughout the company. We met in a conference room on Monday mornings at 8 am sharp. We all sat around a very large table with Melvyn at the helm. One of the first topics discussed one morning was the need for a lock on the back door of the warehouse, the door used by all of the warehouse workers. The conversation revolved around what kind of lock to choose. This was when electronic locks, where just a swipe of a card gave you access, were first being developed. The second choice open for discussion was to possibly use a combination lock that would have to be changed if and when an employee was no longer with the company. The third choice was a good old-fashioned dead-bolt lock with a key. The first conversation was about the different options, the conversation a week later about costs as well as the pros and cons of each option. This went on, week after week, to the point where we were on our sixth meeting and still talking about the lock.

At the time, the expense of the lock would have been a maximum of about $5,000 for the most sophisticated one. After six weeks, we still hadn't made a decision. I was stunned by the lock saga. While watching what was going on, I couldn't help but add up the time it was taking from the people who were sitting there bored to tears because it had no relevance to what they did at the company. Retail managers tend to work inordinately long hours, and this continuous discussion was disrespectful of their time because store and sales managers were not concerned about the lock on the back of the warehouse.

Since I had enormous respect for him (and felt like I *must* be missing something...) I asked Melvyn to explain why he would spend so much time on such a small matter. He's a smart man, runs a very successful business, and makes good money, so I was at a loss as to what he was thinking. When we were alone after the meeting, I said, "Melvyn, I'm sure you have a reason for doing this, I'm just having trouble figuring it out. Would you share with me what the logic is of tying all these people up over a lock?"

He said, "If everybody sees how much I'm agonizing over the lock, they will understand they have to really think about what seems to be a relatively small expense and be cognizant about how they consider it in the future."

After explaining that he was leading by example, he said to me, "Well, how would you have handled it?"

"Very differently."

"Really?" he said, "Tell me what you'd do."

"I would assign one person, maybe two, to study our needs and the different locks available to us. They'd understand all the pros, cons, expenses, and costs and then come back with a recommendation. Then I would ask them to defend their recommendation, while I did everything possible to poke holes in it. Afterwards, if I felt satisfied they had thought of everything and made the right recommendation, I would approve the purchase of the lock." It would have taken me about 30 minutes and them about four hours, and it would have been done weeks ago. Meanwhile, we had a warehouse that still wasn't secure because we still hadn't made a decision. Plus we made everybody feel like we were overly concerned about something very trivial and, in doing so, showed no respect for their time.

He said, "Well, that's another way to look at it. But I want them to really understand that we can't spend money frivolously."

This kind of thought process wasn't unique to him or Star Furniture; it happened at Simmons as well. While in the number two position, I also watched Bob Magnusson make, in my opinion, critical management mistakes. One time, while in the midst of developing a new product, an issue arose. After taking over the product development committee I had initiated, he challenged one engineer with getting a certain project completed. When it didn't get completed, Bob got involved in the project and started to tell people what to do and how to do it. He basically saved this engineer from failure. Again, being the intrusive, inquisitive person that I am, I asked him about it in private. "Why in the world are you imposing yourself in this conversation when you've already told this guy what you expect?"

His answer was straight to the point: "Because I don't want him to fail."

I said, "Well, I don't want him to fail either, but how do you hold him accountable for something when you impose yourself and then you become the one who causes it?"

"Well, I'd rather cause the problem than him."

"But you'll never get him to be accountable," I insisted.

"Well, maybe," Bob said. "How would you do it?"

"I would say 'Paul, here's the project and I'm counting on you to get it done within four months. If you need some help, be sure to call me. Maybe we'll meet once a month just to make sure everything is going well, but here's the date it needs to be completed by.'" I paused, as Bob studied me intently. "'This is what I expect, Paul. Are you okay with that? Does that work for you?' And that's the end of the conversation. He's an adult and a responsible executive in this company and if he's having trouble getting it done, I expect him to come to me. That's the risk of giving him a job, but at least I know that he can't get the job done or he isn't strong enough to figure out how to find solutions to achieve the goal that he set for himself. That's not only empowerment, but accountability and making people responsible for their achievements. If and when he finishes, I would acknowledge his work and praise him for a job well done, but I'm sure as hell not going to do his job for him. If I do his job for him, what do I need him for?"

While both Bob and Melvyn perceived themselves to be tough managers, in my opinion they were not. Their weakness was that they didn't want people to fail. It was not my wish for them to fail either, quite the opposite. But I was willing to hold them responsible because I didn't think it was unreasonable to expect a senior-level person, who is paid a lot of money, to get a specific job done.

I give them both the benefit of the doubt: Maybe that's all they knew. In those days—30 years ago—it was customary for the boss to be involved in every little detail. The traditional management style was command and control—you do this, you do that— telling everybody what to do, when to do it, and how to do it.

My management education and experience taught me that, especially in a larger organization with more complexities, it's very difficult to grow if only one person makes all the decisions. You're limited by the capacity of that individual to make smart, well- informed decisions. If you take a retail business like Sleep America, where we eventually had 47 stores, I could probably have been involved in everything in the beginning when we had only a few locations. However, my vision for the business was that we were going to have dozens of stores. It was my plan to give people room to make some decisions, and even some mistakes, in order to help them develop their management skills, allowing the business to grow, expand, and flourish.

*My experience has taught me
that even a weak plan well-executed will succeed,
but a great plan poorly executed will never succeed.*

The added benefit of trusting others to make decisions is that their job satisfaction goes through the roof. As a middle manager in an organization, it becomes exciting to see tangible results based on your own decisions. It encourages you to make well-informed choices when you have a vested interest because you're going to be held responsible for the results. It compels the individual to be extremely thoughtful. Keep in mind that most people need training to learn how to ask the right questions and become analytical, and not reactive or impulsive. Training and experience help create a culture of competent decision-making.

TIME TO MOVE ON...

Moving to Houston required me to fully immerse myself in my work with Star Furniture. Taking on this new challenge was complex, stimulating, and interesting, but it was a difficult time for me on a personal level.

Again, work was my highest priority and my explanation to my wife was, "This will just be for a short period of time. I need to really understand what's going on here and the faster I can do that, the better." But the more time I spent at work, the less time we spent together, which eventually led us to drift apart. She craved more attention than I was able to provide and it wasn't long before we were moving in different directions. I could no longer deny the fact that, had I not been rebounding following the end of my first marriage, Bette and I might never have married in the first place.

Maybe it was my health scares and how they made me realize how short life was that motivated me to face the fact that, after just five years, this second go around at marriage wasn't going to be the successful, fulfilling relationship I had hoped for. We called it quits and painfully went our separate ways.

For the first and only time in my life, I felt depressed, insecure, weak, and incompetent. One may think that being a successful businessman provided me a certain level of confidence that dictated that I could pretty much fix anything. Having played a part in significantly impacting Simmons' turnaround made me feel like a master of the universe. It filled me with confidence and strength, and although surely I wasn't Superman, it made me feel as though it was possible to accomplish almost anything I set my mind to. Until that point, at least. Finding myself in a relationship without any control over the outcome *and* knowing that my business sense couldn't fix it was extremely frustrating for me. I said to myself, *There's got to be a way to fix this. I just haven't thought of it or done the right thing yet.*

There has to be an approach to fix it or there's something I'm lacking. There was a lot of guilt and I did a pretty good job beating myself up. Never one to give up, it seemed logical that if it was within my power to fix almost anything in business, it must be possible in my relationship. My inability to make it better was the most difficult aspect for me.

There is usually a time in all of our lives where we need help and there is no shame in that. I'm a big advocate of therapy when we need it. Talking to a therapist was good for me, providing me with the ability to see things a bit more clearly and objectively. She gave me a great piece of advice that has stuck with me to this day. We were discussing the buildup of anger and hostility I felt towards my second wife, which evidently is quite natural, when she said, "Your best revenge is finding your own happiness." That really helped.

The therapist's advice makes me think of the poem, *The Guy in the Glass*, again. I think we all need to focus our attention on our own self-image. How do we deal with ourselves? What is the relationship we have with ourselves? From what I discovered over the years, it is a critical issue.

We have to be congruent with our self-image, and from my perspective that is where most of us get confused—including me. Sometimes we don't have a clear perception of what makes us happy. It is so important to know yourself, but unfortunately it appears that many of us are in denial about who we are. Who we *really* are. One example of this that comes to mind is when you see women who are thin but become anorexic because they don't *see* that they are thin. It could also be why severely depressed people take their own lives, because they can't deal with who they are and lack the hope they need to do that. Sadly, in many cases, it may just be that their own self-image is so negative that they can't live with themselves any longer because it is just too painful. At some point in time, I think to become a healthy person it's important to say, "I may not be perfect. I may not be the prettiest, the smartest, the most handsome or the strongest... but I'm okay."

Have you heard the saying, *I'm okay, you're okay*? I have learned, for me, that it is imperative to be at peace with yourself. I challenge you to ask yourself: *What gives anyone the right to say you're not adequate because your skin isn't perfect or your hair is not right or you're a little overweight—or whatever it may be? Who are they to influence your self-image?* Even if the "they" is you. I used to say to myself, "You better like the person you see in that mirror because you're going to wake up every day and it's that person who is going to be there looking back at you." There's no getting away from yourself. Ever.

HEAD-ON COLLISION

One evening in Houston, while trying to get back on my feet, I went on a date. We planned to meet at a restaurant because we thought neutral territory was a good first step. Upon arriving, I realized that a woman and I had both pulled up to the valet parking from different directions at literally the same exact moment. The front of our cars met and we got out simultaneously and looked at each other. "I think this is my lucky day," I said to her.

With a fabulous smile that lit up her entire face, and mine, she said something to the effect of: Well, it's very nice to meet you too. It was a beautiful moment that still makes me smile, and for which I will be eternally grateful. Little did I know at the time how lucky that day would be for me, or how prescient I was.

I wanted to buy my new friend Debbie a drink, so we sat down together at the bar. To my surprise, the bartender refused to serve us saying, "Nobody buys Joe's girlfriend a drink." So we chatted for a few minutes instead, just long enough for me to explain why I was in Houston and my position as president of Star Furniture. Working in real estate, Debbie was familiar with the company since it was some of her client's favorite furniture suppliers. The conversation ended quickly because she was there to meet her boyfriend and my date had arrived.

Several months passed before Debbie called me and asked if I had remembered the encounter. *"Yes, indeed,"* was my answer. We went out a few times and although I immediately felt profoundly drawn to her, my focus to repair my second marriage won out. I said to her, "I love your company and would love to be with you, but my wife and I are trying to work on our marriage to see if we can revive and rebuild it."

"I understand and respect that," she said. And that was it. We didn't see each other anymore.

Six months went by before I finally came to terms with the fact that my marriage to Bette wasn't going to last. Compartmentalizing problems in my personal life was not my strong suit and after four years in Houston, reality set in that my marriage had crumbled and was beyond repair. In turn, it began affecting my ability to work productively. It became obvious that this wasn't a healthy place for me, personally or professionally, so I left my second marriage and my position as President of Star Furniture to move to Chicago to get a new outlook on life and work.

By the way...in 1999, a few years after I left, one of Warren Buffett's companies purchased Star Furniture for an undisclosed amount of money. Melvyn continued to run the business, and he still does today. The fact that Warren Buffett bought the company tells me what I knew all along: Star Furniture was extremely well-run and profitable venture.

Chapter 14

Being a Mensch

"For me, the concept of being a mensch is one of the best tools I've used to find happiness within myself."

I knew that getting back into the furniture business was the fastest way to getting my life back on track and I took a job with a furniture company in Chicago. My understanding was that it wasn't a long-term opportunity, but it did keep me busy for a year until we agreed to part ways. Despite dabbling in quite a few areas, my primary business focus was on finding an entrepreneurial opportunity that really piqued my interest.

Chicago-Bound

A friend of mine, Earl Kluft, owned a mattress factory in California. He had visions of buying another one and asked me if I wanted to partner with him. That conversation led us to initial investigating into a business opportunity in Cincinnati. After studying it for a time, it was clear to me that it wasn't something that intrigued me for numerous reasons. The opportunity did lead to some consulting work for Earl in Los Angeles. It was a busy time for me, full of travel and contemplating my next business venture. Having my own business had always been a goal of mine, although I didn't have anything specific in mind.

I had never been terribly fond of Houston, so it was exciting, on a personal note, to move to Chicago on my own. My apartment, on the 80th floor overlooking Lake Michigan, offered a spectacular view of this beautiful city. Not only did I enjoy the fine restaurants and lifestyle, but it was also a time when I could focus on becoming the person I wanted to be. Although the end of my second marriage had initially been frustrating and very challenging, it led to a time of introspection and significant personal growth.

THE MENSCH MENTALITY

Healthy relationships can be one of life's greatest joys, but I've learned that it has to begin within you. No one can come in and love us enough to make up for our own lack of self-love. It is also self-destructive to feel inadequate, feeling that you don't meet someone else's standard. You've got to meet your *own* standard, the most important bar against which to measure yourself.

> *The concept of being a mensch is one of the best tools I've used to find happiness within myself.*

Mensch is a Yiddish term that means to "be a good person" or "a person of integrity and honor." In Judaism, it's an important concept that poses the questions... What do you do when nobody's watching? How do you handle yourself? How do you respond to challenges and temptations that always present themselves?

I'm proud to be a mensch and although no one, including me, is perfect, it was—and is—always my intent to do the right thing. Being a mensch is a cultural concept that is ingrained in Jewish boys from an early age. It was something to strive for as you grew up, eventually treating your spouse and children that way.

In fact, there is a movie called *Supermensch: The Legend of Shep Gordon*, about a friend and college roommate of mine. Directed by his friend Mike Myers, it's a wonderful movie chronicling Shep's life. He managed numerous musicians and chefs, including overseeing Alice Cooper's career for more than 45 years. It was interesting to learn that Alice and Shep never had a written contract. Why? They were both mensches. To be able to have strong, enduring a relationship in such an intense and volatile world— and never have a written contract—is a true testament to living your life as a mensch. The title of the movie says it perfectly. You can live your life beyond just being a mensch, you can even be a supermensch.

In a recent conversation with Alice Cooper, he told me, "Shep and I never had a contract. If I had money, he had money. If he had money, I had money. We took care of each other; we always trusted each other."

When you're being a mensch, your word is your bond and it's not important who gets credit or who is looking over your shoulder. Remember: It's what you do when nobody is watching. I've challenged people to be a mensch throughout my life, and to live up to a higher standard than they might otherwise have aspired. In my opinion, there is not a right or wrong way to do this... but, let's say, a *better* way.

ARE YOU A MENSCH?

It was 10:00 at night in Dallas, Texas when I arrived at the front desk to check into the Adolphus Hotel. *Stately* is the perfect word to describe this beautiful classic hotel. I had a reservation, so I expected a quick check-in and retiring to my room to unwind after a long day of travel. The gentleman at the front desk said, "Mr. Gaby, we don't have a room for you. It's after 6:00 and you didn't have your room guaranteed, so it is no longer available."

"My secretary made the reservation. I assumed she guaranteed it," I told him.

"I'm sorry, sir, but we don't have a room. We hope to see you again on your next trip."

I was incredulous! *"Really?"* I said. At that moment I saw a sign behind the desk and pointed to the hotel's mission statement that was on the wall behind him. It read: *Be a Mensch.*

"Do you know what that means?" I asked him.

"Yes, sir, I do," was his reply.

I said, "You're telling me that this is the hotel's mission statement, but although I had a reservation, you don't have a room for me and you're going to turn me away at 10:00 at night. Just like that, with no alternative?"

"Mr. Gaby," he said, "you are absolutely right and I apologize."

Not only did he apologize, but he found a room for me at another fine hotel and comped the room. It was wonderful. I didn't have to explain to him what was wrong with what he was doing. Merely reminding him of their mission—*Be a mensch*—nudged him to do the right thing. I never even raised my voice.

It's such an important concept and although its roots go back culturally for centuries, you don't have to be Jewish to be a mensch. The other interesting aspect is that, typically, when you challenge someone to be a mensch, most people will rise to the occasion. It is much more effective than threatening someone with bodily harm, cruel names, or embarrassment because then they're likely to react out of fear and you won't get the end result that you are looking for. People tend to respond much more favorably when you ask them kindly to do the right thing. It is a simple but different approach, and not the one most people take when they are frustrated or disappointed by others. Many people's first reaction is to lash out with anger and expect to get a positive result. In most cases, that's not going to happen. It was late and my initial reply could have been to get upset with him, right? If my reaction had been to start yelling at him, most likely he would have turned a deaf ear, but when I asked him to do the right thing, he did—even though he wasn't obligated to.

MOVING FORWARD

It took a little time, but I did get my footing back and became secure in myself again. It was at that point when life gave me the best surprise of all.

Although I was enjoying my time in Chicago, my thoughts continued to return to the unforgettable woman I'd met in Houston. Debbie. I called her one day and said, "I've moved up to Chicago. Would you like to come and visit?"

"Absolutely," she said.

After sending her a plane ticket, she came to Chicago to see the big city and me. She thought I was terrific and the feeling was mutual. Along with Debbie, excitement, enthusiasm, energy and vitality entered my life, for which I am eternally grateful. After reconnecting at the right time, her love was enormously helpful to me as we looked forward to the future together. It was and still is a wonderfully fulfilling relationship. It's so important for each of us to feel positive about our own future, and having wonderful supportive personal relationships is critical to accomplishing that.

BREAD OF LIFE

On a subsequent visit to Chicago, we went out for dinner at one of my favorite restaurants. I tried to nonchalantly push the bread basket toward her, but she ignored it. I said to her, "Don't you want some bread?"

"No. Bread's too fattening."

"You really should try some of this bread, Debbie, it's the best bread ever."

"Okay," she said, as she reached in and took a piece.

After a few minutes, I said, "Get another piece."

Confused as to why I was pushing her to eat bread, she reluctantly said, "Okay," and reached in and found the gold necklace and bracelet I had hidden in the bread basket.

She was overjoyed. "Oh, I love it—and I love this restaurant!" she was so excited. "I definitely want to come back *here*."

From her very first visit, I knew we had found something special together. We had so much fun, talking and laughing and enjoying one another's company. We agreed that we made a great pair, visiting each other and traveling together frequently. Debbie brought such joy to my life that I felt the transformation almost immediately. Something inside me had changed.

Debbie has such a great spirit, making everything more fun for anyone lucky enough to be around her. It was such a pleasure to experience together all that Chicago had to offer. We had magnificent times visiting art museums and once even joined a sailboat race in Lake Michigan. Navy Pier had a huge Ferris wheel we rode in the summer. It was just a beautiful time getting to know one another. Once, when Debbie brought her 8-year-old son JJ with her, we all went to the *Taste of Chicago*. The annual festival featured thousands of food vendors, which was thrilling to JJ who considered himself a connoisseur of pizza. We suggested that he try all the different pizzas to determine which was the very best pizza in Chicago. He ate so much that he ended up throwing up. It was quite an experience, but he really enjoyed it.

In March of 1996, for her 40th birthday, Debbie and I went on a dream vacation to London and Paris. It was an unforgettable first-class celebration. We spent five days exploring London before taking the new bullet train from London to Paris under the English Channel. It was amazing! Traveling at 180 miles an hour, the train allowed us to have breakfast on the train in London and then, just a few hours later, lunch in Paris. We stayed at Plaza Athénée Hotel in Paris right near the Champs-Élysées. The day we checked into the hotel happened to be her birthday. That evening the hotel had brought a bottle of champagne, flowers, and candy to our room. Debbie said to me, "How thoughtful of you to do all of this."

I said, "I didn't do this, the hotel did. They must have seen it was your birthday on your passport." To this day she gives me a hard time for admitting that it wasn't my idea. It was the first time Debbie saw the Eiffel Tower—and the first time I saw it with someone who seemed to be as excited as I had been years ago on my first visit to Paris. It was very romantic, and my greatest joy came from sharing it with somebody I loved. Although traveling had always been enjoyable for me, experiencing the world with her was so much more gratifying, and a pleasure to be with somebody who was so appreciative of everything.

Spoiling Debbie taught me that
we gain so much more from what we give,
than from what we receive.

Celebrating life with Debbie brought me more happiness than I'd ever experienced and I found that I was thinking of her and what would make her happy, instead of just concentrating on myself. This led to my discovery that it isn't nearly as cool to give yourself a gift as it is to give one to someone else, especially when they are so grateful.

HEARTS AND HEADS TOGETHER

Although we knew that we wanted to build a life together, Debbie maintained her residence in Houston while we contemplated where to start a business of our own.

We weren't quite sure what we would do, but Debbie and I continued to toss around ideas. At first, we thought about staying in Chicago and opening a design store with mattresses, furniture, and accessories. The early stages of local companies like BevMo!, and other specialty stores in warehouse environments, thoroughly intrigued me. We had quite a few ideas, but not many really solid ones that were compelling enough to pursue. That is, until one day when I was talking with an old friend, Bob Cook, who I helped start his retail mattress business in Seattle. He was a Simmons customer and at that time he owned a company called Sleep Country in Dallas, Texas. We had a long relationship with him while his company continued to grow and do very well—until it grew too big and too fast. He ended up filing for bankruptcy and, at the time, he owed the Simmons Company a large amount of money. It's not a pretty story, but it happens.

Bob Cook had come to my boss at Simmons, Bob Magnusson, and said, "I need your help to get back into business." The implied quid pro quo was that we could count on his support for Simmons and our products.

We were pretty excited about that opportunity because he wanted to open retail mattress stores. So Bob said, "We don't have any distribution up in Buffalo, New York, so we want you to open some stores there."

Soon after that meeting, he went to Buffalo at our expense. After a week, he came back to Atlanta and said "Buffalo is awful; it's not a good market at all. I just don't see us opening stores there."

Bob said, "Well, we need stores in Buffalo and that's where it has to be."

I said, "Well there is another market, Seattle, where we have a big department store." It was called the Bon Marche at the time. I continued, "We don't have a furniture business or sleep shops clients there, and it's a more substantial and healthier market, I think, than Buffalo."

Reluctantly, Bob agreed that we would look seriously at the Seattle market for Bob Cook's new venture.

This time Bob Cook and future wife and business partner went to Seattle. Their first reaction was the same as it had been in Buffalo, but since they had planned to be in Seattle for a week it gave them time to study the market and its potential. On their third day, they started to realize that not only was it not as bad as they originally thought, but there was a massive amount of opportunity to be had there. We agreed on Seattle for the first store and helped them get started. The business became wildly successful and, we gained a loyal customer in Seattle who was doing a large amount of business and—having a wonderful time of it. Eventually, they opened more than 50 stores and continued to prosper.

When we reconnected eight years later, I said to Bob, "I've left Star Furniture and have some retail background now." When I told him I was looking for my next big venture he invited me to Seattle to see his operation there.

Shortly after that conversation, Debbie and I went to Seattle. After extensive conversations, we decided that Sleep Country was the perfect business model for what Debbie and I needed to do. My five years of retail experience with my previous mattress business background, convinced us that we were more than competent—and ready—to enter the world of mattress retailing. Debbie's years of real estate and design experience complemented my abilities perfectly. It made sense. The question then became, *Where were we going to start this business?*

THE VALLEY OF THE SUN

We looked at a number of different markets, including my current home base of Chicago, but it turned out we didn't have enough capital to get started in such a large market. After considering Atlanta, Denver, and Phoenix, we had a strong inclination about Phoenix and decided to investigate further. Debbie had never been to Phoenix and I knew she was in for quite a shock to her system. As we were landing, at 10:00 in the evening, the pilot commented that we were "Landing to clear skies and 104 degrees..." Debbie looked at me and said, "It can't be 104 degrees."

"It must be an old report they haven't updated yet," I replied, putting off the inevitable.

When we left the terminal and were walking to the car rental area, she noticed that because it was so hot the big gold bracelet she was wearing started conducting heat, burning her wrist. From our vantage point, the little bit of the desert we could see appeared to be endless dirt and dust. She was not happy.

The next day we woke to a breathtaking sunrise. Debbie has always had a wonderful way of finding something positive about everything, and she began to warm (no pun intended) to the "Valley of the Sun," as the locals called it, and find beauty in the desert.

We decided that Phoenix was *the place* to start our life together—and our business. The following month, in September 1996, we moved to Arizona, rented a house, and got married in the backyard and enrolled 10-year-old JJ in school. The next step: figuring out where our retail stores were going to be located.

At first, our friend Bob Cook from Seattle wanted to be our business partner. But since he had sold the trademarks for Sleep Country to a firm in Canada, he no longer had the rights to the Sleep Country name. One of the partners in the Canadian firm was responsive to Bob's request to meet with me in Phoenix. A short time later, he came to Phoenix and spent the day with me, seemingly very interested and positive. Several days later, he called me and said, "We've decided against licensing the Sleep Country name to you, or offering Bob Cook an exception to his non-compete agreement." He added: "I know this is a disappointment to you, but I promise someday you will appreciate that this is the right thing for both of us."

"You're right," I said. "I am disappointed." We had already worked our way through our business plan as an extension of Sleep Country, but we decided to go ahead and start a business of our own anyway.

Chapter 15

The American Dream

"Sleep America,
where America goes to sleep."

*T*here are many schools of thought in regard to how to name a business. And we weighed many ideas and names—and the type of experience and image that each option brought to mind. Initially, we decided we were going to call our company Sleep City, instead of Sleep Country. It seemed like enough of a play on words to be different. And we knew that differentiating ourselves for other mattress retailers was critical.

The Name Game

We also decided that we would only advertise on radio and TV, and that Debbie would be our spokesperson. The idea was we would have a female entrepreneur talking to our predominantly female customers. While she had never done that before, she was perfectly willing to try and give it all her energy and talent.

One of the new suppliers we were dealing with was Spring Air, whose national spokesperson at the time was Vanna White, from the television game show *Wheel of Fortune*. Spring Air offered to shoot a commercial in Los Angeles with Vanna and Debbie to lend some credibility to our new venture and capitalize on Vanna's enormous popularity.

Before we even opened the first store, she went to Los Angeles. All of the scripts for the commercials were already written as Sleep City. While literally driving home from dropping her off at the airport, I saw a sign for a company named Computer America. I thought to myself, *Computer America sounds like an important company.* It dawned on me, at that moment, that Sleep City was not a great name—but that *Sleep America* was. It was bigger, more sophisticated, and representative of a national brand. I got Debbie on the phone when she landed I said, "Let's not call ourselves Sleep City... let's go with Sleep America."

She said, "I've memorized everything already. I'm going to say Sleep City because I know it, and it's imbedded in my brain."

I said, "Well, please try to forget it because it's not nearly as good a name as Sleep America." She did end up using Sleep America in the television spots and the rest, as they say, is history.

THE BUSINESS OF BRANDING

Our original plan was to work with a local advertising agency in Phoenix, so we could meet with them frequently and start to build a long-term relationship. But we couldn't find an agency in Phoenix that matched the caliber of the agency in Seattle that had worked with Sleep Country. Sadly, no one in Phoenix at the time seemed to understand the business, nor did they appear to want to learn. Many of them approached the advertising with cartoons, animation, and so forth, and although nobody suggested Debbie as the spokesperson, we were inclined to take that route because of the success our friends had with that strategy in Seattle. The concept of a female entrepreneur talking to female customers made such great business sense.

The agency in Seattle, Destination Marketing, gave us 50 different tag lines to choose from. We started debating all of the merits of our top ten. Then one day it just hit me, the way things do sometimes: "Why don't we just say *'Sleep America, where America goes to sleep'?*" Everyone agreed that it seemed logical, straightforward, and compelling. So: decision made. In the months and years that followed, the agency built the jingles around the tagline incorporating holiday and seasonal themes—all variations on *Sleep America... Where America Goes to Sleep!*

The man who owned Destination Marketing, Dan Voetmann, became an important part of our success as a trusted friend and eventual partner in the business. One of our points of differentiation in positioning the company was that we developed Sleep America as a brand, as opposed to a single retail store. Most independent retailers usually don't consider themselves a brand by valuing and reiterating what they stand for consistently. We had a core list of principles that we stressed in all of our communications with our customers and associates, which distinguished us from our competitors. Over the years, as we invested in our brand through signage, jingles, and Debbie as the spokesperson, we created a brand consistency that became ingrained in the public's subconscious. People recognized Debbie's distinctive voice from our radio ads, so much so that at times when she called a restaurant for a reservation they recognized her before she told them who was calling.

Even when we developed our logo, we anguished over it, spending weeks revamping different iterations before getting to the point where we were happy. I've always said that in the development and the design of this business, from agonizing over the logo design to the jingle, absolutely nothing can be left to chance. Each aspect of our brand was given thoughtful consideration, with no detail too small for us to pay attention to during this process. Using constant repetition across all channels of advertising is what eventually creates brand recognition. After we were well established, there were times when we didn't have time for the entire jingle in a radio ad, so Debbie would simply end her message by saying, "...where America goes to sleep." People knew that *where America goes to sleep* was Sleep America, even without saying it. That is the payoff for the investment in brand building when it's done to such an extent that a tagline didn't even need full explanation.

In the wake of our success in branding Sleep America, I heard a story that has stayed with me all these years. Apparently there was a speaker at a marketing luncheon in Phoenix and in his presentation he asked the 400 people in attendance, "How many of you have heard of Debbie Gaby?" Almost everybody raised their hands. He then asked, "How many have heard of Sleep America... and can sing the jingle?" Four hundred people sang the Sleep America jingle in unison and it was the powerful, real-world example to demonstrate the importance and power of branding.

STORY OF A START-UP

In March of 1997, after nailing down our name and message, we rented a warehouse. It was far bigger than what we needed to begin with, but fortunately it had a wall down the middle so we could divide the space into two separate areas. My plan for the first year was to use half of the space and find a tenant to lease the other side. The tenant wanted an 18-month lease, which we agreed to, figuring it wouldn't be a big deal. But after a year, we were out of space.

In typical "start-up" fashion, we were cramped for those next six months, but the warehouse offices we worked in were not finished anyway. Our "office," in a warehouse with unfinished cement floors, held only a couple of TV trays we brought over from our home and used as desks. An exposed light bulb hang from the ceiling and our phone was hooked up in the room next to us, so we had to pull the cords through a hole in the wall. Although it wasn't pretty, it got the job done and we were very excited.

Next, we employed a real estate group to find the ideal locations for our future stores. We thought we would eventually open eight stores, maybe 10 to 12 max. That was the extent of our original business plan. The goal was to have a store within a five-mile radius of 90% of the Phoenix metropolitan population. The real estate team helped me create a map with eight circles drawn on it representing the locations and covering most of the key metropolitan area. After identifying the eight general sites, we were finally able to start hiring.

Although we hadn't yet opened our first store, we began to hire warehouse workers and a sales team. We had nothing other than our map to share with them. Instead of pretending they didn't exist, we chose to cherish the challenges under which we were working. I said to the people we hired, "Embrace this moment because you're at the beginning of something that's extremely exciting. I want you to remember my TV tray desk and this exposed light bulb because in years to come we're going to have quite a few stores and be very successful." With confidence I assured them that, "One day we're going to smile about where we are right now." It was an approach that allowed people to understand our vision.

Initially we operated with a small team, and, at first, no one had a job title or a description. We laughed about it, although it wasn't a joke. When asked, "What's your job?" The answer inevitably was, "I do whatever it takes." We were all equal and in it together, agreeing to do whatever it took to make it work. There was no jealousy or defensiveness. We weren't competitive. We were a collective, working together as a team. Each of us embraced what we were doing and found joy in celebrating in the simplest ways. Buying pizza for everybody was our first awards dinner. When you're starting up a business, that's the excitement of it.

THE EXPERIENCE OF PERCEPTION

Before opening a single store, Debbie and I shopped every retail store that sold mattresses in the Phoenix metropolitan area. If a company had eight stores, we went to all eight of them. The beauty of it was that no retailer had more than a 10 percent market share. This meant that there were no dominant players in the marketplace—which was attractive to us. We knew that a dominant player and position would be more difficult to challenge. While studying the other retail stores, Debbie turned to me one day and said, "I think I've made a mistake, I don't really want to be in this business." This came as quite a shock to me... until she explained what drove her to that statement. "This is disgusting—the stores we're visiting are filthy and the salespeople are not well-groomed. I don't even like lying down to test a mattress because it's so dirty." Ah... now we were getting somewhere.

Debbie also shared this comment: "If I was alone, I wouldn't even walk into these stores because I feel so uncomfortable."

"So," I said, processing this... "What we need to do is create an environment that you're comfortable in. If you're comfortable in it, every one of our female customers will be too."

That's when Debbie started to realize that she could design the store she wanted to shop in. Paying attention to every tiny detail, she started the store design phase by using pillars and archways in each store—symbolizing traditional architecture that represented integrity. She chose dark blue, or what we called an *admiral blue* color for the walls. The carpeting was the same dark blue allowing the white mattresses to be the focus of the store. We referred to the countertops as *antiseptic white* as a reminder that they would always be pure white and sparkling clean. This is where creating the culture began because we needed people who were committed to maintaining this cleanliness, this pristine atmosphere. In creating the first store, we included the associates we had already hired in the design process. One of them asked, "What's the carpet going to look like?"

We said, "We could have gray carpet that will never show anything, or we could make it very dramatic have the dark blue carpeting to match." We shared samples and examples of the products merchandised against the dark blue as well as the gray. "You decide," we said to the newly-hired associates.

It was unanimous: "The dark blue is much better."

We agreed, but there was a caveat, "OK... as long as you understand that dark blue carpeting will be harder to keep clean and will have to vacuumed twice a day."

They answered, "No problem."

I said, "Okay, we're never going to have a conversation about vacuuming the floors again. You all need to maintain these stores and create the environment that says to the next person we hire that this is the job we're all committed to. I'm not going to carry that on, you are. Can you handle that?"

They said, "Absolutely."

And do you know what? We never had to have another conversation about vacuuming the floors. It wasn't necessary because of initially charging them with the responsibility of carrying on the commitment to the dark blue carpeting and white aesthetics. The culture was transmitted and perpetuated by the associates themselves. The mantra we shared was that we had an *irrational commitment to cleanliness*. Everyone understood what that meant.

Debbie was fanatical about touching the five senses of potential customers, creating a pristine environment that was welcoming on all levels. If you walked into another mattress store, the glass door was often covered with fingerprints and you were assaulted by a boom box blaring hard-rock music. The salesperson was usually unkempt and didn't even bother to look up at you. The air was stale, the floor was dirty, and you just wanted to run away—and put off buying a new mattress until another day. When you walked into a Sleep America store, you entered through a clean glass door. Instantly, you inhaled the welcoming aroma of a fragrant candle. Equipped with Muzak® systems, quiet and peaceful music floated through the air. After a few moments, the well-groomed and sharply-dressed salesperson offered a kind smile. Within 15 seconds, you felt comfortable. Now we had an opportunity to make a sale. It didn't mean we were going to make one, but at least we had a fighting chance.

SIGNING UP FOR SUCCESS

Our very first store was in the Paradise Valley Mall on Cactus and Tatum in Phoenix. It was May 1997 and although we were hard at work inside the store, we hadn't opened yet. The day the company came to hang our first sign is still so clear to me it seems like yesterday. I watched them putting it up while having a cup of coffee on the patio of the coffee shop next door. Out of nowhere, a flood of emotions started to well up in me. When they finished and the sign was hung, it occurred to me that tears were running down my face.

Crying into my cup of coffee, I wasn't prepared for such an emotional outburst at seeing the sign hung. It was one of the most exciting moments of my life, and although it felt like it came out of nowhere, I came to realize that it was the symbolic nature of the fact that Debbie and I were finally in business. We had spent so many months agonizing over the logo, the sign, and every other detail. We still have a file with all the work we did to develop the logo and the evolutions it went through before it came to fruition. I can't tell you how often I asked myself, *Do most small retail businesses spend the amount of time we did attending to every single detail?* I don't know, but we knew we were building a brand so everything seemed so much more important than if our focus had been on just opening a single store. The brand also helped define the culture, so every aspect of the business worked together positively.

SELLING SLEEP

As Sleep America, we wanted to be in the business of selling sleep, as opposed to just selling mattresses. All of my previous experience gave me an understanding that if people were really interested in the quality of their sleep, they were willing to pay more for a great night's sleep, versus just buying a mattress.

Most of the people we came in contact with asked, "Why do we need another mattress store?"

We explained, "These are not typical mattress stores. We are going to open beautiful stores and do things differently. We are not selling mattresses, we are selling sleep... and here's how we are going to do that."

READY TO PLAY

The quality of the sales staff in most of the mattress stores was another aspect we wanted to approach differently. At the time, none of the other stores had a dress code for their employees and if they did, it consisted merely of wearing a tie... any tie. Most of the salesmen we came into contact with appeared to be completely uncomfortable in a tie. Not to mention many of them looked as if they had worn their ties during several meals involving greasy pizza. It didn't appear they were required to have their shirts tucked in, pressed, or clean. It became evident to us that business casual attire was better suited for this type of environment and market.

Our initial dress code was to wear either a golf shirt with the Sleep America logo embroidered on it or a clean and pressed shirt with a tie, and a pair of khakis or dress pants, whichever they felt most comfortable in. Whatever they chose, we made it clear that it had to be clean and pressed. That was always a part of the culture in our stores. If someone came to work dressed in any other fashion, we immediately corrected it by requiring them to go home, change, and come back dressed appropriately.

The next way our sales team differentiated themselves from the competition was in how they were taught to approach customers. We noticed that typically when you entered a competitor's mattress store, the first thing the salesperson would say was, "What size are you looking for?" The second question was, "What's your price range?" Then they found something around that size and price range to recommend. From that point on, it was a hard and usually unpleasant negotiation. The salesperson would try to wheel and deal by saying, "I've got a special on this one this week," even though the customer didn't even say they liked that kind of bed.

In our stores, the conversation went very differently. When someone entered *Sleep America*, we would say, "Hello, how are you today?" After exchanging pleasantries we would ask, "How did you sleep last night?" And then more specifically, "Do you have trouble falling asleep? Or do you wake up before you'd like to?" We'd start a conversation about their sleep quality and patterns and what was not working well for them. We would ask, "Do you have any physical issues such as back problems? Do you suffer from allergies? Do you have any kind of chronic pain or anything else bothering you?" We would even ask, "How many hours do you sleep a night, typically?"

If they said, "I only sleep five hours a night," we would ask "Why is that?" We would continue to dig deeper, asking more questions. "If you only sleep five hours a night, do you start to get a little drowsy in late afternoon?"

Some would say, "Sure, but I just fight through it."

Our mission was to get people to talk about themselves, which in my experience is their favorite subject. We were empathetic because everybody has a story to tell and it's not always pretty. Many times it involves pain, discomfort, and suffering. When we finally arrived at the point where we were about to suggest a few options, we would excuse ourselves for a moment. We would come back with a bottle of water and say, "Here's a bottle of water for you. We've got work to do because we're going to find the right mattress for you so that you get seven or eight hours of healthy, uninterrupted sleep every night." We'd smile and say, "It might take a little bit of work and you're in the desert so you need to stay hydrated."

While shopping competitor stores, we found some salespeople asked, "Would you like some water?" The typical response was, "No, thanks." Why? Because people don't want to feel obligated, right? If you take something from the salesperson, then you have to give them something. At Sleep America, we didn't ask, we just gave them water and they took it immediately. After this we continued by giving our undivided attention to each customer. In return, we wanted them to take the discussion seriously because we had some work to do. We were not negotiating for a mattress. There was a huge difference between buying a mattress and talking about their well-being. It was a completely different dynamic, driven by having a completely different conversation. The water was such a well-received gesture that Debbie had the bottles labeled with our Sleep America logo, choosing the no-drip "sport cap" style, which we felt created a greater perceived value. Customers would walk out of our store with their bottles, proud to have been shopping at Sleep America. We even spotted our bottles around town, refilled—and advertising our brand.

THANKS, BUT NO THANKS

All the major retailers in Phoenix advertised in the Saturday edition of the newspaper, so readers would see every mattress retailer in town vying for attention and offering the "lowest prices." When the newspaper heard that we were going to open stores, they came to us and said "We'd like to talk with you about advertising your Grand Opening and a program for weekly ads."

I thought about it for a moment and said, "I don't think I can afford to be in the newspaper."

They said, "We can come up with a program that won't be a burden to you—and you can't be the only mattress retailer in the Valley who isn't advertising."

"I don't think we're going to run ads in the paper," I repeated.

The sales rep repeated her pitch, and said, "You cannot be in the mattress business in Phoenix, Arizona and not be in the Saturday paper."

I said, "Really? I don't get that."

They repeated themselves yet again.

I said, "You know this is a new business and we're going to make many mistakes. There are numerous things that I don't know yet, but there's one thing that I know already and that is that I am *not* going to be in the Saturday paper with everybody else shouting about mattress prices." I paused before adding, with too much arrogance, I'm sure, "I'm certain of that."

I took a breath and delivered my closing punch: "If there's a time that I should ever do that, you should not take the ad or you should demand cash up front from me to run that ad because that will be a clear indication that we are in trouble."

They were convinced that I wasn't going to be in the Saturday paper but they weren't convinced that I wasn't going to advertise in the paper because they came back with an offer, which I have never seen before or since. They said, "We will run whatever newspaper advertising you want or you feel you need and we will charge you seven percent of your sales per month. If you do a hundred thousand dollars in sales, we'll charge you seven thousand dollars, no matter how much advertising we run. If you do two hundred thousand dollars in sales, we'll charge you fourteen thousand dollars and we'll run as many ads as you want."

It was an unprecedented offer. In retrospect, maybe I should have taken it. But, instead, I said to him, "You know what, I appreciate the offer. I'm impressed, but I'm sure you knew that I wasn't going to accept this offer. If I accepted it, you would be in trouble." I think they threw it out just to see if I was really serious or not. I added, "I don't know what I would run. A big picture of my wife?" In their newspaper, all you could do was display the item and a price. Your competitor the following week was going to have a bigger picture with a lower price. The next week after that it's going to be a bigger picture with a red price that was even lower. Everything deteriorates to price and item. We didn't have any interest in advertising either one of those things, because we were selling sleep not mattresses. Our business had nothing to do with an item or a pillow-top mattress at a specific price.

THE AMERICAN DREAM

Two days prior to opening our first store, we received a citation from the Vice Mayor of Phoenix thanking us for our donation of mattresses to a homeless shelter, Andre' House. We had donated all of the mattresses they needed before we had even sold our first mattress. We had no right to claim success because we hadn't sold anything yet, but the first impression we made was that we were a generous and thoughtful company. What does it say to a consumer when you are gracious and involved in your community? We felt it said that we were good people, generous and kind—and also successful. I bet you'd agree. And isn't that the kind of company you want to do business with? With people who are kind, generous, and successful.

Our first three stores opened in May of 1997, all within two weeks of each other. We created the perception that our company, Sleep America, was already successful. The first question people asked was, "Where are your other stores?" They thought we were a successful chain. (I was always tempted to reply: From your mouth to God's ears!)

We'd say, "This is our first store."

"You're kidding," was the typical response, with people unable to believe that it was only the first or second store. To them it seemed like we had been in business forever *and* that we were a large, thriving business. We had been congratulated by the mayor's office for community service, hadn't we?

The response we received to our new and creative approach to buying a mattress was immediate and dramatic right from the start. We had a consistent strategy for customers, and we treated them very well whether they bought during their first visit or not. Most retail salespeople believed when the customer said, "We'll be back," they were just empty words. We didn't believe that. In fact, our position was just the opposite.

We believed that if we treated prospective buyers exceptionally well, by welcoming them and helping them to feel comfortable, when they walked out with our bottle of water and the information we gave them they *were* likely to come back. From our data, we believe half of the people who left without purchasing, came back. We may not have made every sale, but in the process we created a great reputation and a large referral network. By taking all of the principles [not the ideas, but the principles] I had learned over the years in corporate environments, I knew we, as entrepreneurs, would be successful in creating Sleep America.

Chapter 16

SUCCESS BY DESIGN

*"Over the years, it became clear to me
that in an organization everything flows from the Top Down,
and then exudes from the Inside Out."*

*K*nowing that a culture would grow within our company whether we were in control of it or not, we asked ourselves the big question: Are we going to be the architects of our own culture, or the victims of it?

As we started to grow, opening eight stores that quickly turned into 12, it became obvious that we were going to be fairly successful. That said, we knew that there were certain aspects of the business that we needed to approach with caution. One of them being that although the warehouse operated 24/7, we weren't always able to be there. It was imperative that we had people we could trust so the merchandise wasn't going out the back door.

Investing in a superb software program helped us create internal controls from the beginning. Not wanting to reinvent the wheel, we simply followed the guidelines that were already built into it. Every store was connected to this one central program that we used to manage the entire process from beginning to end. Providing us with the ability to ascribe discipline to a third party non-entity if you will, we always focused on following the steps according to "the system." The system provided all the structure and processes we needed; we needed only to commit to it and use it meticulously.

And so we embraced an internal culture that aspired to the performance of every task at the highest quality level—all the time. This required that we follow the system's internal controls exactly. Not as Dick, the store manager, or Tom, the warehouse manager, told you, but how *the system* forced you to do things.

CUTTING-EDGE CULTURE

Each store began the process by entering a new order into the system, specifying the merchandise the customer purchased and their requested delivery date. The program managed the inventory by locating and transporting the merchandise from the warehouse to the store. It created a transaction trail for that order, eliminating a need for a mandate from me to avoid transferring merchandise without the proper paperwork. This process required us to create a document that said we were taking these 10 mattresses from the warehouse to Store 15, for example. After arriving at Store 15, the employee there had to sign and verify receipt of the 10 pieces of merchandise. The driver then returned to the warehouse and reported that the transaction was complete. If there was ever a discrepancy about where those 10 pieces were, we knew that Jeff at Store 15 signed for them on a certain date and time.

In an organization, everything flows
Top-Down... Inside-Out.

These were the internal controls, but the culture we nurtured was that you absolutely must follow the guidelines of the system that we put in place. All that we had to focus on was getting everybody to commit to *not* work outside of it. Of course, this was tested at times because people, being people, had a wide variety of excuses for not following the process. We always—always—corrected it. This created a disciplined environment, which is what we needed with such a large amount of merchandise going in so many different directions.

Looking back, it seems to me that people were more inclined to follow those rules because they were tied to a culture where we strived to be the best, not just meet the demands of the program. From the beginning, we managed this on a formal basis and although the approach was much larger than our initial needs, I believed we were going to be successful and ultimately grow into it. Typically, small businesses start out with no structure until their growth demands they implement one. We started out believing we were large and structured ourselves that way, eventually growing into it. It was a different way of looking at the business, which I believe was an element that contributed to our success.

One of our original goals was to become the dominant mattress retailer in the state of Arizona. Not only because we wanted to capture a large share of the market, but because, from a defensive standpoint, we wanted to be able to protect that market share. If somebody was going to come into the marketplace and challenge our position, we wanted it to be evident that it would be extremely costly to do so. Not that they couldn't, but it certainly wouldn't be easy because we had such a strong brand and hold on the market. It worked that way for quite a while.

We also applied the same high standards to our interpersonal relationships within the company. Eventually we had sales managers who talked to prospective associates and remained selective in their own right, but once they said, "We're ready to hire this person," I would interview them. Although at times it was challenging, I always made time to spend an hour with each prospective associate, never hiring a salesperson who wasn't interviewed by me first.

The reason for spending an entire hour with each person was because over the years it became clear to me that during an interview, it was very likely that I was going to either fall in or out of love with someone pretty quickly. When you start talking to someone and hit it off you may think, *Boy, I really like this person. They're my kind of man or my kind of woman. They seem to be perfect.* Typically, if a conversation continues for an hour, something was going to shake loose, possibly leading to second thoughts or confirming that we'd found a great match for our business and our culture. If we spoke long enough, it would either reinforce or change my original impression. Conversely, you could start a conversation with someone where you didn't hit it off well. Maybe they were nervous or uncomfortable and initially they didn't show you their best or true self. By giving them some time, people often opened up, relaxed, and you were able to get a better sense of their strengths, weaknesses, and whether or not what they were capable of performance that was a good match for our needs. It also gave me time to set the tone and the opportunity to share some of our philosophy and culture to see how they reacted to it.

Originally, Debbie screened prospective employees as well, but eventually she was no longer part of our interviewing process. She had one rating for everybody: Amazing! This optimism was a wonderful quality on her part, but not at all helpful in interviewing for our business. If we were looking for a receptionist for the warehouse to greet people and take in the mail, she would interview them first and then come to me and say, "This person's fantastic! She is the most wonderful person I've ever met." Then she'd speak to the next candidate and say, "She's even better than the last person... she was phenomenal!" One of Debbie's many redeeming qualities is that she finds beauty in everybody, but it didn't always mesh well with what we needed as it related to hiring. Not only are some people better choices than others, some are not good choices at all, even if they are exceptionally nice.

THE VOICE OF AMERICA

Over the years many people have asked me, "How are you successful in business with your wife?" I can tell you the first few years were tough, because we were stepping on each other's toes a great deal, while we were dealing with obvious challenges of getting started. It was nothing serious, we were just bumping into each other too much. At some point, we both agreed on one another's strengths and weaknesses. The beautiful thing is that her strengths are my weaknesses, and my weaknesses are her strengths. We thought, *Wouldn't it make sense for us to just stick to what each of us does best?*

Debbie has a gift that allows her to connect to people almost immediately on a personal level. It's quite unlike anything that I have ever witnessed before. It's hard for me to remember someone I met a week ago, let alone his or her name. Although it is in my nature to be caring and kind, my personality doesn't dictate that I'm the warmest person in the world, but Debbie truly is. We had a good basis for a partnership because we were each willing to accept that we weren't great at everything. Individually we may not have been successful, but together as a team, we were. We complemented one another perfectly and both of us have acknowledged that we couldn't have done it on our own.

*Complementary strengths
are one of the real keys
to successful long-term partnerships.*

Borrowing the idea from our friend's business in Seattle, it seemed to make sense for us to have Debbie act as the spokesperson for Sleep America. For me it was great because I didn't want that role, and we never competed for the limelight. I readily stood on the sidelines while she took the spotlight, which was not the easier road for her by any means. While filming commercials, she had to stand under hot lights in the middle of the summer with no air conditioning, because you were able to hear the fans in the background. Debbie stood for 10 hours reading lines off of a teleprompter, trying to look fresh, cheerful, and energetic when that was the last thing she was feeling. Eight hours in, someone would say to her, "We need some more enthusiasm and excitement," and Debbie would summon the strength to do just that. Motivated to do her best, she dug deep and found the tenacity to pull it off—and beautifully, I might add— while I stood in the wings and watched in awe.

Debbie has a wonderful way of speaking that involves her own unique Texas twang. We questioned whether we should try to break her of it and at first, we tried to have her change it, quickly realizing that wasn't going to happen. We didn't have any choice but to embrace it, but in doing so, it became a great success in its own right. It definitely made her more likeable because it was evident that she was being herself. Her voice was also very high-pitched and initially some people made jokes about it. In addition to her pitch and accent, her smile was unforgettable. It was not only memorable, but likeable and the camera easily captured her beautiful genuine qualities.

We made a conscious decision to never put her in a position where she sounded like a huckster. Instead, always positioning her as the consumer's advocate. She worked on behalf and for the benefit of our customers. In other words, she never went on camera and said, "I'm slashing prices this week." It was always, "If you're not picky about color, we can save you some money because the mattress and the box spring won't match." That made sense and she gave potential customers a logical reason to save some money. She wasn't just a pitch woman, *she* was the brand. I don't believe she ever wore out her welcome in homes by over-emphasizing that. People knew her voice, what she did and why, and they saw that she was a wonderful person who had logical reasons for offering special deals. That was important in communicating great authenticity.

Did we get push back from some people? Sure. We had an occasional person who'd say they couldn't stand her voice. They were one in a million. Once, a woman called and said, "We just can't stand that Debbie person."

"What seems to be the problem?" I asked.

She said, "Nobody here likes her."

I said, "Where are you?"

She said, "At the park."

I said, "What park?"

She said, "The trailer park. Everybody here at the trailer park can't stand her."

I said, "I guess you have the choice to turn it off if you want to."

Anyone who meets Debbie finds that she is just what you'd expected—gracious, genuine, warm, interested in other people, caring, thoughtful, generous, and kind.

All of the traits that she was able to communicate through our Sleep America commercials and advertising. Whether in jeans and a nice blouse or a Sleep America shirt and a baseball cap, she was always relatable to our customers, and completely authentic.

THE MAGIC OF MISTAKES

Another way we empowered our team and contributed to our culture of success was by encouraging them to make mistakes. That may sound counterintuitive, however, whether we wanted them to or not, everyone messes up at some time or another. Knowing that it was inevitable, it was my intent to create a culture from the beginning where it was not only okay, but *better* to make a mistake—rather than doing nothing at all. During my years managing the teams at Simmons, I learned that if it were acceptable for people to make mistakes without fear of any fatal backlash, the associates would extend themselves further and independently try more creative approaches to problem solving. In order to make mistakes permissible and create a culture that encouraged people to "try things, even if it means making a mistake," we needed to be explicit about what that meant to us.

My belief is that there were two different types of mistakes in the world: one that is tolerable, and one that isn't. The welcomed ones were made in the act of doing something, as opposed to the impermissible blunders that were an unintended consequence of doing nothing. Let's use falling down as a metaphor. When you make a mistake and you fall on your face, I'll come over, pick you up, dust you off, make it better, and work with you to find the best solution to fix things. It's okay to fall on your face. However, it's *not* okay to fall on your butt. If you fall on your face, it means you're moving forward and doing something. You're in the act of trying to make something happen. That's a good thing. If you fall on your butt, that means you're standing still or you're going backwards. It's imperative to make a mistake in the act of doing *something*. It's unacceptable to be paralyzed by a problem or a challenge because you don't want to mess up.

In many organizations, you will find people who become completely debilitated by the fear of doing something wrong. Often they have a shoot-the-messenger syndrome because when a mistake is made, you often hear from the top down, "I'm going to find out who did this and they're going to pay." That's an unfortunate culture that exists more often than not. In that environment, it's very difficult for people to try to extend themselves by believing in their own creativity and ability to handle a problem. Our team was told when they encountered a customer with a problem, they had the power to take care of it, as long as they kept the customer's best interest in mind, while using sound business practices. Their directive was to always make sure the customer was happy first. If it was a problem they hadn't previously dealt with, they were able to consult with someone if necessary, but they were to immediately do what they thought best solved the customer's problem. Maybe they gave them a new mattress, which may not have been my first choice and possibly a mistake in my opinion, but I didn't care. It made me happy that they did something, which is always better than doing nothing or handing the problem off to someone else.

Not only did this allow our team members to feel valuable and capable, it also created a culture for our customers in which they were assured that if they had a problem, it was dealt with quickly *and* to their satisfaction. Internally, after the situation was handled and if necessary, I may have said to the associate, "Next time you come up against that issue... you might try this or that. Or here is another way to handle it." However, I was always thrilled that they took care of the customer. In a typical corporate setting, you often find that there are hard and fast rules about how to handle things. The culture dictates how to handle every possible situation, with no deviation allowed. The problem with that is not every situation will fit into the corresponding "correct" way to respond. This doesn't allow associates to feel empowered to approach the situation on a case-by-case basis, which is how to truly make each customer happy. Instead, they think, *What am I supposed to do?* Nobody wants to intentionally break the rules, so they are unable to react appropriately.

At Sleep America, the rule was to take care of the customer based on their specific need. We used to say to our people, "Look, if that customer gets all the way up to Debbie or me because they're frustrated by some experience, we're going to cave in completely and give that customer whatever they want. We're going to say, *'What would you like us to do?'* and then we'll do it. Whatever they say they want is what we're going to give them." Once I was sure that point was crystal clear, I continued: "If you would like to find a solution that's not that simple, you have to do something else to make that customer happy. You have the authority to make a better business decision as long as you are sure that customer is happy with it." Not only were we empowering them, we were imploring them. This was how we created a culture where people felt comfortable with making decisions and mistakes, allowing them and our business to grow. By giving them that power, they were much more thoughtful about their decisions and they thrived when this responsibility was bestowed upon them.

Creating this type of environment took my involvement in the beginning by talking explicitly about different scenarios *before* they happened. As part of their training I would say, "I expect you to make some mistakes. It's going to happen. If you're not making a mistake, you're not trying. Let's decide how we're going to deal with that beforehand so you know what we're comfortable with and how we want to treat people." After building on that over the years, the culture began to transfer internally. Somebody would ask a seasoned colleague, "What do I do?" Having experienced a similar situation previously, they said, "Well, you're expected to make a good business decision *and* take care of the customer." The culture grows internally, vertically, then horizontally—top down, inside out.

My position was simple: The road to satisfying the customer was not set in stone, but taking care of the customer was non-negotiable. In many companies, the person in charge wants to control every tiny detail, but when you make all the decisions, the ability for the organization to grow is limited by your capacity to make those decisions. If you really want to grow and prosper, you've got to empower other people to do that. The trust comes in when they make what you consider to be a mistake and you don't shoot them. Before that, it's just conversation because many people say one thing and do another. The challenge for the leader is to be consistent and trustworthy with what was promised. When we first started the business we had one rule—*Do whatever it takes*. This communicated to our team that they could figure it out, but they needed to do *whatever it took* to make the customer happy. It also spoke volumes to team members when we trusted them to make appropriate decisions. If we specified every detail including a million *dos* and *don'ts*, it meant we didn't trust them to be an intelligent adult and a responsible citizen of our company.

That's a culture of not only empowerment, but respect. It told our employees that we had confidence in them and the decisions they would make. Where are you going to get better customer relations? In what kind of environment are you going to get better employment satisfaction? This culture flows top-down and exudes inexorably from the inside out. Once an organization gets large enough, not only can it not be contained, but it is difficult to stop. That is why it is imperative to create the culture that you want from the very beginning.

REAL HAPPY CUSTOMERS—REALLY!

From there, the culture will extend past your team and directly to the customer, impacting their satisfaction and eventually your overall success. We found in the retail mattress business that typically, competitor stores were most concerned about their closing rate. The *closing rate* is calculated by how many people actually buy on their first visit. Research indicates that most people buy a mattress every eight to 10 years, so if we didn't sell you a mattress on your shopping experience today, we are not going to see you for another eight years. Therefore, collective wisdom dictated it was imperative to sell that customer on their first visit. You may notice, as you're walking out of mattress stores, that the salesperson magically finds a new incentive or discount for you to buy that day. You could liken the approach to that of a used-car salesman. We worked hard to avoid that process and perception. Our belief was that if we could take care of the customer by having a conversation about their sleep and their well-being, they would understand that we were truly interested in their health and, thus, quality of life.

Upon walking into another mattress store, most likely the first question would be, "What size are you looking for?" The second question would be, "What is your price range?" Using that information they would try to sell you the deal of the day because that is where they are making the most profit. At Sleep America, we wanted to know how you were feeling. After we talked, if you said, "I want to think about this a little bit," we felt it was inappropriate to say, "Before you go, I want you to know I'm going to drop the price $100," just to try to close the sale that day. Since the other stores were basing all sales on price alone, they felt that once the customer left the store, they would go to another one that would make a sale on the spot.

We actually measured this and we closed 50% of the people who walked through our doors on their first visit. Of the 50% that left, 50% of those people came back after visiting another store and realizing, I believe, how special we truly were. We were not selling commodities, we were selling quality of life which interests people much more than a deal on a mattress. Today, people are captivated with this aspect because they are more aware of its impact on the quality of their life. If I can help you find the right mattress that will improve your sleep, thereby positively influencing your quality of life, you've have a wonderful experience. The interesting part was not only did we not have to play the price game, but we charged for delivery—which was free at most of the other stores. In the competitive world, we were proud of that because it was a significant part of the success of our financial model.

People would ask, "Why would I pay you for delivery when everybody else is giving it away for free?"

We said, "With the other stores, you *are* paying for it, it's just built into their price. We don't build the delivery into the price because many people want to pick it up, or they understand that there's a cost to deliver it."

Although it probably was in the industry, it was *not* unusual for people to pay more than the $50 we charged to deliver it. It begs the question: Why would somebody choose to pay more than we charged them for the delivery? They were so delighted with the service, they tipped the delivery people on top of the regular delivery fee. They had a sense that they received much more than they actually paid for. Our delivery drivers were well compensated and there was never a mention of a tip for the delivery team. If customers felt like they wanted to, that was certainly their option, but there was no obligation or expectation. If someone asked about the delivery fee when purchasing a mattress, we would say, "We charge the $50.00 for the delivery, but what I'll do is call you after the delivery, and you can tell me whether it was worth it. If you tell me it was worth zero, we'll completely refund your $50." We never had to issue a single refund for a delivery.

Always promise less and deliver more.

MANAGING EXPECTATIONS

A large component of a successful and positive retail experience is managing expectations. Our goal is to have you say, "Wow, we really accomplished something wonderful together." Although internally I may know that we can likely exceed the goal that we agree on, I will understate what can be delivered to tamp down your expectations. Not to be dishonest or avoid hard work, but setting the bar lower and achieving more will result in your being delighted with our experience together.

Why? If we set the bar too high and don't reach the goal, most people will find it disappointing, even if we've attained a great deal. They'll feel that they didn't get quite what was promised. If we say we're going to reach for this and we exceed it, we're thrilled—and so are the customers. Even if we didn't accomplish as much as we might have, had we set a higher goal. The psychology of it is more important than the actual goal. Feeling that you've surpassed your goal is the key to maintaining a positive outlook and fueling continued success. Success becomes habitual.

If you were a customer of mine, here is an example of how I might manage your expectations. Knowing fully well that I can have your mattress delivered to you tomorrow, initially I would say, "I'm not sure that we can get it to you tomorrow." Then, I would come back and say, "You know what, we *are* going to be able to get it to you tomorrow after all." Now you are delighted. If my initial message was that we could get it to you tomorrow, there's no excitement when you are told you will be getting it then. With this delivery, we are merely fulfilling what we said we would do to begin with. By giving you the "good news" after setting a lower bar, you felt you received more. I created anticipation that it might not happen, so when we were able to get something that might not have been the case, you are delighted.

---

*Always set expectations low
so that you can consistently exceed them,
delighting customers rather than just satisfying them.*

In every interpersonal relationship we have, the quality of that relationship is dependent upon the caliber of the relationship we have with ourselves. Obviously this can be positive, negative, or neutral. That personal relationship we have with ourselves starts at the top with our head, working its way down through our being, eventually exuding from the inside out and affecting others. The concept of Top-Down... Inside-Out is very much a personal phenomenon, as well as a larger organizational one.

Chapter 17

PAINS OF GROWTH

"Whatever it takes."

A lthough we started out strong, we were fully prepared [or so we thought] to make an impact in the industry, it was not a time without challenges. For quite a while during the growth phase, we were chronically understaffed. To top it off, sometimes we didn't know what we were doing. Quite often we referred back to our mantra—*Do whatever it takes*. If Debbie or I said, "I don't know what to do," the other very often said, "I don't know what to do either." We decided that our answer to that question always was, "I'm going to do whatever it takes." I can't tell you how often we asked ourselves, *What does that really mean?* We don't know what to do, but we're going to have to figure it out. We had to trust ourselves to find the best answer and in the end, we needed to do whatever the situation required.

Although it may not have been what we thought fell under our job description, we needed to be fully open and committed to getting things done by doing whatever was required at that moment. It was interesting to watch people respond to that when things would come up. For example, we had to pass an inspection with every store before we could open our doors for business. Once, the inspector came in and said, "You don't have an exit sign here, so I can't give you your occupancy certificate."

If we would have stopped there, the store wouldn't have opened on time because the inspector didn't give his approval. Instead we said, "Well, what do I need to do to get an exit sign up there? How do we do that? Who do I call?" Instead of panicking because we had already advertised our grand opening date, we did whatever it took to make it happen. We asked the inspector, *"Can you give us a temporary sign off?"*

"I can do that," he said. "I will give you three days to correct this."

"Wonderful," we said, "we'll have it fixed by then." We committed to completing the task at hand, even though we had no idea why we needed an exit sign or where to get one. When opening a new business, those are the type of things that come up over and over again. Our *do-whatever-it-takes* philosophy was something that was part of our culture within ourselves as well as our employees. Everybody was charged with figuring out a way to get the job done. It wasn't considered a negative or a bad thing, it was just part of the joy of opening a new store. We told them that we had no idea what was going to come up next, but something surely would. They weren't going to have the answer and neither would I, but we were going to have to figure it out. Empowering them to use their own capabilities, creativity, and ingenuity to get things done without looking to someone else was a very unusual approach for most, but it worked.

THE ADVERTISING EFFECT

Along with recognition and success came unwanted attention as well. One month, we ran a big sale because we had purchased a large amount of discontinued stock from Simmons for an extremely low price. In 60-second radio spots, we were able to tell our story to potential customers. On the last day of the sale, we had advertised over the radio, "Be sure to get in before Monday night at 9:00 p.m. because this is going to be over and when they're gone, they're gone!" The urgency and repetition created significant traffic and excitement in the stores. That evening at 7:30 p.m. a man came into one of our stores with a gun and said, "Give me all your money."

The employee said, "We only have a hundred dollars here. That's it. It's all credit card and checks, there's no cash."

"That's ridiculous. You have this big sale going on that's over at 9:00 p.m., so that drawer must be full of cash."

"Sorry, there's no cash here," our employee told him.

After taking the small amount of cash in the drawer, the robber went to another one of our stores, believing that he had been lied to. Fortunately nobody got hurt and it didn't cause any real problems. That's the power of advertising—it even inspired somebody with a sinister intent. He was convinced that the sale was so big that there must be drawers full of money waiting for him to scoop up at the end of the day. That's one of the ways we knew our advertising was highly effective.

THE WORLD ON 9/12

After our first few prosperous years of rapid growth, we went through a tough time along with the rest of the country following September 11, 2001. Understandably, our nation was traumatized and nobody was thinking about going out and buying a mattress—or anything else for that matter. It was as if everything stood still.

My early projections were that things would get back to normal rather quickly, but they didn't. It took at least a year before business was back up and running at the prior pace. During that year, we were cash-poor and living hand-to-mouth, financially. Every month we had overhead of a half million dollars, just for the rent on the stores. On top of that we needed to meet payroll every two weeks. There were many instances when not only did we not have enough to pay Debbie and me, but we didn't have enough to pay our controller. It was stressful. Fortunately, I knew Debbie and I could forgo our checks for a time, but we couldn't miss sales or warehouse employees who probably didn't have enough of a cushion to survive.

Previously, we had a banker who was always calling to lend us money, so we thought about taking out a line of credit for $100,000 to get us through. Now, when we really needed money, suddenly he didn't know who I was. I said, "You've been talking about how we would be a good client and that you'd be happy to lend us some money. Let's have a conversation."

He looked at a few numbers and said, "We can't lend you any money because you don't have any money."

"If I didn't need money, I wouldn't be here. What do you suggest?"

He said, "Well, I would close some stores because of your overhead issue."

I said, "But I will still owe the rent regardless. Nobody is going to forgive the rent."

That's when I decided banks weren't for me because they only wanted to be helpful when you didn't need them. We had some partners in the business, but everybody was strapped as well. The only place left to look to stay solvent was with a few of our suppliers. I told them, "We're having a tough time of it and I owe you $200,000. I'm not going to be able to pay you right now."

Several of them said, "That's okay, we'll write you a note." By communicating with them and sharing our challenges because of 9/11, they worked with us. Not only did we *not* have to close any stores, we opened more. Everyone was paid on time after that, and we forged even greater partnerships with those who helped us when we needed it most.

FRIENDS AND FOES

From my experience, even a relationship that potentially begins as an adversarial one, can become mutually fulfilling with a simple approach. Many times, our first instinct isn't always the best course of action when "doing whatever it takes," to achieve success. Throughout the years, it has occurred to me that there is an art to the practice of conducting oneself as a mensch. Operating from this mentality isn't about domination, control, or undermining one another, but instead, holding oneself to a higher standard and inviting others to rise up and do the same.

This approach worked better than expected for me on more than one occasion. A wonderful example that stands out occurred at a time when we had a letter of intent (LOI) to rent a piece of real estate for an additional Sleep America storefront. Unfortunately, the owner sold the property before we signed an actual lease. Shortly after the sale, a representative for the new owners called me in for a meeting to discuss the impending lease. After exchanging pleasantries he said, "We don't have a signed lease, and the letter of intent is not legally binding. We have been approached by one of your competitors who has offered to pay us 25% more than what you've agreed to. Obviously we're inclined to talk to him."

When he was finished I asked, "When you purchased this property, were you aware of the letter of intent that we had?"

"Yes," he said.

"And you bought the property anyway... fully aware of this?" I confirmed.

He responded affirmatively again: "Yes."

"Then I would assume that that letter of intent represented an acceptable agreement, although I understand it was not a legal contract," I said. After a short pause, I continued, "I'll tell you what, I'm going to let you go and talk to your associates. I have full confidence that you will do the right thing." Then I shut up and didn't say another word, making a conscious decision to refrain from elaborating.

As if on cue, he began, "We're Weingarten Realty, one of the largest real estate trusts in the country. We pride ourselves on operating from the highest ethical standards, and we will eventually figure this out and do the right thing."

I continued sitting quietly. It was a bit of a struggle, requiring me to speak silently to myself saying, "Keep your mouth shut, Len."

He continued, "When we come to the final conclusion, we're going to do the right thing. I realize that significant work and effort went into this. In fact, the *right thing* in this case is to execute the lease just as you had agreed. And, that's exactly what we are going to do."

After thanking him, the meeting adjourned. My real estate agent, who had joined me for the meeting, could barely contain himself until we reached the parking lot. In awe, he said, "I've been doing this for 30 years and I've never, *ever*, seen that happen."

Scenarios such as this made it clear to me that by simply offering people the opportunity to do what they believe is the right thing is usually more than enough incentive for them to rise to the occasion. Most of us want to be the best person we can possibly be. If we are not accused, threatened, begged, or belittled, but instead simply given the space to come to a place of integrity, it seems that we innately gravitate towards this.

Notice I didn't leverage my statements while trying to accomplish this. I did not say, "I expect you to live up to your agreement," or "I demand you to live up to this Letter of Intent," dictating what that meant to him. My calculated silence was to intentionally leave him on the hook to internally conclude what he knew to be the right thing to do. Well, to my delight, he exceeded my expectations during that meeting. The most I expected was possibly an agreement that he would discuss it with his superiors. Originally, I didn't think he had the authority to make a decision on his own right, then and there, but fortunately, he did. The real estate company indeed honored the letter of intent at the originally agreed upon lease rate. The store became one of our best performing locations. We were loyal tenants. How wonderful is that?

If you give people an opportunity to elevate themselves to a higher level, they will most likely accept the challenge. On the other hand, if you allow yourself to give into your anger or feel slighted, they will quickly follow you down into a hostile confrontation. Gratefully, it became clear to me that it was in my best interest to focus on making partners instead of adversaries out of everyone I dealt with. This experience, as well as many years of interactions with business associates, in varying forms, reinforced my belief that by simply changing our mindsets just a little, we can find that staying calm and working together, even when we feel attacked, benefits everyone involved.

Mastering this strategy and approaching your interactions this way is really an art form. The tools are varied but simple. You can take a deep breath, count to ten in your head before responding, or just keep your mouth shut. From my view, the key to success is to broaden our thinking. Approaching situations from a more expansive perspective affords us the unique opportunity to see the "bigger" picture, and therefore choose the most beneficial approach. That *is* the art of being a mensch.

HOW CLOSE IS TOO CLOSE?

Previously, while still with Simmons, we had done a research project that told us that 80% of all mattresses are purchased within a five-mile radius of a customer's home. When we worked on our original map for our Sleep America stores, we thought if we had a store within five miles of most everyone's home that should be sufficient. In a neighboring city named Mesa, we already had two stores that were exactly 10 miles apart. Literally the circles on the map touched each other, but a third location became available right in the middle of the two of them. Vestar, one of the largest real estate developers in the Phoenix area, was opening a power center right between them. We were already great tenants of theirs and they came to us and said, "We're going to give you the right of first refusal on this power center. If you're not interested we'll lease it to another mattress company, but we want to give you the first shot. If you're interested, we'd love to have you and we won't talk to anyone else."

We looked at the center and although theoretically we didn't need a store there, I knew that if we didn't, a competitor was going to sell mattresses at that location. Whatever the volume of business, we would rather it be ours than a competitor's, so we took the store. Long story short, all three stores ended up being very successful *and* we didn't notice any changes in sales volume at the original two. It was an interesting lesson for me that when you build a brand and become more convenient to people, adding more locations *is* beneficial. We actually tried to "cannibalize" our own business, but were unable to do so.

One of our original eight stores was located in Glendale, Arizona. It did a phenomenal amount of business and was one of our best stores, if not *the* most profitable store. Ironically, it was tucked behind a restaurant called Mimi's Café so you couldn't see it from the main street. About seven years later, a major storefront opportunity—right on the street—opened up. Since it was visible from the street and you couldn't miss it, we decided to lease it with the intent of using the new location and letting the other store's lease expire. There was some overlap time, since the old lease didn't expire for another eight months, so we opened up the new store while the old store was still open. Guess what? Those two stores were the number one and number two stores in sales volume for the entire company. They weren't five miles or even a mile apart—they were one *block* apart. We thought, *Why close either store?* So we didn't.

This is a lesson I learned from a man named Bruce Halle, the CEO of Discount Tire, a multi-billion-dollar company based in Scottsdale, Arizona. We spent some time together and once I said to him, "I believe we're in the same business."

"Well, you're in the mattress business and I'm in the tire business," he responded.

"Yes," I agreed, "but I think they're really the same thing."

"How do you mean?" he asked.

"Well, nobody wants to buy a new set of tires and nobody wants to go out and buy a new mattress. You do it because you have to when you realize that whatever tires you're riding on or whatever bed you have is just not good enough anymore."

He seemed to consider this as I continued, "There is no ego satisfaction that comes from your new tires or from your new bed. You can't show it off to your friends and it doesn't feel like it does anything for you. It's a grudge purchase. Our pricing is even similar—new tires probably cost you eight hundred to a thousand dollars, and a new mattress is at least a thousand dollars. It's not a small purchase so people view them as commodities. A tire is a tire and a mattress is a mattress, but we all try to convince them that this tire is better or that mattress is better. Our shared skill is in helping people understand the different qualities available and helping them find the best solution for their needs and budget."

After a while he said, "You know I guess we *are* in the same business." Then we started talking about real estate. He told me that he had a store on Scottsdale Road, just north of Shea Boulevard, a high-traffic street that runs east and west in North Scottsdale. A new piece of real estate had become available on Shea, just west of Scottsdale Road, literally around the corner from his other store. His people came to him and said, *"When do you want to close the old store?"*

He told them, "Let's keep both and let the customers tell us when it's time to close the old store." For at least 20 years, they profitably operated *both* stores even though one was just around the corner from the other. This was a big lesson for me, and taught me that it's okay to be close.

It's Always Something

In 2005 and 2006, life was good. The business continued to grow and prosper and we had reached what many call *a peak of success*. However, just four months after my memorable 60th birthday soirée, I was faced with my own mortality yet again. Finding myself short of breath often enough to take notice, motivated me to get a checkup. Fast forward a few appointments, and a probe through my arteries revealed blockages in my heart. The doctor informed me that heart bypass surgery was necessary, which was performed by one of the cardiac surgeons at Mayo Clinic. Unfortunately, I'm not sure who had it harder that day, Debbie and Rebecca, or myself. Originally, they were told that the doctors anticipated they would be in the operating room with me for about three hours. After five hours had passed, no one had come out to talk to them. Both Debbie and Rebecca relayed to me later that they were extremely apprehensive and nervous as the minutes and hours ticked by. Finally, approaching the sixth hour in the operating room, two surgeons emerged from the OR in blood-covered scrubs. One of the doctors said, "He's on the table and his chest is open. We're just making sure that everything is working well and that there are no leaks. We're going to close him up very soon." Rather than feeling comforted by the news, Debbie and Rebecca were more focused—and disturbed—by the sight of all of my blood on the doctors.

As I reflect on that time, it was difficult for me. It was also tough on Debbie, my daughter, and the rest of our family. It must have been quite frightening for them to see someone they care about going through a life-threatening situation. I found myself suffering, but not wanting to complain because it was apparent to me they were suffering too. Love and empathy aren't always easy when you love someone. This taught me that when we start getting wrapped up in our own problems, we can easily forget that other people go through challenges in their own way as well. It's not always easy. When we find ourselves in disconcerting situations, feeling insecure and frightened, sometimes we think only of the worst possible outcome. That's a terrible place to be. The impact of trauma in our lives can inflict damage that may seem difficult to recover from. It can take a while to get over these types of scares and sadly, some people never do. Something that helped me immensely to sort through this was this prayer.

SERENITY PRAYER
By Reinhold Niebuhr

*God, grant me the serenity
to accept the things I cannot change,
The courage to change the things I can,
And the wisdom to know the difference.*

I've always embraced this short but powerful prayer. For me, it's a roadmap for a happy life. It helps us understand that there are things we can impact, and indeed we should, if we can. But there are also things that we cannot. Most of us get hung up on things that we cannot affect, frustrating ourselves and our loved ones. As it related to my health, there were some things that I could do to help myself, which I did to the best of my ability. But there were other things that were beyond my control. If there wasn't anything I could do about something, it was my intent to spend as little time as possible worrying about it. That is the best tool I can offer. Some of us ascribe the things we can't control to a higher being by saying, *It's God's will.* You can choose to handle it whatever way suits you best, but for our sanity, I believe it is important to let go of those things that are beyond your control.

*To move ahead,
sometimes we just have to let go.*

Letting go is a really important concept. There's a true story I heard once that illustrates this perfectly. In a remote part of the world, a tribe of monkeys lived on an island. They were able to take a coconut and break through the shell to carve out the coconut meat to eat. Afterwards, the monkeys understood the empty coconut shell could then be used as a vessel or a jar for storage. During the appropriate season, they collected nuts and saved them in the coconut shells, demonstrating highly evolved behavior. When it was time to eat the stored nuts, the monkeys put their hand into the coconut to grab one. In the process of picking the nut up, they made a fist. When they attempted to pull their hand out in that position, while holding the nut, they found they couldn't. It was quite a bizarre scene and, at first, nobody could deduce why all of these monkeys had coconuts stuck on their hands. After studying them, they finally figured it out. The key was that the monkeys needed to let go, but obviously they really had trouble with this. And don't we all?

Although the surgery and recovery were taxing, it never occurred to me that it might be the end. Another challenge? Yes, but never the end. Maybe that's part of my personality and optimistic nature. My feeling was, *I'll get over this. It's just another challenge, another adversity to face and overcome—and I will.*

*The ability to think positively
about outcomes,
literally influences the outcome.*

I often remind myself how lucky I was to have a superb support system. Debbie was comforting and optimistic, as she always is. My kids, associates, and everyone who surrounded me brought positive energy to me and, thus, my healing. Those who encircle you have a big influence on your attitude and happiness, so it's my hope that you choose well. Because of them and my determination, it wasn't hard for me to believe a favorite expression of my mother's from the works of Persian Sufi poets, *"This too shall pass."* It's extremely important to stay positive even when faced with challenges. It doesn't mean that you're assured of the outcome you're envisioning, but in my opinion, it just gives you a better chance. Have you ever noticed that when you're really pessimistic about things, those thoughts can end up being self-fulfilling prophecies?

SEEKING CHALLENGE

Many people fear challenges, spending a considerable amount of their energy trying to avoid them. Others, like myself, love challenges. Why? Because they test me, and typically bring out my best. Not only do I love them, but throughout my life I've actually sought out difficult tasks. Always wanting to learn something new, master it, and then move to another level was how I stretched myself. What is more stimulating than to continue to challenge yourself?

There could be any number of reasons people try so hard to sidestep challenges and obstacles. There is the dreaded fear-of-failure thinking—*I just don't want to fail, so I don't want to try. If I don't try, I'm not going to fail.* There's also the fear of disappointing yourself or others, stemming from a lack of self-love or healthy self-esteem. Whatever the cause, trying to avoid difficulties is a definite roadblock to finding your happiness in life. There will always be struggles and unwanted circumstances, so I suggest that we not worry about whether or not those scenarios will happen... because they will. They don't need any encouragement. Instead, I put my focus on believing in myself. Believing that you *can* make it through, and perhaps even happier than before the dreaded challenge.

I admit, some challenges are much more difficult than others. Sometimes, health issues are fear-inducing because we may not have direct control over the outcome, but they're still challenges, right? We still have to deal with them by trying to find good information, help, and support. It really comes down to perception. I truly believe that growth and development do not occur unless you overcome some hardship or adversity. Until you've faced it, dealt with it, and overcome it, there isn't usually very much personal growth. There's no question that everybody *will* face adversity. The true test is how we handle it.

Maybe you are a person who continues to try to avoid it because you don't feel that you have the tools to deal with it, and you feel ill-equipped to face the tribulation. Many people run to their family members or partners for the answers, always seeking help from outside themselves. Learning to take on your own challenges by yourself is part of maturing and growing. We all have problems and we have the freedom to make choices and mistakes, but we also have the opportunity to overcome them. Not only do we have the opportunity, but I think they can be part of a healthy growth process for each of us.

My approach has always been to welcome challenges and seek them out instead of running and hiding from them. It is exciting to try new, interesting, and difficult things. Writing this book has been a challenge. How many people are willing take that on? Is it because I'm a writer? Not at all. Instead, I tried to figure out how to accomplish my goal by enlisting help from people who know more than I do. On the other side of that coin people may say, "Well, that's too much work and too difficult because I can't write." You can find dozens of reasons why you don't or won't do something, but there's only one really good one for trying new things: because you love overcoming challenges.

Chapter 18

THE POWER OF JOY

*"Success is never realized
from the actions of one individual."*

S leep America's success didn't materialize merely from the actions of
one or two of us. It culminated from the support of the numerous
associates who came in every day and offered their high level of service, as
well as every single team member that helped us in our collaborative effort.
Without their commitment and willingness to embrace our mission and
culture, there is no way we would have met and surpassed our goals. I think
one of the big keys to success is being able to engender a real enthusiasm
for what you are doing, followed by continuously appreciating the people
that dedicate themselves to assisting you in getting there. It requires a rich
mix of respect and gratitude, along with some good old fun.

Many times we expressed our gratitude through sales contests. On one
occasion, we created a competition for the salespeople where they could
earn a weekend trip to Cabo San Lucas with their significant other. That
was a big deal, but to add to the fun I promised to come down to the
pool in a Speedo. It was the most self-deprecating vision I could think of,
believing if they could laugh at me, it would motivate them even further. It
turned out to be quite an inspiring and amusing experience. At the end of
the contest, we went to Cabo San Lucas and they waited by the pool with
a *cerveza* in hand. When it was time for me to make my grand entrance, I

appeared wearing a bathrobe. After descending the stairs to the pool area, I sat down on my chair, took the bathrobe off, and smiled wearing my regular swimming trunks and a cap on my head that read... *Speedo.*

Not only were they rewarded for their hard work, we showed them that they were abundantly valued and cherished. It was so much more effective than if we had just given them a cash bonus, equivalent to the amount of money the trip cost and it was our hope that the trip would be something they would remember for the rest of their lives. During the trip, we took the time to commend and thank our associates in front of their spouses. We also acknowledged the sacrifices that spouses make related to "working retail"—the weekends, evenings, and holiday hours. It's really a tough job. We understood that and expressed our appreciation for everyone's efforts, even presenting a gift to the spouses to thank them for their patience and support. We were building a business together and this helped them to feel that they were an important part of that.

One of the things that Debbie and I found most gratifying was that so many of our associates were on board with us for more than a paycheck... they were committed to what they were doing. Our principles included three imperatives—we asked them to be honest, respectful, and have fun. We tried to demonstrate the concept that if you wanted to be successful, you had to enjoy what you were doing. If you didn't, it would get to you. There were many times when a sales associate was alone in a store for 12 hours, days when not one person would come through the door. As much as we would like to have avoided that situation, we knew it was inevitable. If that person didn't have enough internal strength to sustain his or herself during those periods of time, they would fall apart. Retail sales require special people and once found, we believed it was imperative to embrace and show appreciation for them.

*Success is never realized
from the actions of one individual.*

INFINITE WEALTH

My theory of infinite wealth is an understanding that really good ideas, executed with great follow through, create enormous opportunities for *everybody* involved. This thinking is directly opposed to a *zero sum game*, in which there is a finite amount of wealth. For example, if you and I are working together and you get one dollar, then I must lose one dollar, equaling zero. If you see the pie as finite, then we're all jockeying and competing for our portion of that pie. If we have the mentality that we are always competing for our share, it may seem as if there's always only a certain amount available. Unfortunately, many people still operate from the zero sum game perspective. If you embrace the fact that the pie can continue to *grow*—infinitely—and there's no problem with us *both* benefiting, you will start perceiving opportunities as limitless. If we believe that both of us (all of us!) can have a dollar, it simply means there is more to be had.

Embracing infinite wealth says, *I can really do well and help you be successful too.*

Digging a bit deeper, many people have issues with incremental goals. In other words, they may say, "You're benefiting more than I am, so I'm jealous of your success." Or "I'm doing really well, but you're doing even better, so I've got to be worried about that." Even if someone is doing well themselves, other people always have their eye on them because they perceive them as doing better than they are. From my perspective, this is a short-sighted viewpoint—and one that gets in the way of people feeling gratitude for their own beneficial circumstances.

No one can be responsible for everybody's success in life, but they can show concern for the people who are supporting their endeavors. My goal has always been to put any thought of worrying about myself aside. It has been my view that if I take care of you, I'm going to get taken care of as well. In other words, if my main focus is to make this a beneficial experience for you and for you to prosper in a certain environment or situation, at the end of the day I'm going to come out okay as well. If you are doing well, selling a great deal of product, and making plenty of money, then guess what? I'm going to do fine as well. My primary approach was to show people that I was sincere about doing everything in my power to support their success. Maybe that's why it's so strange to me that some business owners are oppressive to the associates that work for them. It doesn't make any sense because if their prosperity is based on the performance of others, it would benefit them to encourage and invest in others' success.

In a venture, if we all do well, we will *all* benefit. This aligns with the concept that "a rising tide lifts all boats." If I can understand that and help you achieve what you want, you're going to help me achieve what is important to me. It is a win-win scenario. When we utilize this type of thought process, we are both pleased with the experience and most likely we will want to continue to work together. This creates an incentive to perpetuate what we've done rather than to terminate it and just go count our share. If you feel like you were screwed over by me, and I was the only one who benefited, what motivation do you have to continue doing what you have been doing? You wouldn't. Instead you would think, *You're selfish and self-centered and you don't care about my needs.*

A rising tide lifts all boats.

During my time at Simmons, quite a few of our retail customers looked out for themselves first, never giving a thought to looking out for us. They took advantage of us at every opportunity, in any way they could. When starting Sleep America, we decided to change that paradigm. We frequently asked our suppliers, "Are you happy with our business? Is this relationship profitable for you? I want to be your most lucrative customer, so if you'll tell me what it is you need to be successful, I'll do everything I possibly can." I wanted them to know, in no uncertain terms, that in our business relationship, "I'm going to ask you to help me and you have every right to ask me to help you. Wherever it is possible for me to be accommodating to you, I will, so we can both have a business built on mutual strength. I'm proud to have you as a supplier and I want you to be proud that you have me as a customer."

It could be something as simple as timing. For example, let's say it is typical for me to place my order at 10 a.m., but if I got my order to them two hours earlier, by 8 a.m., it would be extremely beneficial to their work flow and process management. It may not be apparent to me, but if I ask and learn that something this minor would be advantageous, I would do everything in my power to figure out how to help. These types of scenarios wouldn't cost me a thing, and simply by being sensitive to a business partner's needs, it could deliver immense value and strengthen a relationship. By putting in a little extra effort toward making your life easier, we could change the dynamics and create a mutually beneficial relationship.

This same premise applied to our team members within Sleep America. If someone asked, "It would really help me with getting my kids to daycare if I could come in at 9 a.m. instead of 8 a.m. Is there some way you could help me with that?" If it was possible to accommodate them, we would because we knew that person was working on our behalf. We always tried to be flexible and if we couldn't, we explained, "I'm sorry, we wish we could do that for you, but here is why we can't." It was important to us to be open to that conversation so people felt free enough to say, "I have a favor to ask," or, "I need some help here." I would say, "You come to me if you have a problem and I'll do what I can to be helpful."

This extended, at times, to money as well. If a team member needed money, I tried to lend it to them or at least help them figure out a way to get it. It was my preference to give it willingly [even if I didn't receive anything back] rather than have it taken surreptitiously.

In my opinion, it is acutely important to approach people with empathy. When you show someone that you understand their pain, and that you will do everything you can to be helpful, they are much more apt to do the same for you. It is simply exercising respect for one another. Where most people fall short is not with their intent, but in the communication aspect. To circumvent that I would say, "You need to tell me what you need because I'm not going to be shy when asking you for what I need. I will tell you the truth, and I expect you to do the same for me." I drilled down even deeper, to be sure that my position was crystal clear: "If you're harboring some kind of resentment because I'm unknowingly doing something, you can't fault me for not knowing. I'm counting on you to tell me what you need, otherwise, I'm going to assume that everything is okay."

By making that clear from the beginning, it sets the stage for how we're going to operate, and alleviates any surprises. Respecting our individual differences, while putting in the minimal effort required to communicate and help one another, builds a solid foundation for obtaining infinite wealth. Not only do you learn and grow from this approach, but it will benefit you throughout all of your relationships and interactions.

JOY IN GIVING

Another advantage of treating our vendors and suppliers with respect and thoughtfulness was our ability to say from the beginning, "Part of our culture is our wish to help our community. From time to time, we're going to ask for your assistance with giving away some mattresses, and helping others. We need you to understand that we are not going to ask you for many other things, but we are going to be asking you for assistance with community outreach programs."

Much of Debbie's time was spent vetting organizations by visiting and having face-to-face meetings with them. Primarily, she wanted to be assured the organizations we committed to were legitimate and sincere. Typically, we concentrated on teaming with smaller local charities where we could offer hands-on support. Most of them were extremely appreciative for our involvement, expressing that even humble efforts made a huge difference for them.

Giving back with gratitude was of the utmost importance to us. Not so we could say we gave to charity, but because we wanted to play a role in changing lives for the better. Drawn to certain issues, a large part of the support we lent was assisting people who were struggling with challenges that were beyond their control—single mothers, victims of domestic violence, and so forth.

Many times we hear discussions or comments about the *appropriate* amount that a person should donate based on a percentage of his or her income. We didn't want to be obligated to do something based merely on a percentage of our earnings or profits, because it felt like an artificial commitment. Although giving anything to those less fortunate is noble, we decided to take it a step further by finding ways around putting limits on our ability to give based solely on our profits. This goes back to the culture we established from the beginning with our vendors and suppliers. They knew going in that, in doing business with us, we expected them to be a part of our charitable endeavors. So they were not surprised when we asked them to donate mattresses for a worthy cause. We spent a good amount of time as the facilitator between different organizations we worked with that were willing to donate to any number of charities we supported.

Since we wanted to be a company that said "Yes" more often than we said "No," we needed to figure out a way that made sense for us. We tended to look at community outreach opportunities on a case-by-case basis, evaluating our support and contributions based upon whatever made sense at the time. If we couldn't afford to donate money, we would said to them, "We're sorry that we're not in a position to help you in that way right now, *but* it is a wonderful idea and we'd like to help. Here's what we *can* offer you." By trying to find other ways of saying "Yes" to them, we rarely said "No." From the beginning, before we even sold our first mattress, we tried to support not only the people we worked with, but we reached out to our community. As our business became more prosperous, our financial capacity to give back grew, but it never really changed the generosity we were committed to sharing from the start. We are so proud that through all the work that Debbie did with establishing the Sleep America Charities, we were able to create positive situations for many thousands of people.

AN ATTITUDE OF GRATITUDE

Obviously, when things are going well, it's easier to be generous, but if we gave away mattresses before we even sold our first mattress, giving back quickly became part of our DNA. This was part of the culture with everyone connected to Sleep America. Even in the beginning with our employees, when we couldn't afford to send them to Cabo San Lucas, we always treated them with respect and gratitude. Buying them pizza was quite a bit different than a trip to Mexico, but under the circumstances, they sensed our appreciation for them by our commitment to spending time with them while enjoying pizza. You do the best you can with what you've got. If it's a principle that you live by, you always do that.

It was second nature for Debbie and me to say to our associates, "You are amazing. I love what you're doing." And "Thank you. It's because of your help that we're going to be successful with this." We were generous with words of appreciation and encouragement, in lean times and in flush ones. The dinner might be a little bit better and more expensive than pizza, but, conceptually, it's the same emotion that you are sharing. We're telling those on our team how grateful we are for their support and commitment to what we're trying to accomplish together. It's a product of the kind of relationships you choose and the dynamics you create.

There are so many ways to demonstrate your thankfulness. Simply putting my hand on the shoulder of an associate who has been working extra hard and looking him in the eye and saying, "You've really helped so much today, thank you," can be more rewarding than anything material. Sincerely appreciating someone by acknowledging them and their commitment doesn't cost a thing. And from what I've seen, it can be one of the most powerful expressions you can make.

Maintaining the Bar

At the peak of our success, we recognized one of the biggest threats to our business was our *own* arrogance. It was my concern that if we started to get "full of ourselves," we would let our guard down and not be as steadfast with all of the day-to-day details. As the number of stores grew, it became evident that sales managers were hiring people that did not embody our original high standards. Concerned primarily with finding somebody to open the store and covering all of their bases, they were looking for what's called a *warm body* versus a competent, dedicated associate. At the time, it felt as though it was my primary job to keep the bar up, making sure no one tried to crawl underneath for the sake of convenience or expediency. I don't believe the sales managers acted out of indifference, but simply found themselves challenged to find quality associates to fill the positions in all 45 stores.

Wanting to ward off the prospect of mediocrity slipping into the organization, it was evident to me that we couldn't allow the standards to fall or they would quickly reset and settle there. If we didn't maintain and aggressively defend our standards, we ran the risk of allowing that to happen. As an observer of other organizations, I'd seen the attention to detail drop off drastically in companies that had grown large and successful. In my opinion, this happens from a combination of arrogance and convenience.

For me, it felt like one of the worst things in the world to allow mediocrity to slip in because of its insidious nature, evading scrutiny until it is too late. Then, you look around and say, *"What has happened here?"*

Avoid mediocrity at all costs.

Although a strong culture and values direct the flow, inevitably in times of growth, something is going to test what you'll tolerate. Whether that is through execution, commitments to delivery schedules and inventory levels, or something as simple as the dress code or showing up on time for work. It could even begin with the level of cleanliness in the stores. Inadvertently, when somebody is in the store every day, they may not notice that it's not as clean as it used to be, so the standard slowly starts to drop and complacency creeps in. Every time you let somebody slip under the bar, you've eroded the standard. You have probably heard the saying, *You are only as strong as the weakest link*. Well, the weakest link will often test the boundaries—unless you are vigilant about reinforcing the culture.

As our success grew, my role and, subsequently, my priorities changed. It was a natural evolution of any organization. It may not seem like a very important part, but it is.

My role of maintaining the bar, ensuring we were not going to get sloppy, lazy, or complacent, was incredibly important (if not the most important) consideration for the continued success of Sleep America. In fact, in order to maintain our edge, I created another aspect of our culture I like to refer to as "controlled paranoia." The premise was, if we always maintained a sense that competitors were trying to attack our leadership position, we would stay vigilant and sharp. If we were over-confident or became cocky, we would inevitably let our guard down and one day find ourselves in trouble.

It all begins from the Top-Down... Inside-Out. We were committed, and we were sure as hell not going to become arrogant and set any of the aforementioned perils into motion.

Chapter 19

ADAPT OR DIE

"A business is an amorphous entity that needs to progressively move ahead, building and growing upon itself."

After my cardiac bypass, I was reminded yet again that I was mortal and that each day, was indeed, a blessing. This experience, like my other health challenges, increased my sense of urgency in taking stock of my life and business.

If something happened, it was important to me to have a succession plan in place for Sleep America. As things stood, there wasn't anyone within the company who could immediately step in and take over my position. This would have left Debbie and everyone else in an extremely difficult and vulnerable situation. The thought of her being forced to sell the company under duress, diminishing its value and possibly having someone take advantage of the situation, made me realize it was time to seriously consider our options and put a plan in place.

FORK IN THE ROAD

In assessing our position strategically, it was clear that we were at a crossroads. We had basically expanded as much as we could throughout Arizona with the exception of a few additional real estate opportunities.

Knowing that the continued success of a business like ours hinged on sustaining growth, it was important to look at our alternatives. From my perspective, a business is an amorphous entity that needs to progressively move ahead, building and growing upon itself. If it stagnates and ceases to grow, costs still continue to rise even if the topline volume doesn't follow suit. Eventually the margins start to dwindle, rents rise, inflation comes into play, and expenses continue to increase. If you're not growing at the top of the business, you're going to start getting squeezed—and you will see a steady decline of profits. Another important but often-overlooked aspect of growth as well is the fact that when you have a young workforce, they need the opportunity to grow professionally and personally.

Sensing that it was imperative for Sleep America to continue its growth, the next logical step would be to expand outside of Arizona. Knowing that this would take an enormous initial investment of capital as well as an abundance of energy, that neither Debbie nor I were equipped for, we knew that it was important to consider selling. As good fortune would have it, a short time later I received a call from Dale Carlson, the owner of a company in California called Sleep Train.

Dale and his partners expressed an interest in purchasing Sleep America. We engaged in numerous conversations and after he visited, it was apparent his interest was serious. This prompted me to immediately do two things. The first was securing an investment banker with an expertise in managing these types of transactions because of my lack of experience in this area. The second was contacting the CEO of Sleep Country in Canada to make him aware that we were considering selling the company in case they were interested in acquiring us. Having met them previously when we were interested in using the Sleep Country name they purchased from our friends in Seattle, it occurred to me to offer them a chance to look into using our brand to expand into the United States.

Being a relatively small industry, word got out that we were contemplating selling, and that is when we heard from Mattress Firm.

They were in the midst of acquiring companies across the United States, prompting them to inquire whether we would consider an offer from them. This created a bit of competition because we had other alternatives, but we never moved forward with an auction as our advisors suggested. After discussing details with all three entities, the opportunity with the Canadian company, Sleep Country, was the most appealing to us. Their offer was fair and generous, and it was my belief from our conversations that they would do their best to maintain the culture we had built so meticulously. Not only were they planning to continue using Sleep America as the name of the business, they were going to retain Debbie as their spokesperson. Their strategy at the time was to take over, using our model for expansion, because they didn't want to present themselves as a Canadian company coming into the United States. Instead they wanted to appear as an American company simply expanding from Arizona throughout the United States. Because Debbie personifies the quintessential American woman, they loved the idea of retaining her as the spokesperson. Additionally, they intended to maintain most of the strategies we employed to successfully build the Sleep America brand.

Although I had been friendly with Dale from Sleep Train in California, he understood that it was a better fit for us to pursue a deal with Sleep Country from Canada. He made out extremely well in the long run, recently having sold his business to Mattress Firm for over $400 million.

SOLD!

Part of the sales contract with Sleep Country included my commitment to stay with Sleep America for three years following the sale. For the first two years, I continued to run the day-to-day operations for them, although my new position required me to report to senior management in Canada. Sadly, within a year of their purchase, Sleep Country found themselves deeply affected by the recession that hit the United States. When it reached its peak in 2008, the housing bubble and its impending burst was increasingly problematic, forcing them to change their approach with advertising and sales. Many people have asked me if I had any idea there would be a recession in the near future, a factor that prompted us to sell when we did. The truth is, we had no idea. All of our projections appeared to be heading straight up, without an end in sight, so we were blindsided along with most people. Of course, it would be nice to take credit for brilliant timing, but I like to call it simply good fortune that Debbie and I sold prior to the recession.

Like everything else, Sleep Country was well-intentioned in wanting to continue Sleep America's distinct approach to branding and marketing by helping our customers obtain exceptional sleep comfort, thus improving their quality of life. In hindsight, it didn't happen as we would have hoped, but there isn't much doubt in my mind that if Debbie and I had still owned the company, we would have been in trouble ourselves. It was a traumatic financial crisis that impacted the business to such an extent that we would have found it extremely difficult to survive that time period. I expect that we would have definitely downsized and sales would have significantly declined just as they did for Sleep Country.

During the recession, volume stagnated or declined for several years. In this type of business you don't even have to sell less merchandise to lose volume. Instead of spending $1,000 for a mattress, people may choose one for $800. Each person spending 20 percent less results in a 20 percent decline in sales, even if you are serving the same number of customers, which we were not. If this continues for any period of time, you can find yourself in a real predicament.

There is no question, this turn of events called for a different strategy, prompting Sleep Country to respond to the financial crisis by becoming very aggressive on price. Whether that was right or wrong, I can't argue with their decision. My guess is they probably chose the right strategy to employ at that time, given the circumstances. Where we differed in opinion related to their choice to continue in that vein after the recession started to abate. It would have been my first instinct to revert back to what made the company unique by refocusing on the brand and what truly mattered.

Understandably, it had to be frustrating from their point of view having entered the market just before the economy crashed. However, my perspective on their continued decline was that it was, in part, a result of choosing to stay in the rat race, playing the price game with everybody else—even when it was no longer necessary to do so. This removed the distinction that made the Sleep America business so wonderful to begin with. It is my belief that it wasn't that they didn't understand *what* we had done to become the dominant brand in Arizona, but I don't think they understood *how* to execute it.

A NEW SHERIFF IN TOWN

During my third and final contractual year with them, they sent a young man from Canada in to run the company. Upper management asked me to mentor and guide him through the final year of the transition. I not only agreed to this, but was eager and willing to do so. Upon arriving he asked me, "What is your agenda here?"

I said, "I want to help you become so successful that everybody says, 'Len Gaby must have been playing golf all of the time and neglecting his business.' That's my goal: to help you do better than I could have ever imagined. So much so that it makes me look like I was relaxing." Although I was being completely sincere, I'm pretty sure he didn't believe me. With money in the bank and grateful for my life and family, I was happy and fulfilled. It was my intention to do everything possible to be helpful to him and Sleep Country.

When management asked my opinion about what title would best demonstrate to everyone that he was in charge, I said, "I would call him the Executive Vice President and General Manager." They asked what else we could do for him so his position was clear. I said, "Let's give him my office so everybody will relate to the fact that the boss is in that office."

It was my intent to do everything I possibly could to demonstrate my dedication to his success. My main perspective was to think, *If I was in his shoes, what would I want from somebody else?*

For the following year, I was there with him offering my counsel and guidance on a daily basis. I said to him, "Everything we did in this company, we carefully considered, analyzed, and came to a conclusion about what was best for the company. Of course you can change any of it that you want, but if there's some aspect of what we're doing here that you have a question about, come to me. I'll explain to you how we got to where we are. Then as you move forward, you can decide whether you want to continue to do that or you want to do it some other way."

With the exception of a question about what made an advertisement successful, he never came to me with questions or asked me to explain anything about how or why we did things the way we did. Never. Not once. And I'm not sure why. Maybe he felt like the new person who wanted to make sure everybody knew he was in charge instead of me, leading him to be more concerned with establishing his turf instead of using me to his advantage. Who knows? But, he made it very clear that he didn't want to be involved in discussions with me. Maybe he doubted my sincerity. Sadly, he never gave me the chance to prove it. From my point of view, it was to his detriment because he had the opportunity to learn from somebody who had a plethora of experience building a thriving brand from the ground up. Concerned that Sleep Country was missing out on the knowledge I was willing and able to share, I mentioned to senior management that he wasn't asking many—any!—questions. His boss said to me, "He feels like you're forcing information on him."

"I'm simply volunteering information," I assured him.

He said, "Well, I guess he would like to be knocking on your door rather than you knocking on his."

"Okay," I said. "Let him come and knock on my door. I'm here." But even after that conversation, he never knocked.

A GREAT MATTRESS = A GREAT LIFE

Although the new EVP and GM never took advantage of my offer, he did absorb some of what I shared with him. He made this apparent when he presented me with an etched glass award displaying the diagram I created to explain the importance a mattress plays in our daily lives. His inscription read,

Len Gaby
Thank you for creating a vision for the future.

It was a kind gesture that meant a great deal to me.

My diagram, titled, "A great mattress = A great life," may sound absurd at first, but if you think about it, your mattress *is* the foundation on which you begin and end every day. It occurred to me at some point in time that most people don't fully appreciate the significance their mattress holds in their overall well-being. Typically, people look at it as a commodity, something that they need to have, but not something that is life-altering. To me, a mattress is much more than that. We as human beings struggle on a daily basis to not only get by, but to function to the best of our ability in the world. Ultimately, our mattress impacts everything.

Picture this if you will. You're leaving work, let's say in downtown Phoenix. You get into your car and you are immediately hit with heavy bumper-to-bumper traffic. People are honking and frustrated, creating more stress for you in the midst of the chaos. There's an accident on the freeway, causing you to be hyper-aware of the constant stopping and starting. Other drivers become frustrated...even angry. When you finally exit the freeway and enter the smaller roads approaching your home, you may begin to feel less stressed.

As you anticipate arriving home, you begin to emotionally decompress. Pulling into your garage, you watch the door close behind you when you hear the welcomed sounds of your dog, spouse, and maybe even children. Hopefully that allows you to let go of more stress as you leave the outside elements—the heat, potential crime, and the threat of bumping into another car—outside the closed and now locked door.

In your home, hopefully you are greeted by a family and an affectionate dog, all glad to see you. You're feeling better now. After enjoying dinner with your family, you relax watching sports or a favorite show on television. You are feeling comfortable as things begin winding down. After tucking your kids and dog into bed, you anticipate getting into yours while brushing your teeth and changing into your pajamas. When you finally enter the place of ultimate security for you and your spouse, where is that? It's your bed. What do you find there? A comfortable space, that is warm and hopefully full of affection with your spouse. It doesn't always have to lead toward amorous relations, it could simply be holding hands or a kiss good night. There it is. That's the ultimate peace that you experience as a human being—in your bed—where you end and begin each and every day.

I can't think of any place more important than that. It's not your car, your office chair, your couch or anywhere else. There is no physical space in your life more important than your bed. That is why I believe your mattress is the foundation of your life.

At Sleep America, we treated your search for well-being with the value it deserved, explaining its impact on your everyday life. When you realize that your chosen mattress is one of the most vital foundational aspects there is, it no longer enters your mind to ask about the cheapest queen-size bed that's in stock. Although it was my wish to offer as much insight as possible, it was fulfilling that the man who was in my old office appreciated my diagram and how we had built Sleep America on this premise.

MIXED EMOTIONS

Change can feel difficult no matter what position you are in during a transition. I'm sure we all had our own struggles and perspectives. For me, letting go of something I poured myself into for years wasn't without mixed emotions. Although we showed every care and concern we could think of to our team members, they too had to deal with the change of ownership and the new owner's methods of operating. Upon deciding to sell, we told our team with all sincerity that we believed it was the best thing for Sleep America because the Canadian company had the resources to expand into markets outside of Arizona. We felt that the sale had the potential of providing amazing opportunities for them.

After the market eventually recovered from the recession, some of our associates became disgruntled with the lack of expansion and opportunities, as well as the way the management chose to operate moving forward. Debbie was still employed for four more years, therefore, many of the associates regularly voiced their concerns to her. This was especially difficult because she had been with some of them since the beginning. Although there were extenuating circumstances that helped lead to the deterioration of the culture we had built for Sleep America, it was difficult to watch. There wasn't blame from our end, just sadness. It wouldn't be fair to judge given the pressure and challenges they had to deal with. With great humility, I can say they tried their best, worked hard, invested a great deal, and didn't give up right away.

My part in the transition came to an end in 2010, although Debbie stayed on as their spokesperson until Sleep America was sold to Mattress Firm in late 2014. With the acquisition by Mattress Firm, the name and brand Sleep America was retired as were its founders, Len and Debbie Gaby. Our dream of growth beyond the borders of Arizona was never realized.

SAYING GOODBYE TO SUSAN

Sometimes, goodbyes are extremely tough. During the sale and transition of Sleep America, another life-altering event occurred for me. This one was unexpected, swift, and cut even more deeply.

My sister, Susan Pamela Gaby, was born three years after me on November 11, 1948. One of my earliest memories of us as young children was when I was working on building a model airplane. The paint I was using had an exceptionally strong odor, which we called *dope* because it was so foul when you breathed it in. We lived in a very modest apartment at the time, so when I accidently spilled some paint on the sofa, my sister was beside herself. My parents were sleeping late on this particular Sunday morning so they weren't yet aware of my blunder. Susan cut right to the chase: "Dad is going to kill you."

"Probably," I agreed.

She truly believed he was going to *literally* kill me, which caused her to become awfully upset. In her young mind, she was genuinely frightened, thinking my actions that day were going to be the reason for my death. Trying to calm her down, I kept saying, "I don't think he's going to kill me, but he is not going to be happy."

We lived in Queens in a very small two-bedroom, garden apartment. Susan and I shared a room, with all four of us sharing one bathroom. There seemed to be an ongoing fight over who was going to use it first. Although we didn't have much, we also didn't know what we were missing—without a television showing us how the truly affluent lived in our culture, we were doing fine.

Later in life, she once told Debbie that I bullied her when we were young. Bigger than her and in good physical shape, I'm sure at some point or another, we had altercations. Although it escapes my memory, she said one time I hit her, after which, she ran and told my parents. Apparently, my response was a made up story about how Susan just happened to run right into my fist. She held her own during our childhood though.

My recollection is of her as a strong, smart young girl, physically as well as mentally. As an exceedingly bright teenager, Susan was voted by a local publication as the "ideal youth." Besides having exceptional grades, she never found herself in any trouble. In her teen years, she figured out how to needle me. Competitive was an understatement when it came to her interest in besting me by receiving higher marks in school. Saving my report cards hadn't held any interest for me, but to my amazement, Susan kept all of mine along with her own. Evidentially, she took the same courses I had, always checking my old report cards to make sure that she received higher grades in each course. Not only did her grades top mine, she never failed to remind me of it each semester. "Well," she'd say, "I took English in high school and got an 'A' and you only got a 'B'."

I really didn't care at all how she did. There was no jealousy or envy on my part that she received better grades. I'd say, "Well, that's good for you." It took me a long time to figure out why she was doing that. With a much higher maturity level at a younger age, she was overtly competitive and interested in performing well, long before me. Playing sports and having fun topped my priority list. I'm not sure if it was fortunate or unfortunate, but I was able to do moderately well without putting in much effort. My curiosity was never piqued until college. Smart enough to pay attention in class, regurgitate it on the test, and get by with above average grades was fine by me. I didn't feel a need to get an 'A' or have any requirement for myself to excel. Quantity of life was much more important to me then quality grades.

It seems that Susan either saw my lack of initiative or thought *Boy, I'm not going to do that*, using it as an example to do better or she may have matured earlier. Unlike myself, she loved school. After high school, she went to college and eventually became a teacher, which was a perfect fit for her. In her early 20s, Susan moved to California, where she finished college, married, and started a family. Eventually she took her career to another level, becoming a guidance counselor. Ultimately, her specialty became nurturing gifted children by helping them find the perfect school and the right scholarships as a college counselor. It truly was a fulfilling calling for her and she was superb with her students.

During the last years of my mother's life, she lived in California where Susan took on the role of watching over her. After my mother passed away, Susan and I found ourselves closer than ever. In my mother's personal belongings, Susan found a shoe of mine that had been crushed by a trolley car and she used it to create the special gift for my 60th birthday. Always great council for me when I had a problem, she possessed crystal-clear reasoning, which made her the perfect person to seek advice from. Her considerate and thoughtful nature made it easy for me to share my insecurities and fears with her, knowing that I could entrust her with anything.

A couple of years after my big party, on a Sunday morning in May of 2007, I was in a sales meeting at one of our stores when a call came in from Susan's husband, Frank. Evidently, she hadn't been feeling well. Thinking she may have strep throat, she went to the hospital. Her husband Frank said to me, "They just admitted Susan into the hospital."

"What's the matter?" I asked.

Frank said, "They believe she has acute leukemia."

That afternoon I flew to Los Angeles to see her in the hospital, but unfortunately she was only semi-conscious. They were trying to literally wash her blood, but the leukemia was so virulent they couldn't keep up with it. It was destroying her blood cells faster than they could clean them, attacking her in an extremely aggressive way. I don't think she ever knew what had happened to her.

The doctor said to me, "Don't expect her to go home."

I said, "Well, where is she going to go?" She was trying to tell me was that Susan was not going to make it, but I wasn't ready to hear that. Sadly, she never regained consciousness and within a week she passed away. To my heart's dismay, Susan never made it to *her* 60th birthday. Although grateful to have been by her side, it was devastating not being able to say goodbye, reminding me of my father's all-too-quick departure from our lives. My only solace was in knowing that she didn't have to endure long periods of suffering. It was a huge shock to everybody in her family, especially her two daughters, Stephanie and Nicole. There isn't a doubt in my mind how proud Susan was of them. Her eldest, Stephanie went on to become a hairdresser for celebrities, traveling all over the world as a personal hairdresser to Steven Tyler, Mariah Carey, and many others. She seems to be thoroughly enjoying life, and recently had a baby girl. Susan's youngest daughter, Nicole, graduated from Stanford and is working on her PH.D while working for the State Department. She also traveled the world doing research in several countries in Africa.

There is a story that Susan once told me that sums up how many people's lives she positively affected. While counseling one of her pupils who was having some trouble, she shared a story about me. She said to him, "Well, don't worry about it, you'll be fine. My brother wasn't a very good student either, and he is much more successful than I am."

Apparently, the student pondered that and came back a day later and said to her, *"What did you mean when you said your brother is more successful than you are?"*

She said, "Well, he's made much more money than I have."

He replied, "You shouldn't measure success with money. You're probably much more successful than he is because of all the lives you've helped."

She shared that with me, stunned that a high school student understood that success wasn't just about financial rewards. It was a beautiful gesture, wanting to make sure that she didn't feel second-rate because she hadn't made as much money as her big brother. Although it is always nice to hear, she didn't need recognition for that because she understood her accomplishments were different than mine—and just as important, if not more so. Regardless, when Susan shared this story with me, I knew she was exceedingly touched by his comment.

Standing on the leading edge of feminism and dedicated to what she was doing, Susan shared that with her children, her pupils, and everyone who was lucky enough to know her. Her death was exceptionally tough on me. It seems like just yesterday when there were four of us in a two-bedroom apartment. Now, I'm the only one left. This reality has caused me to ponder my own mortality more than ever, driving home the fact that nothing lasts forever. Additionally, it made me even more grateful for the time we spent together, especially over the last several years of her life. It's hard to believe that it was only 18 months after my 60th birthday when Susan passed. Reflecting on what a big part of it she'd been made me even more appreciative that we had been able to celebrate it together. Without saying it directly, it was clear she too had felt the magnitude of the moment. There is a special bond with a sibling who has been with you forever, who understands things about you without having to say a word. Death is so complete and final, and I miss her very much. But through her sentimental gifts and my memories, she lives on.

Chapter 20

GREATEST GIFTS

*"Life isn't perfect,
but it is grand."*

A s I sit here, having passed my 71st birthday, it has occurred to me that one of the most meaningful statements anyone can make is that *They love their job so much they can't believe someone pays them to do it.* That is exactly what my son Jonathan said to me.

PROUD PARENTS

Without any preconceived notions about what career path he should follow, my son picked one that would have undoubtedly never crossed *my* mind. He works in technology, in the television production trucks that produce live sports telecasts. And he loves it. To hear him say that fills my heart with immeasurable satisfaction. As a parent, your greatest wish is for you children to find what makes them the happiest. The funny thing is, his job is so incredibly demanding [they can't even leave to go to the restroom during the live broadcast] and so high pressure that I could never do it.

I asked him once, "Why can't you go to the bathroom during the commercials?"

He said, "We're busy preparing the replays, commercials, and so forth."

It wouldn't have been something I would have chosen, but it is the perfect career for him, first and foremost *because* he loves it. There isn't much that he could say to me that would make me happier. To have so much passion for what you do that you would do it for free if you could, means that you've found your calling. Not only does that make me ecstatic, but he is also happily married and recently welcomed a beautiful daughter into his life. Her name is Elizabeth Mae Gaby, and she is (indulge this grandfather!) the cutest baby ever!

It is also with great pride and enthusiasm that I was able to walk my extraordinary daughter, Rebecca, down the aisle last year. How lucky am I? It is quite an honor to have watched my children grow into capable, smart, and independent adults. To have the privilege to celebrate with them as they begin their own families is priceless. You hear people say that true joy lies in the little things, but that statement is so full of truth. Some of my most cherished memories and the moments most important to me have to do with spending time with the ones I love.

Debbie's daughter, Tobie, is also happily married and doing very well in Houston, Texas. Tobie's son, Cameron, who just turned 15 years old, is a tall, handsome, and very bright young man. He has wonderful aspirations and will undoubtedly do very well as he is anticipating college in the near future.

Our youngest, James—JJ—has relocated to Los Angeles to pursue his dream of dominating the real estate world in that very competitive market. He has paid his dues and is well on his way to realizing and exceeding his personal goals. Having found a wonderful young woman, they've recently become engaged to be married.

Seeing all four of our children moving in different, but very positive directions is very fulfilling to Debbie and me. We are truly blessed—and most importantly—we know it!

LOVE & MARRIAGE

Even after 20 years, every day I find myself more in love with and in awe of my wife Debbie. One of her many endearing qualities is her genuine positive outlook towards every person she meets. It is baffling to me how this rare trait seems to be an innate part of her makeup. I have such admiration for her ability to ingratiate herself with just about anyone, possessing a natural talent for bringing out the best in people. When she gives someone her attention, she is all in, making that person feel as though there is no one more important to her in that moment.

Debbie truly focuses on whomever she is with at any given moment, connecting in a way that conveys how interested she truly is. Time after time, I've seen her engage with a waitress in a restaurant that she never met, and by the end of the evening they're hugging each other. It is a talent and gift that is obviously beyond my reach.

Debbie will tell you that she gets it back tenfold. Her generosity, the help she offers to others, and her efforts to make people feel welcomed and valued are sincere and integral part of her personality. She refers to it as the *law of reciprocity*.

NO STRINGS ATTACHED

From my experience many people struggle with this concept of giving something without completely understanding what they will get in return. This can be tough for people and leave them wondering—how do we give of ourselves and balance that with the selfish instincts we have?

Most of us are willing to give some of our time, effort, talent, or skill but, typically, there is always a sense of, *What do I get in return?* We're taught from an early age that we all need to get a return on our investments. If we go to work, we need to get paid. If we invest money in a business, we need to get a return on our investment. These are business concepts and most of the time, they're important principles. However, there are times when we cannot define what the return will be. Ironically, that time may end up being one of your very best investments.

Many young people have said to me, "I'm making a lot of money, so this is a good investment of my time." Maybe... maybe not. Debbie gives of herself with no expectation other than the intrinsic value and joy of helping others. How do we measure that? How do people grapple with that dilemma? I think it's an important issue and one that becomes clearer with experience. Part of becoming successful is learning to trust yourself to the extent that you can embrace the unknown and a future without certainty. In my opinion, that's what defines a mensch and an entrepreneur. The entrepreneur says, "I have an idea that I want to bring to reality, and although I don't know how it's going to work out, I'm going to try." The mensch says, "It's the right thing to do."

WORKS IN PROGRESS

It has occurred to me that part of the continued success that Debbie and I enjoy in our relationship stems from our complimentary skill sets and personality traits. We are compatible, as well as dedicated to putting forth the effort needed to sustain our partnership. As you've probably surmised, it is not in my nature to sugarcoat anything so I won't start now. Nothing is perfect. Our marriage is not perfect, and it can't be because *nothing* is. If anyone tells you otherwise, you may want to dig a little deeper because that is the reality of life. But, if you were to ask me if it is pretty good, my answer would be, "Yes, it's darn good and I'm a very lucky man." Is it as good as it could be? "Not yet, because we are all works in progress." There will always be room to grow and improve, and we will.

From what I've experienced, a successful partnership allows you both a place where you are cherished so much that you make continued efforts to support one another's personal growth. It is a synergistic relationship where the whole is greater than the sum of the parts—where one plus one equals three. Together, you operate at an entirely different level than you would individually. We have both given to the best of our abilities and, in return, we've been blessed with this extraordinary relationship.

Green and Growing

Enhancing any type of relationship always begins with adding value to yourself first. It is a lifelong process to continually improve upon yourself. I'm still learning, hopefully, getting better, and heading in new directions. It has occurred to me that once you shut that off, you stop growing, and when you stop growing you start dying. There is an old expression for this: "When you're green you grow, and when you're ripe you rot."

If you stay green, continually learning and absorbing new information and ideas, you begin to see more clearly that you are not perfect and constantly evolving. As a result, the more you experience and are open to learning, the more you're going to realize all of the things that you have little to no knowledge of. There are a vast number of subjects that I don't know much about. Many times I've said to people, "I know an awful lot about very little." Yes, my knowledge about a narrow piece of information in this world [the mattress business] essentially makes me an expert, according to the definition of an expert in a given field. If you want to talk about that, I can talk forever, but if you want to discuss something else, I may only have a cursory knowledge. The more you learn, you begin to realize just how little you know.

There are few people who motivate and break down the steps to achieving your ultimate happiness like Tony Robbins. In fact, there's an interesting YouTube video I recently watched where he was asked, "What's the most important thing that you can do to be successful?" His answer: "Success begins with the work you do on yourself." His message was about how imperative it is to perpetually add value to yourself by continuously making yourself more of an asset, regardless of what it is that you are doing. The investments you need to consistently give to yourself are learning, growing, and doing the best job you can possibly do. It is a brilliant way of looking at it.

Friends to Treasure

After building a solid foundation by continually investing in yourself, you have the tools needed to create lasting friendships. For me, the term *friend* is often overused today, along with other adjectives and superlatives such as: amazing, insane, crazy, unbelievable... and on and on. It's a simple fact that not everything is *amazing* or *insanely wonderful*. The whole concept of *friends* on Facebook and people thinking they have so many can be deceiving. Although it has its upside to offering a vehicle for people to express themselves and seek solace where otherwise they may not have been able to, it can also mask what a deeper friendship requires. Is this truly friendship or something that develops over time and through shared experiences?

I guess, to me, the definition of a friend is someone you're close enough with that if you don't connect for an extended period of time, months or even years, they are delighted to hear your voice and experience a reconnection. This all happens without judgment and without the need for explanations on either end as to why you haven't been in touch. The minute you ask for some justification for the lack of communication, it seems to me to imply that this is not a true friend. Don't get me wrong, it takes two people with a mutual commitment to be friends. If either of you fails to reciprocate or offer feelings of good will, it will obviously fade away.

Friendships are such a treasure in life and it is definitely worth the effort to get together, have dinner, talk on the phone, and spend some time when you can. It feels like a gift to me to have friends that I've known since I was a teenager that I'm still close to today. It is wonderful to have people in your life that you can be honest with, share each other's life experiences and challenges, travel together, and trust one another. With gratitude and certainty, I can say my friends and I would do anything for one another.

BEYOND FRIENDSHIP

Partnerships in my opinion go beyond friendship, requiring a deeper commitment and understanding. Can your friend be your partner? Yes, but I strongly suggest people choose their partners wisely. It is imperative to be extremely careful about who you create a partnership with because by nature they are challenging and require mutual responsibility and commitment to building a foundation based on shared values for that partnership to thrive. This is applicable whether you are talking about life partners or going into a business partnership with someone. Either way you've agreed to commit to and trust each other.

Regardless of the type, it is important, in my opinion, for partners to care about one another's outcomes. If I'm always taking from you, you're not my partner. Many people felt that it wasn't in my best interest to become partners with my suppliers because it wouldn't allow me to squeeze them for everything possible. The mindset that one has to *get-one-over* on the other is the opposite approach used in my theory of infinite wealth. Instead, it has always been my belief that real success must be shared. Whether *you* choose to believe the mindset that it is safer to keep a distance between yourself and your partners, or you feel the benefit of embracing the theory of infinite wealth, it is important to search your own soul to decide what works best for you. A relationship is going to develop one way or the other, making it important to be mindful about the direction you want your partnership to grow. It is in your best interest to strategically create what you are wanting instead of having a culture created by accident.

DEALING WITH DISAGREEMENTS

My experiences have taught me that success in relationships or business hinge on creating a solid foundation with a partner. I believe that the best partnerships are based on bringing people together that absolutely complement, rather than duplicate, one another. This goes back to another favorite expression of mine from Dale Carnegie, "When two people always agree, one of them is not necessary." We must accept the fact that we're going to disagree, and that's a healthy situation. The question is, *How do we deal with those disagreements and what comes out of it?*

Inevitably, partnerships have to be strong enough to handle tension and challenges. Many people go into partnerships or business with the illusion that it's always going to be easy and everyone will live happily ever after. That's so far from the truth that it's a ridiculous notion. Getting comfortable with the fact that sometimes things will work out well and other times they won't, is part of life. Even if someone appears honest and forthright, they may not be. This is where, for me, a healthy dose of skepticism keeps you on your toes.

However, even complementing one another by offering different skill sets and strengths cannot work if the partnership is not built on a foundation of mutual core values. This requires both parties to clearly articulate their beliefs so nothing is left to assumption. As long as we can fundamentally accept each other's principles, trust can grow. It may go without saying but it is important to genuinely like one another. It can be extremely difficult to forge a strong partnership with someone you don't like, even if you share the same core values and their skill sets complement yours. Search for the mensch.

LEN'S SIMPLE TRUTHS

As far as sharing my conclusions for finding your own success and personal bliss, let me share some simple truths that I've learned throughout my life. Mind you, it isn't the end of my life yet, nor the end of my stories, but there are a few consistent and simple truths that have become clear to me thus far.

The first simple truth...

> *The happiest people I've ever known are the ones who are*
> *the most grateful, no matter what their circumstance.*

If there is one thing that you could do for yourself to vastly change the trajectory of your life, be grateful for what you have. Whether that is for your health, your children, or whatever it is that brings you joy. Gratitude is a secret ingredient.

The second simple truth...

Do the best you can.

What more can we expect of ourselves? It's so simplistic but if you can say, I do or did the best I can, you can't do any better than that. How inordinately basic but true this is. I have the freedom to do less than my best, but it is impossible to do any more than give it my all. What more can we ask of ourselves? I think we're all looking for a little internal peace and for me that is the ultimate peace. It seems that the most prophetic words of wisdom are the most straightforward. It doesn't have to get much more complicated than that. Be grateful for what you have and do the best you can. If somebody has a better list than that, I'd love to learn about it.

It almost seems absurd that the keys to success are so elementary, but they are. Life can feel immensely difficult with so many different things going on at the same time, but changing your perspective can provide much needed clarity.

Think about what we say to our children before a test or sporting event: *All I want is for you to do the best that you can. You don't need to be perfect, just give it your all.* It's sound advice, in my opinion, to spend your energy trying to do your best up front instead of beating yourself up afterwards for getting a 90% on the test. Did you do all the things that were necessary to prepare for it? Did you study the expected information, using all of your abilities? If you can honestly answer *Yes* to those questions, then feel comfortable with the fact that 90% was the best you could do. Next time you might want to try something else, but that doesn't mean that you should be unhappy with what you accomplished.

To round it all out, after you have attempted to give it your best shot, let the rest go. Recite the *Serenity Prayer* if it helps, but it is imperative to allow yourself the freedom to relax, knowing your best *is* good enough. If everybody accepted that simple truth, they'd be much happier. There is no sense in knocking yourself out over things you can't change, because it isn't going to help you. Instead, work on the things that you have the ability to impact by doing the best you can. Truly, the wisdom *is* knowing the difference—when you can change something and when you can't, and accepting that. These are staples of mine for living my most fulfilling life.

EMBRACING CHANGE

Lastly, keep in mind that especially in this day and age, it is crucial that you embrace change. Even if we go back nearly 200 years, the message was clear: "It is not the most intelligent of the species that survives; it is not the strongest that survives; but the species that survives is the one that is able to adapt to and to adjust best to the changing environment in which it finds itself," said Charles Darwin in his book *The Origin of Species*. That's why you hear that, if an atomic war hits, the cockroach will survive because it can adapt to any conditions. Scorpions as well. Believe it or not, I picked up a scorpion one day, put it in a jar, and placed it in the freezer. To my amazement, after opening up that jar months later and putting the scorpion on the ground, it got up and ran away. Your ability to adapt to change is a huge determining factor in continually finding places, people, and situations that will sustain you.

GIFTS OF LIFE

Have you ever heard someone say, *Have a blessed day* or *Have a blessed life*? I'm not quite sure I know what that means frankly, but I believe I understand what they are trying to convey. However, for me, life *itself* is the blessing. This is a core concept of my infinite wealth philosophy. Once you understand that you've been blessed with this gift of life, everything else falls into place. Gratitude and doing your best are extremely important, but it begins with realizing there is a blessing that's been bestowed upon you, and it is this life. No matter who you are, where you are, what you're doing, where you're going, what you've endured, and what you've been fortunate to experience, just the fact that you're experiencing *something* is a blessing of infinite wealth. As long as we're alive, we are always receiving some of this gift.

ENJOY THE RIDE

Many times people have asked me if I think I would be just as happy if I'd chosen a different path. With all sincerity, my answer has always been *Yes*.

There is no doubt in my mind that on any road, I would have been fulfilled, challenged, and made a good living in a stimulating career. This could have been an entirely different story had my choices been different. What if I never went to work for Simmons? What if I went to law school and became an attorney? Would things be any different for me today? I don't think so. My approach would have been the same—digging in and figuring it out. My personality and drive would have given me the opportunity to be successful no matter what path I walked, even if my career hadn't begun at Simmons. The only distinction would be that my days may have been spent doing something very different. Certainly, I wouldn't have been less interested or found myself indifferent to what went on around me because of my personal passion for life.

My advice, as someone who has traveled an interesting road for move than seven decades: Don't get hung up on wondering if you made the right choice... embrace what you have chosen. Live life to its fullest and enjoy it. There isn't so much a "right" choice as there is deciding to take *your* choice and make it the best you can. How did I know if Simmons was the right choice for me? I didn't, but it worked out in all likelihood because I fully embraced it, immersing myself in doing the best I could. Had it been my choice and I didn't give it my all, we could sit here today and say that I made the wrong choice. Yet, in my estimation, the fact would not be that

I made the wrong choice, but that I chose not to give enough of myself or apply myself to the best of my ability. The same goes for the moment Debbie and I started our business. Was it the right decision? We loved and cherished every moment and everyone we were able to touch. We are so grateful for that journey.

So as I found myself nearing this end of writing this book I asked myself an important question: *What do I hope readers will glean from this book?*

Mostly, I hope you smiled quite a few times and enjoyed it. A critical component of living a life of infinite wealth is having fun and enjoying what you're doing. It is also my hope that you found a few small elements that can be useful for you. In the end, my reason for writing this book was to share my experiences with the goal of offering something that could enhance your own journey.

I've relished the process of writing this, even though the outcome was unclear to me from the beginning. No matter what, it was worth it because I've benefited in many ways already. It is my wish to leave you with some gift, whether that is from demonstrating the benefit of remaining curious about life, or merely offering you the opportunity to learn from my mistakes and successes. Sharing information is my way of letting people know how much I care. There are many times, while reading *The New York Times* each day, I find myself drawn to articles that seem interesting—and especially when one strikes me as something a friend or family member might like. I save the article and send it to them. It is a simple pleasure of mine and that's a reward in itself.

Time seems to have passed by entirely too quickly, but as the years flew by, it striped away any of my illusions about what is really most important in life. Sitting here today with the most of my life behind me, I'm filled with immense joy and certainty, knowing that I did the best I could and that...

Life isn't perfect, but it is grand.

~~The End~~

To be continued...

ABOUT THE AUTHOR

Leonard Gaby's professional career began and continues by putting the customer first... anticipating their needs, exceeding expectations, delivering both a quality product and a quality experience.

It shouldn't be surprising that, after 50-plus years and a career that included the launch of a business that would rank among Arizona's most admired, Len has taken some time to reflect.

After 13 years as Chief Executive Officer of *Sleep America*, the company he co-founded with his wife, Debbie in 1997, he retired in 2009 to focus on consulting work with entrepreneurs and business leaders. He currently serves on the Executive Board of Directors for The Sandra Day O'Connor Institute.

Sleep America, which the Gabys grew to 47 locations and over 150 employees statewide, was the largest mattress retailer in Arizona. In launching that company, Len and Debbie blended their previous experience—his in the mattress manufacturing and retail furniture industries and hers in interior design and real estate. In 2005, *Sleep America* was voted Best Place to Work in the Valley by *The Phoenix Business Journal*. The company also received the Scottsdale Chamber of Commerce's Sterling Award and was a proud finalist of the National Better Business Bureau Torch Award. The company was acquired in 2006 by mattress retailer Sleep Country Canada, which operates over 230 stores across Canada. And, in January 2015, *Sleep America* was acquired by Mattress Firm.

Early in his career Len learned the ropes of the mattress industry with the Simmons Company, and his career with Simmons continued for 20 years as he held various senior level management positions, including president and general manager of the mattress division. Gaby received his BS and MBA degrees from The State University of New York at Buffalo.

The Art of the Mensch is Len's first book and he anticipates that highlights of his "retirement" will include speaking engagements, mentoring, and business coaching based upon his book.

MEET THE MENSCH!

LEN GABY

SPEAKING ENGAGEMENTS
MENTORING
BOOK SIGNINGS
BUSINESS CONSULTING

Visit www.TheArtoftheMensch.net
or email: LenGaby@TheArtoftheMensch.net